THROWIM WAY LEG

TIM FLANNERY

THROWIM WAY LEG

TREE-KANGAROOS, POSSUMS, AND PENIS GOURDS— ON THE TRACK OF UNKNOWN MAMMALS IN WILDEST NEW GUINEA

Atlantic Monthly Press
New York

First published by The Text Publishing Company in 1998
Printed in the United States of America

FIRST AMERICAN EDITION

Library of Congress Cataloging-in-Publication Data

Flannery, Tim F. (Tim Fridtjof), 1956–
     Throwim way leg : tree-kangaroos, possums, and penis gourds—
on the track of unknown mammals in wildest New Guinea / Tim
Flannery.
          p.   cm.
     Includes index.
     ISBN 0-87113-731-3
     1. Indigenous peoples—New Guinea. 2. Ethnology—New
Guinea.
     3. New Guinea—Social life and customs. 4. New Guinea—
Description
     and travel.   I. Title.
     GN671.N5F565   1998
     919.5—dc21   98-38435

Design by Chong Wengho
Maps hand-drawn by Norm Robinson

Atlantic Monthly Press
841 Broadway
New York, NY 10003

99 00 01 02 10 9 8 7 6 5 4 3

I dedicate this book to Jim-Bob Moffett, his successors and all the other CEOs of mining companies with interests in Melanesia, in the hope that, through reading it, they will understand a little better the people whose lives they so profoundly change.

CONTENTS

PART IV
OK TEDI AND BEYOND

PART V
NORTH COAST RANGES

PART VI
JAYAPURA AND BEYOND

PART VII
SNOW MOUNTAINS

Throwim way leg

In New Guinea Pidgin, *throwim way leg* means to go on a journey. It describes the action of thrusting out your leg to take the first step of what can be a long march.

For as long as I can remember I have been intrigued by New Guinea. Perhaps it was the stories my uncle 'Gunner' Keith told of fighting the Japs in Dutch New Guinea, of spiders the size of dinner plates, and of fuzzy wuzzy angels, the warriors who used their local knowledge to save the lives of many Australian soldiers during the Second World War. Maybe it was the visit to my school by a group of excruciatingly shy yet fascinating Papuan students. Whatever it was, it worked its magic while I was still a child.

I was twenty-six when I first travelled overseas. I went to Papua New Guinea. I can still feel the wonderment, tinged with excitement—even fear—which flared in my breast. The crisp, cool mountain air, the unfamiliar smells, sights and sounds all embedded themselves deep in my consciousness. Everything was new and strange.

New Guinea sprawls like a vast prehistoric bird across the sea north of Australia. After Greenland it is the world's largest island, and its size, shape and rugged mountains are all the result of its peculiar geological history, for New Guinea is Australia's bow wave. As the continent of Australia has drifted northward it has accumulated islands and fragments of other continents along its leading edge. Like debris swept together by a broom, these have built up into a long, chaotic pile of landforms. This geology also explains why New Guinea's flora and fauna resembles Australia's. Although it is close to south-east Asia, New Guinea has no tigers, rhinos or elephants, but it does have kangaroos. New Guinea's kangaroos, however, live in the trees.

Mi bai throwim way leg nau (I'm starting my journey now) still has literal meaning, for even today walking is the only means of travel in much of New Guinea. The island's topography is so rugged that roads service only a tiny portion of it. There are no roads, for example, linking either Port Moresby (the capital of Papua New Guinea) or Jayapura (the capital of Irian Jaya) with the rest of the country. Furthermore, there are no pack animals in New Guinea and, until the arrival of aircraft, New Guineans living in adjacent valleys, or in the mountains and on the coast, were as isolated from each other as people living on different continents. This helps explain why New Guinea is home to about 1,000 languages—one sixth of the world total.

While New Guinea is still one of the world's last frontiers, its human history is venerable. People have lived there for at least 45,000 years. They arrived by sea from Asia at a time when New Guinea and Australia were joined. As the sea rose and isolated the two landmasses, these immigrants were to diversify into the living Australian Aborigines and the tribesmen of New Guinea.

Nine thousand years ago, New Guineans living in high mountain valleys had already developed intensive agriculture. There they domesticated and harvested the world's most important plant crop—sugar cane—along with taro (a large nutritious tuber), bananas, yams and winged beans. They had begun this process at a time when my European ancestors were still chasing woolly mammoths across the tundra.

Despite its isolation New Guinea has played an important role in world trade. By the sixteenth century, Sri Lankan princes were adorning themselves with hats made from New Guinea's birds of paradise. Before that, it seems likely that Chinese were consuming New Guinean nutmeg, and Indonesians rubbing themselves with oil made from New Guinea's Massoi tree. The ancient Romans flavoured their food with cloves, which are the flower buds of a lilly pilly which grows only on islands just to the west of New Guinea.

During the colonial period, Germany, the Netherlands and Australia all counted parts of New Guinea as their territory. Australia ended up administering the eastern half of the island, which became the independent nation of Papua New Guinea in 1975. The western half passed from Dutch to Indonesian hands, and is now a province of Indonesia.

This brief political history, however, says little of the lives of the village people themselves, for many were unaffected by much of it. Despite half a century of colonial rule, it was only in 1935 that Australian gold prospectors stumbled across the 750,000 people living in the central highlands of Papua New Guinea—by far the largest concentration of people on the island, some of whom live at the greatest rural population density on the planet.

Irian Jaya's major population centre, the Baliem Valley, was discovered even later, in 1938, when the millionaire adventurer Richard Archbold saw what he described as a 'shangri la'

from the air. This was the last time in the history of our planet
that such a vast, previously unknown civilisation was to come
into contact with the west, and it was not until over a decade
later that substantial contact was made with this area.

Biologists have played a leading role in the exploration of New
Guinea. Luigi Maria D'Albertis, a Genoese, was one of the first.
On 6 September 1872, he had the privilege of being the first
European to enter the island's mountains. There he discovered
a biological realm unknown to the outside world. He later
explored the Fly River with the aeronautical pioneer Lawrence
Hargrave, impressing the locals with dramatic displays of fire-
works. Richard Archbold was leading just one of three major
biological survey expeditions which he participated in when he
discovered the Baliem Valley. The fund he established was eventually to sponsor seven major biological exploring expeditions
to the island.

Even contemporary biologists have made significant contri-
butions. In 1974 Jared Diamond explored the Foja Mountains
of Irian Jaya. No European had previously set foot in this vast
range, and no native people inhabit it. The animals were
entirely tame, birds of paradise displaying to Diamond within
metres of his face, while undescribed kinds of tree-kangaroos
stared at him as he walked by.

I was already studying for my doctorate when I undertook my
first expedition to New Guinea. I went there because New
Guinea seemed to be the last great biological unknown, and I
felt that it was on the island's biological frontier that I could
make my best contribution to mammalogy, my area of expertise.

As I studied in preparation for that first expedition, I read
avidly about the island. I found that one had to ferret around
in innumerable musty scientific papers to discover what had
already been achieved in New Guinea mammalogy. There was
no compendium, no single volume where I could go to learn

what other researchers had already found. There were few photographs of the mammals, and everything then known about their ecology could have fitted comfortably onto this page. Here, I felt, was my chance to make a lasting contribution. I could write the first handbook of the mammals of this great island.

Fifteen expeditions, two trips to museums overseas, and countless hours in libraries later, I achieved my goal.

In my naivety, I imagined when I set out on this quest that the world was fully documented, and that the great age of exploration had ended in the nineteenth century. I was envious of explorers like D'Albertis, who walked through entire undiscovered mountain ranges, and who lived for months on end on a diet of rice and newly discovered birds of paradise. My role, I thought, was more humble: to bring together the knowledge previous researchers had gathered, add some photographs and ecological notes, and place it all between the covers of one book. If I was lucky, I might discover some obscure creature such as a rat which had escaped the searching eyes of earlier explorers. My greatest discovery in New Guinea, perhaps, was finding out just how wrong I was.

Little did I imagine then that I was to live among largely uncontacted peoples, to whom, just a few years before, cannibalism had been not a rumour but a way of life. Nor did I think I would climb mountains previously unscaled by Europeans, enter uncharted caves, or rediscover animals previously known only as ice-age fossils. Had someone intimated to me that I was to discover what is arguably the world's largest rat, name four kinds of tree-kangaroos, or stumble on a cave full of the bones of long extinct and entirely unknown marsupial giants, I would have scoffed in disbelief. Yet I did.

I have always worried that my book *Mammals of New Guinea* would lead students into imagining that the age of exploration is finished in New Guinea. The book looks so glossy, so neat and so complete, but it is, in reality, just a beginning. New Guinea is as vast a field for adventure and discovery as it ever was, and even though the cultures of its people are changing rapidly they will offer a very different way of seeing the world for many years to come. I hope that the great island will continue to exert its magnetic attraction on young adventurers and researchers, and that they will continue where I have left off.

PART I

MT ALBERT EDWARD

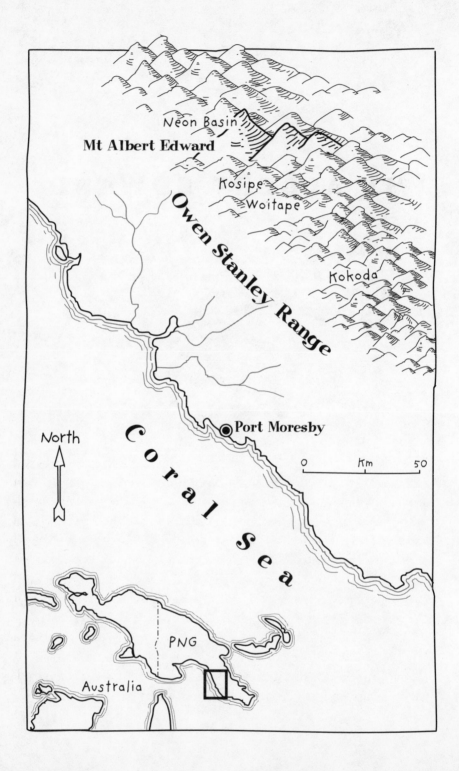

Mt Albert Edward

Neon Basin

Kosipe

Woitape

Owen Stanley Range

Kokoda

Port Moresby

North

Coral Sea

Km
0   50

PNG

Australia

Buai impressionism

The aircraft circled slowly over a parched landscape. Below, the atmosphere was thick with smoke as the rank, brown savannah burned. In the wet–dry tropics, fire rends the landscape the way an archaeologist strips layers of sediment with a trowel. Here it had revealed a dozen old horseshoe-shaped redoubts (once used to shelter aircraft from bomb attacks) encircling the airstrip, vast piles of discarded fuel drums, and the skeletons of armoured vehicles and other such *remanie* of the Second World War.

This was Jackson Airport, gateway to Papua New Guinea, a nation which in December 1981 was less than six years old. It was definitely not the luxuriant, jungle-clad New Guinea landscape I had imagined countless times in my dreams.

My first memories of Port Moresby are still vivid. Dark-skinned women and children sitting on each street corner before piles of *buai* (betel nut) and *daka* (fruit of the pepper vine chewed with *buai*), or perhaps neat bundles of peanuts as I had never seen them before, tied together by their stalks.

At first I took the red stains lying on every footpath and wall to be blood. The result, perhaps, of violent assault and bloody riot. It was only later, after much private anguish, that I learned that the stains were *buai*. When the kernel of the small green nut is chewed with lime (made from crushing burned sea-shells) and *daka*, the mixture turns bright red. Chewing *buai* ends when a great red stream of liquid is ejected from the mouth, often with extraordinary force, accuracy and aplomb.

The first flush of innocent inquiry allows a person a kind of liberty which fuller knowledge denies them. Satisfied that the streets of Port Moresby were not steeped in blood, I felt free to roam where I would—even once as far as the front bar of the notorious Boroko Hotel.

That evening, after I'd drunk a beer or two in a hushed silence and surrounded by dark stares, a couple of young Hanuabada lads suggested that they would walk me back to Angau Lodge where I was staying. It was only as we neared home that, noticing the barbed-wire compounds and vicious dogs surrounding every house in Boroko, I realised they had certainly saved my money, and possibly my life.

I soon found that the best and cheapest places to eat in Moresby were the Chinese cafes. The Diamond Cafe in Boroko became my favourite. Its laminex table-tops and simple menu reminded me of the Chinese restaurants of my childhood, of my father bringing our own saucepans to be filled with fried rice and sweet-and-sour pork. One night, I noticed that a curious addition had been chalked on the menu board. Below the chow mein was written *Papa Fell Over*. Intrigued, and suspecting it to be some exceedingly alcoholic local brew, I ordered a small one with coffee.

Startlingly renamed in Melanesian Pidgin, and transmogrified in a Chinese kitchen, that distinctively Australian dessert pavlova never tasted so good.

Koki Market nestles by the sea near Ela Beach. This beautiful, exotic place drew me daily. A sea of constantly moving black bodies crowded the square, the musky animal smell of humanity blend with the distinctive spice of *buai*. Huge red splashes of the latter seemed to be concentrated around a sign proclaiming NO KEN KAIKAI BUAI HIA (BETEL NUT CHEWING PROHIBITED). Nearby, an old fellow sat each morning, dressed in a simple laplap, with just a few *buai* for sale in front of him, his grizzled head nodding. One afternoon there were only two fruit left as he made a painful effort to unbend his arthritic joints. A woman screamed out in Motuan, 'Hey old man, you've left your balls behind!' and the entire marketplace rang with peals of hysterical laughter.

Gargantuan piles of fruit and vegetables always covered every market bench. Above this cornucopia hung mysteriously shaped bags and bundles, suspended by wooden hooks from the rafters of the tin-roofed shelters. I could see, occasionally, a bewildered-looking cuscus (a kind of possum) peek from one of the string bags, but the contents of others remained obscure. I desperately wished to acquire some cuscuses for our museum collection. Before I realised that the bundles could contain anything from groceries to babies, I sometimes found myself bargaining, in this language I barely understood, for *pikininis* rather than possums.

Near the water one day, a mammoth hawksbill turtle lay on its back in the sun, gulping helplessly, its eyes streaming salty tears. This was the seafood section. Someone had already purchased a fore-flipper. Shocked by the cruelty, I abandoned thoughts of turtle soup and instead purchased two live *kindam*, beautiful painted crayfish, for less than a dollar each. Never did I imagine that my meagre field allowance would extend to such luxuries.

Just behind were the meat stalls. There, piled in their dozens, were the smoked bodies of wallabies. The smell of the smoky wood fire was dense, yet was insufficient to deter the clouds of flies which hovered about. I paid my five kina to an old man, blind in one eye and with his shotgun resting behind him, and at one stroke collected my first specimen in New Guinea and solved the riddle of what to curry for tomorrow's dinner.

Leaving the market that day, I joined an enormous crowd gathered around the entrance of a dingy Chinese trade store. Young and old alike were pressed together, their mouths forming solemn *O*s as they craned their necks upward. Their faces were filled with amazement. After fighting my way through the crowd I discovered what transfixed them—television had just come to Port Moresby.

The twentieth century appeared to be catching up with New Guinea. But Port Moresby was a long way from Mt Albert Edward. This high, isolated mountain was the place where I hoped to encounter the timeless New Guinea of my dreams. I had not seen the mountain when I first arrived, for smoke from the innumerable dry-season fires had obscured it. It remained hidden until dawn on the very morning I was to fly to its base.

The fear of heaven

Flatness trains the Australian eye not to stray far above the horizon, so while I stood in the dawn light at the airport, I missed the massif at first. The jagged, dark green peaks of the Owen Stanley Range receded away to the north, their summits becoming increasingly obscured in dawn-tinged cloud. Through a trick of the atmosphere, a pale blue band of sky appeared to rise over the mist. For some reason my eye made an effort to search above this point—and met with a seemingly impossible illusion. There, as if floating, detached above all, were two further peaks. Not dark green these, but golden and purple from the frigid grassland and jagged rock crowning their summit. I fancied that a lost ice age, a new world, beckoned to me from those two islands in the sky. The furthest, Mt Albert Edward, was my destination.

My journey to Papua New Guinea had been made possible by Dr Geoffrey Hope, a palaeo-botanist. At that time he was almost like a god to me. He spoke Pidgin fluently, he had climbed to the Carstensz Glacier in Irian Jaya ten years previously, and knew more about New Guinea than anyone else I had met. A lecturer in geography at the Australian National University, Geoff is one of the most inspiring of all teachers. A real adventurer, he creates irresistible opportunities for students to travel with him to remote places.

Geoff was mounting an expedition to Kosipe, below Mt Albert Edward, because some ancient stone axes had been unearthed there some years before. He thought that sediments in the region might hold fossil pollen which would give some idea of long-term climate and vegetation change there, as well as, perhaps, some idea of the early human impacts on the environment.

On that first trip, Geoff was accompanied by his partner, Bren Wetherstone; their infant son, Julian; Geoff's mother, Penelope; and his father, Alec. I was also in awe of Geoff's father, better known as A. D. Hope. He wrote the finest modern poetry I had ever read. Strangely, I thought, this great man would actually talk to me, a mere student!

Penelope Hope, Geoff's mother, had grown up in the Gulf of Papua, where her father was a trader. She knew the country well, and told me much of her experiences as a child. For her, this was to be a last trip of reminiscence.

With infants and the elderly, however, it was hardly a party that satisfied my desire to undertake life-and-death adventure in a remote New Guinea jungle. The expedition, was, though, to give me experiences I could never repeat. For through it I saw a little of the *taim bilong masta*—the time when white men ruled New Guinea. I look back on it now as an invaluable peek at the way Papua New Guinea used to be.

A. D. Hope seemed to be quite interested in our work, and was particularly fascinated with the small animals we caught.

One day, I trapped a small carnivorous marsupial, a relative

of the Australian *Antechinus*. A. D. Hope was ecstatic. He questioned me intensively about the beast and its sexual habits,
before explaining that his most recent book of poems was
called *Antechinus*. The work had the sex lives of these strange
marsupials as a major theme. Their reproductive pattern is
unusual in that males live only eleven months, while females
can live years. The last month of the life of the males is spent
in search of sexual fulfilment, an exercise so strenuous that it
inevitably leads to their death. Later I received a copy of
Antechinus, beautifully inscribed by Hope in celebration of our
time spent peering at a tiny marsupial.

Our plan was to fly Hopes junior, senior and middle-aged
to Kosipe, a Catholic mission station at the base of the mountain. Ken Aplin (a fellow student) and I were to be dropped
off at Woitape, some fifteen kilometres away, to walk the rest of
the way in.

Sometimes walking has advantages over flying, for it gives
an entirely different feel for the context of the place you are
visiting. The track from Woitape to Kosipe was a good one,
used for tractor access. Following it, we wound our way for five
hours through forest and regrowth. Someone accustomed to
the open forests of Australia begins to feel hemmed in on such
a track, for the vegetation is dense, blocking out vistas. But
finally a splendid and entirely unexpected scene opened
before us.

The mission station at Kosipe lies in an exquisite mountain
valley, behind which rises, in tier after tier, majestic Mt Albert
Edward. On this clear afternoon its summit glowed purple
against the sky. The valley floor was almost entirely taken
up with a great swamp. This was what Geoff had come to
take a core from, in order to examine vegetation changes
through the ages. Around it was a grassland which rose
and fell in little prominences and flats. The afternoon air was
crisp and cool. There was something distinctly European about
the scene. Dotted everywhere around the valley, but particularly on the higher ground, lay immaculate, steep-roofed,

double-storey Swiss chalets, between which grazed cattle and horses. Further in the distance, hidden in clumps of trees, wisps of smoke betrayed the presence of the villages of the Goilala people.

This beautiful place was the result of the synergy between two superficially different, yet fundamentally similar mountain cultures. The grasslands of the Kosipe Valley were created by the Goilala, the original inhabitants of the place. Before the establishment of the mission, they had lived down the valley. They had made this clearing in just the past forty years or so. Whenever conditions permitted they burned the forest, creating an ever-broadening expanse of grass.

The chalets, cattle and horses, on the other hand, were the work of Father Alexandre Michaellod, one of the most remarkable people I have ever met.

Father Michaellod had been unfortunate enough to be born the eleventh child of a humble Swiss Catholic dairy farmer. In the early twentieth century, there were virtually no prospects for such a child. The time-honoured—indeed only—option was to enter a monastery. Michaellod did this at the age of twelve. There he learned to make several varieties of cheese and, by his own admission, became bored nearly to death. Then the opportunity arose to become a missionary. After a brief period of training, Michaellod was sent off to New Guinea. Even on the ship, he was under the distinct impression that he was bound for somewhere in Africa.

When Michaellod finally arrived at the Catholic mission station on the south coastal island of Yule, he was assigned the near suicidal task of proselytising in the then largely uncontacted Mendi area. According to one account (possibly apocryphal), when told of his task, Michaellod swore, spat on the ground three times, and stamped off to begin his journey.

Despite the difficulty of his task, Michaellod was outstandingly successful in bringing the gospel to the Mendi—so successful indeed that he was sent next to establish a mission among the Goilala.

The Goilala have a nasty reputation. One of the most infamous *raskol* gangs in Port Moresby is named '105', a sort of mirror image of the first three letters of the word Goilala. The daring and brutality of the 105 gang is legendary. Just a year after we left Kosipe a Belgian doctor was murdered while climbing Mt Albert Edward. His Goilala guides, newly out of prison, drove an axe into the back of his head before robbing him. The first aircraft ever hijacked in Papua New Guinea (in September 1995) landed at Kosipe, its pilot making the difficult touchdown at the—by then—abandoned airstrip with a shotgun held to his head.

A New Guinean friend once told me about his grandfather, a police sergeant who worked in the Goilala area in the 1930s. As a Papuan with rank, he could lead a police team when tracking down wrongdoers without the supervision of a kiap (government official). His favourite tactic was to track the miscreants back to their village. There, in the early hours of the morning, he would torch the men's house, then stand at the door with rifle in hand. As the sleepy warriors emerged through the door trying to escape the conflagration, he would shoot them through the head.

In his dotage, the old fellow found his many sins difficult to forgive. He would often ask his grandson about divine justice. Why, he asked, if God was just, would He let an old bastard such as himself live to such a ripe old age, yet see so many good men die young?

Strangely, though, when my friend visited the Goilala area he found that his grandfather's name was common among younger men. Despite his tactics, the hard old fellow had been admired by the Goilala. A generation of young namesakes was their tribute to him.

This story threw some light on Michaellod. He seemed an extraordinary man just for staying so long at Kosipe. Yet I liked him for much more than that. He was a complex and intelligent person who had given his life in the service of a faith he never questioned. But sadly, by 1981, he was something of an anachronism—newer Roman Catholic missionaries tend to see themselves as facilitators who guide rather than rule. Father Michaellod, in his way, was of the older, more authoritarian school. Having spent much of his life in New Guinea highland societies, he had become profoundly affected by them. Many in his congregation expected their priest to act like a 'big man', and in the best traditions of New Guinea big men Michaellod was both feared and respected. This suited the older Goilala, for they were comfortable with such an old-style leader.

Michaellod remembered clearly his first contact with the Goilala. How he had trekked through the dense jungle, alone and clad in black robes, and had terrified the ebullient mountaineers. They fled from their villages, leaving a few frail old women in occupation. Only after some days did the others dare to return. Michaellod, unable to speak the Goilala language, decided that contact with children was the best way to win the confidence of the adults. He would offer a child a boiled sweet, then take it by the hand and lead it into his hut to talk.

Many years later Michaellod at last understood why the mothers had wailed in grief as he led their children away. When a Goilala takes someone by the hand and leads them off to a private place, it is an inevitable prelude to intercourse. For years the Goilala believed that the solemn man with no sexual interest in women was a pederast.

His first attempts at proselytising were a dismal failure. The men refused to allow the women access to religious knowledge. When they finally consented, it was only under the condition that they be taught separately by Michaellod's catechist. This pious coastal man would not look upon the nakedness of Goilala women, and took to holding up drawings depicting Christian doctrine while positioned behind the trunk of a tree. These would then be discussed.

Michaellod was horrified to find that his parishioners all preferred hell to heaven. It took him some time to find out why. On the mission picture card, hell was depicted as a place of eternal fire, peopled by dark-skinned beings with spear-like pitchforks. With these, they occasionally pricked a captive white man. In short, he discovered, the scene bore a close resemblance to the inside of an idealised Goilala hut. Heaven, on the other hand, was depicted as a place of cloud and mist, among which many white people stood, pale and menacing. So—to the Goilala—heaven was too much like the mountain summits, where swirling mists and storms often kill with cold. They feared it.

Even worse in Father Michaellod's eyes, the Goilala persistently (perhaps perversely, he felt) misunderstood the nature of the Trinity. Not long before our arrival, he told us, a group of the most devout parishioners had come to him in a state of great excitement. They said that the Holy Spirit had appeared to them while they were working on the edge of the forest, and requested Father to speak with Him. Michaellod coolly jotted down a few words (in French!) on a scrap of paper, and handed his agitated parishioners the note. They returned some time later, highly pleased, saying that the Holy Spirit had hopped down off His perch, taken the note in His beak and carried it up to heaven!

Michaellod was every bit as tough as his Goilala charges. He told me that a few months after he arrived he saw two Goilala men engage in a duel with axes. The naked men circled each other warily, like fighting cocks. Each held a long-handled axe upright before him, the blade standing in front of his face. Both looked for the moment's opportunity needed to drive the wedge of steel deep into his opponent's skull.

Michaellod rushed forward and put out a hand to separate the combatants. In reflex, one brought his axe down on the unprotected hand, spilling blood onto the ground.

Within weeks the offender was dead, believing that he had released the spirit of the great man along with his blood. The spirit, he believed, would not rest until it had claimed his life.

Father Michaellod, meanwhile, had horrified the Papuan

nuns sent to care for him by propping a spare coffin up against the wall of his house, joking that he had bought it for himself 'in advance'.

This fondness for coffins had, incidentally, rubbed off on his sacristan, who must have been a rum old gent. The devout fellow had visited Port Moresby while his wife was taken ill. He returned home with a present for her—a shiny new coffin. Apparently she was delighted with the gift, and neither seemed to mind when she recovered from her illness and so had to defer its use!

Michaellod's easy European acceptance of corpses was a great advantage to him. He would often take the battered mission jeep to a nearby village to pick up a corpse for Christian burial. On the return trip, he would simply tie it into the passenger seat. Inevitably, there would be a rush of potential passengers wishing to hitch a free ride to Kosipe. Their horror at the discovery of the corpse gave the old priest much mirth.

While such events doubtless gave Michaellod something of a reputation as a black magician among his parishioners, his greatest triumph came when he brought cattle to Kosipe. It is hard for a Swiss dairyman to see a grassy, alpine valley devoid of cows. Father Michaellod had to have them, but in the early days the trek in from Ononge was difficult for cattle.

Michaellod himself drove the beasts endlessly along narrow, mossy paths through dense rainforest, all the while dreading the last leg of the route in to Kosipe, for then it was just a winding track through the thickest scrub. But when he neared the mission he found that his parishioners had built a veritable bovine highway. The crooked path had been widened, straightened and paved with mats in order to make the progression of the 'ancestor pigs' (whose tusks grew impressively from the top of their heads) more comfortable.

By 1981, though, those early days were well and truly past. A few old men in the village still respected the priest who possessed the ancestors of the pigs, and whose blood, when spilt, could kill a warrior in his prime. But the young now grew up in a different world. They knew of Port Moresby and were familiar with European ways. Many knew that the Europeans could be robbed as easily as anyone else. They opposed the old priest and, while they did not yet dare to do it openly, the day would soon come when they surely would.

As Christmas vacation drew near, groups of people began arriving almost daily on the track from Woitape. They were returning from Port Moresby to celebrate Christmas and New Year with their relatives. Many were clearly hard-working government employees looking forward to a welcome break. Others, however, were arrogant-looking young men swaggering under great, apparently purloined bundles of western goods of diverse kinds. Radios, lamps and other electrical appliances seemed to predominate, despite the fact that the Goilala huts were without a power supply.

On Christmas Day 1981 the sound of Father Michaellod's great alpenhorn rang out across the Kosipe Valley to call the faithful to Mass, just as it had done each holy day for the past thirty years. And for the first time in more than a decade, I was drawn to a church—apart from anything else, I wanted to hear the old man hold forth in Goilala.

Much of the service was indeed given in the Goilala language, but the sermon contained a strange mixture of Pidgin and English. After sternly commanding lactating mothers to cease breast-feeding in future during the Consecration of the Eucharist, Michaellod set to work on the most ferocious hellfire and brimstone sermon I had ever heard in my short-lived though unforgettable career as a Roman Catholic.

He began with the warning that this might be the last sermon they would ever hear from him, so they had better listen carefully. He was the only guide the Goilala possessed in following that narrow, winding road to eternal reward, yet he was *klosap long bagarap pinis* (nearing death) and might not last another year. He knew of their slothful, forgetful and downright evil character. He had been there when their grandfathers were still killing and eating each other! Even the new generation was falling away from the faith and into dastardly ways. Left to their own devices the entire tribe would surely perish in eternal hellfire.

The terrible tortures of hell were lovingly dwelt upon, and the multitudinous sins of the congregation spelt out in great detail. Strict, absolute adherence to Christian doctrine, Michaellod concluded, was the sole path to salvation.

I reflected later on the fact that he had spoken partly in English—I was one of the few in the congregation who could have understood a word.

As Mass concluded, even Father Michaellod's thundering words were gradually drowned out by a banshee-like wailing emanating from behind the church. When I asked him about this, Michaellod said that it was all the result of a terrible accident.

The wailer was a poor widow whose only possessions were two dearly loved pigs. One morning Michaellod had woken to find these pigs rooting up his carefully tended vegetable garden. He had previously promised summary execution for any such errant swine, yet was sorely troubled at the thought of depriving the widow of her only possessions.

Eventually he decided to take mercy upon her pitiful state, but still felt the need to teach people a lesson. He pushed his shotgun out of his bedroom window, closed his eyes and, without taking particular aim, let fly from a great distance with both barrels. To his horror, both pigs dropped, stone dead.

On every public occasion since, the widow had taken to reminding the priest of his heartless act. But as sorry as he was for his miscarriage of justice, he felt he couldn't offer the compensation she demanded, for fear of releasing an avalanche of similar claims.

By the time I knew him, arthritis prevented Father

Michaellod from cranking up the generator which lighted the mission by night, and I soon took over this duty. He still managed to work the churn, but appreciated help in making the soft and hard cheeses which he traded with his compatriots at nearby missions for rough red wine.

This simple priest, who was raised in the rural Europe of the early twentieth century, was much happier among New Guinea villagers than among modern westerners like myself. He would be lost and saddened if he were ever forced to return to modern Switzerland.

As we were busy cheese-making the morning after Christmas Mass, I asked Michaellod how he assessed his achievements. He looked remarkably calm as he explained to me that it had taken a thousand years to Christianise Europe. The Catholic Church was in no hurry at Kosipe.

THREE

Out of the ether

Everything was ready for the final goal of our expedition—the ascent of Mt Albert Edward. Early on the appointed morning, Geoff Hope, Bren Wetherstone, Ken Aplin and myself, accompanied by over a dozen Goilala, set off across the valley in drizzling rain. After about two hours' walk, much of it through the fabulous Kosipe swamp, we came to the southern face of the mountain and began a punishing ascent.

By the late afternoon, both altitude sickness and exhaustion began to tell on us. Geoff had vomited up his lunch on the trail some time before, and I was reduced, through sheer exhaustion, to crawling up some impossibly steep mossy slopes. Finally, I lay on the side of the trail, defeated. My pounding head felt as if it would split, my trembling legs would not respond to my commands.

Geoff stopped beside me and opened a can of Ox & Palm

bully beef. Desperately in need of energy, I ate it directly from the tin—skin, fat, the lot—remembering all the while hearing as a child that it was made of beef scraps, mostly lips, ears, scrotums. Revitalised nonetheless, I managed to move forward—and a few metres later the narrow ridge I was struggling up opened onto a broad valley.

A greater contrast with the confining moss forest could hardly be imagined. We had reached the Neon Basin at 3,000 metres elevation, a beautiful, wide, grassy valley perched high on the upper slope of the mountain. Ten thousand years ago it had been a lake, dammed by a glacial tongue coming from the mountain. On this afternoon the clouds lay far below, while above my head soared the vast glacier-carved crags of the summit itself.

On every rise stood clusters of New Guinea's fabulous Alpine Treefern (*Cyathea tomentosissima*), their trunks festooned with brilliant orange dendrobium orchids. The ground was covered with tussock grasses, while every now and then a rhododendron bush stood above the tussocks. The entire scene glowed bronze and orange in the afternoon light.

To this day the Neon Basin of December 1981 remains my enchanted place—the refuge I imagine myself in as a means of escape from the interminable boredom of committee meetings.

As I stood contemplating this wonderful landscape, the vision was suddenly snatched from me by a dense fog which came sweeping up the valley faster than I could walk. Soon I could barely see my hand in front of me. I felt the chill of water vapour on my skin and the silence of the enveloping cloud.

Losing all bearings in the mist, I *knew* the Goilala were right in believing that *masalai* (spirits) inhabited this place.

Lost and alone, and fearing heaven as Michaellod's sermon penetrated deep into that part of me where the lessons of my Catholic childhood were stored, I vomited Ox & Palm onto the alpine tussocks.

The sound of an axe biting into dry wood came, and guided me.

Our shelter, when I reached it, turned out to be a fine hunting lodge, constructed with treefern trunks, roofed with the leaves of the mountain pandanus and lined with the soft fronds of the Alpine Treefern. Around the walls hung the trophy bones of animals caught during previous hunts.

It was in this magical place that the unmistakable, slightly acrid smoky smell of a New Guinea hunting lodge first permeated my being. Even now I sometimes pull on a jumper in which the scent lingers, and am instantly transported to New Guinea.

In the middle of the hut lay a long fireplace, now blazing. Filled with smoke and decorated with animal bones and the sleeping brown bodies of our Goilala guides, the hut did somewhat resemble hell as I'd imagined it as a child. I lay down by the fire, and slept off my deep exhaustion.

The fire had died down before dawn, and I awoke shivering with cold, awaiting the sun. Our Goilala hunters and their dogs were also up. After eating a few baked *kaukau* (sweet potatoes), they headed out across the wet grass to the forest edge. I sat admiring the piccaninny dawn. White clouds lay evenly spaced, like ripples on a beach, against a pink sky. A bright moon still shone out over the Neon, frosting the grass with silver.

My first day on the job as a *real* field biologist in New Guinea was rather deflating. While Geoff and Bren sounded the old lake-fill, Ken Aplin and I had a very large basin to reconnoitre, and several hundred rat-traps to bait. We set out.

Our traps were aluminium box traps, which catch animals without harming them. They are, however, cumbersome and heavy. In our rat-trapping we were accompanied by Victor, a ten-year-old Goilala boy who had instantly adopted us. As I was still suffering from altitude sickness, any physical exertion left me quickly exhausted, and it was tiny Victor who, after a time, took up my heavy trap box, and to my amazement carried it effortlessly along. As I set the traps in promising places off the track, Victor would follow behind, whispering spells into the open trapdoors to enhance our success.

At the end of our line, when the trap box was empty, Victor shouldered a huge lump of timber and lugged it back to camp. I experimented furtively with the lump, and was embarrassed that in my reduced state I was barely able to lift it.

By afternoon, the camp had been put in order, the traps were in place, and we finally had time to explore our surrounds. In the middle of the basin we found a rock overhang which had been used as a shelter by human hunters and grass owls for generations. Its soft dirt floor was littered with small bones, giving us a good idea of the kinds of animals that inhabited the valley. Further afield we found the remains of a great grass nest made by a farrowing sow, while everywhere lay the droppings of wallabies and New Guinea wild dogs. The place was indeed rich in wildlife.

That evening the hunters returned loaded with possums. They were anxious to eat, so Ken and I had to work fast extracting samples and labelling specimens. One of the possums, a Coppery Ringtail, was brought in alive. We had never killed an animal before and wanted to dispatch it humanely. Fortunately, Ken and I, anticipating such occasions, had brought a bottle of ether along with us.

After allowing the possum to inhale what I thought was enough ether to fell an ox, Ken and I set to work. There were testicles to be cut out for chromosome studies and liver and kidney samples to be taken. To my horror, when we were nearly finished, our possum began to show signs of life. Quickly I fastened the ether-soaked rag to its muzzle and held it there until I was sure it was well and truly defunct.

As the hunters began their evening meal, excited chatter broke out among them. Finally, Andrew Keno (a Goilala who spoke a little English) came up to me and explained that the hunters had misidentified one of the possums. It was not the common *Kovilap* (Coppery Ringtail), but another, very rare kind. Indeed it was one of the very rarest and most delicious possums of all. They brought me a piece of the meat of this marvellous animal, which I tentatively bit into.

Immediately my tongue was afflicted with an appalling dead palsy.

Ether fumes assaulted my nose and stung my eyes. The gas had travelled throughout the body of the massively overdosed possum, and a brief roasting had done little to abate its potency.

Horrified by the thought of what the ether might do to the Goilala, I spent a largely sleepless night. As the hours passed, I monitored the snorts and groans of my companions. Finally, to my enormous relief, they all awoke fit and well in the morning.

After this, I learned to kill the larger marsupials with a sharp blow to the back of the neck. It brought virtually instantaneous death if done correctly and I was certain that the animal felt very little pain. It also ensured that the meat eaten by my friends was untainted.

I have often mused upon the differing concepts of animal cruelty possessed by tribal people and westerners. New Guinea villagers seem not to have our concept of animal cruelty. During my years of fieldwork I have been brought possums and wallabies with all limbs broken, with intestines and eyes hanging out. When I requested a hunter to put the suffering animal out of its misery, I was often told that it was already dead! In truth, the longer an animal lived the better it was for the hunter, for the meat did not then rot in the tropical climate.

I vividly remember one early morning at Telefomin, high in the mountains of western Papua New Guinea. I had gone to check a mist-net for bats which may have been caught during the night. Much to the disgust of my Telefol helpers—who accused me of wasting precious food—I released the bats not needed for research. But my helpers absolutely refused to allow me to free a small honeyeater that had got caught in the net.

One Telefol man took it back to camp, cradled gently in his palm. On arriving, he began casually to pluck it. *Alive.* I protested, but the man did not seem to understand. When all of the feathers had been removed, the naked atom of flesh looked quite ridiculous: a pink blob sitting in the hand of its plucker. The man picked up a tin with the lid partly open, placed a little cold water in it, dropped the bird inside, closed the lid and put it on the fire.

The chirping of the bird was almost unbearable. Finally, the tiny, naked body forced its way out of the tin and ran around the hut, much to the mirth of the Telefol. When it was recaptured I begged the fellow to kill it, but was told, as he replaced it in the tin, *No ken wari, masta, em bai dai* (Don't worry, it will die soon). I listened with dismay as the chirps became weaker and weaker, until they were overtaken by the sound of boiling water.

The morsel of protein hardly seemed worth the effort—it was eaten in one bite.

These cruelties, as we think of them, were countless. Pigs were castrated with slivers of bamboo in operations that took ages, the testicles being removed piecemeal and the remains used as bracelets. These same pigs were then blinded with lime rubbed into their eyes so that they would not wander. Some months later they would be killed by being stunned, then thrown live into a fire. Their charred yet still breathing bodies would be loaded onto canoes for the long journey home to the feast.

But the very people who did this could be highly solicitous of the health of their fellow humans. Nothing was too much trouble to help relieve the suffering of another person, even a stranger like myself. At times, they risked their lives to protect me from injury.

Just as challenging are some Melanesian ideas relating to environmental conservation. One morning I went to set up a camp at the edge of the forest about an hour's walk from Kosipe so that I could trap in the primary forest nearby. A few Goilala youths accompanied me and, as I set about straightening my camp, they began chopping at an enormous old *Libocedrus*, a native pine tree. This ancient relative of the cedars was a true patriarch of the forest, and was at least two metres thick at its base. After an age spent hacking away at it, the giant finally fell to earth with a deafening roar, preceded by the excited whoops of my Goilala companions.

To my amazement, they casually stripped a piece of bark from one side of the prostrate trunk with which to roof their makeshift shelter, then left the rest of the majestic tree to rot.

There were five hundred growth rings on the severed stump. The tree was at least half a millennium old.

Such behaviour made sense to the Goilala. For them, the forest was endless. This was simply a good opportunity to make a garden where none had been before.

As I sat counting the rings, my companions continued to fell the trees around me, expanding their new garden. My nervousness that a tree might fall on me became the basis of a great joke among these expert axemen. As a tree began to creak and groan, they would scream out to me to run to avoid being crushed.

First left!—no, right!—no no no, left, left!!!

As I dashed back and forth while the tree fell harmlessly away from me, they would all collapse screaming with laughter. Soon they had exhausted the local supply of standing timber and moved to a more distant place, but all afternoon the sound of falling trees reverberated through the forest.

FOUR

Life above the forest

As the days wore on atop Mt Albert Edward, our hut on the edge of the treefern-studded basin gradually filled with specimens, and we began to understand a little of the environment which surrounded us.

During our first excursions into the nearby forest we found the decaying trunks of the Alpine Treefern just inside the margin. This beautiful and distinctive species of treefern, with its finely divided leaves, can grow only in grassland, for it soon becomes overshadowed in forest.

Here, then, was clear evidence that the forest was advancing, smothering the tussocks and treeferns as it went. In places, the margin had all the appearance of a battle zone. Fires, lit by hunters, were slowing the advance of the alpine scrub, giving the tussock grassland a respite, or even winning back a few metres from the forest. On the whole, however, the forest seemed to have the upper hand.

Was this evidence of the greenhouse effect, I wondered, or just less use of the basin (and thus less burning) by people? Certainly, the last time the earth had warmed markedly (following the last ice age), the tree-line advanced from 2,100 metres to about 3,900 metres elevation. It remains lower, of course, in frost-hollows like the Neon.

We found that the innumerable tiny trackways running through the tussocks were made by two species of small rat. The more common was a drab little thing with a distinctive mousy odour. Known as the Moss-forest Rat (*Stenomys niobe*), it takes its scientific name from Niobe, a tragic figure from Greek mythology who lost her six sons and six daughters. It was perhaps the dense, blackish fur of this small rat that reminded some nineteenth-century naturalist of formal Victorian mourning dress, and prompted him to associate it forever with this figure of sorrow.

The other rat was beautiful, an inoffensive little red creature known as the Mountain Melomys (*Melomys rubex*). I became very fond of these mice as the days wore on. It was always a pleasure to feel their soft red fur, and to smell their pleasant scent after opening a trap, when the ten before had held only the more olfactorally challenging Moss-forest Rat. We would measure and weigh the animals, killing a couple to be kept as museum specimens, and release the rest.

Our hunters and their five dogs returned early one day, carrying a heavy sack. The highlight of our expedition had come.

They emptied the sack and I saw before me for the first time a living Long-beaked Echidna (*Zaglossus bruijnii*).

Long-beaks differ from the smaller Australian echidna in their denser fur (which can be so long as to obscure their spines), and their extended, down-curved bills. Long-beaked

Echidnas can weigh seventeen kilograms, and measure almost a metre from beak to tail tip. They are the very largest of the egg-laying mammals. Little did I realise then that this would be the first and last time I would see these majestic creatures in the wild.

We built a sturdy corral for our lovely female echidna—of palings two metres high. I hoped to deliver her alive to Baiyer River Sanctuary (near Mount Hagen) so that she might help found a breeding colony of this highly endangered animal. She, though, had other ideas. I was amazed, passing the corral a few hours after we had placed her inside, to find our echidna balancing precariously on top of the paling fence. These wonderful animals possess almost unbelievable strength and agility.

Our echidna did eventually reach the sanctuary—by way of Father Michaellod's toilet (it had a cement floor through which the animal could not burrow) and then a temporary cage in Port Moresby.

Several years later, while working on a wildlife documentary, I visited Baiyer River Sanctuary and became re-acquainted with my old friend. During filming, I had to enter the echidna enclosure at night. The echidnas remained immobile as long as the lights were on. But, when the lights were turned off to save power, things changed.

The first I knew of my old friend's approach was a wet, worm-like thing entering my boot. Then I felt a great, curved beak plunge down almost to my sole, so that the extraordinarily long pink tongue could tickle my toes.

The echidna and I were soon on terms of considerable intimacy, a state doubtless precluded during our earlier association by her fright on being captured. Long-beaked Echidnas really are the most remarkably intelligent and affectionate animals. Their bird-like faces allow no show of emotion. But they can show their feelings in other ways.

For many years Taronga Zoo in Sydney had a huge old male which was on very good terms with his keepers. Whenever he heard the lock turn in the enclosure door, he would trundle towards the entrance, then lie on his back like a wombat, waiting for his stomach to be scratched.

When a sprinkler system was installed in the enclosure, he would lie belly-up, ecstatic under the misty spray, his four-pronged erection startling passersby. Although already adult when captured, he had survived nearly thirty years in various zoos before his untimely death—from pneumonia brought on by his beloved sprinkler.

Were they more plentiful, and perhaps less powerful excavators, Long-beaked Echidnas would make companions as fine as dogs. But they may well be extinct before too long.

Reproduction in Long-beaked Echidnas presents a bit of an enigma to most New Guineans. Like all monotremes, or egg-laying mammals, they have no externally visible genitals (except when the male has an erection) nor even secondary sexual characteristics such as nipples. Furthermore, young ones are never seen. Presumably they remain hidden in burrows dug by their mothers.

The Goilala told me that echidnas did not breed like other animals, but that they possessed drills, rather like miniature rigs (some Goilala had seen these working at mining exploration camps), which they used to generate young. These drills, they told me, would be used to penetrate the forest floor, and when they had reached a suitable depth, a drop of blood would be secreted from the tip. This would eventually form itself into a young echidna. The parent would then visit the site regularly to feed the young with urine produced from the end of the 'drill'. When it was of almost adult size, the young would emerge.

At first I regarded this story as nothing more than a flight of fancy. It was only when I saw a male echidna rampant, so to speak, that I realised where the notion of the 'drill' had come from. The penis of the Long-beaked Echidna is a truly impressive organ. Ten centimetres long, it is surmounted at its head by a coronet of four large papillae which do indeed give it something of the appearance of a drill bit.

The Neon Basin also abounded with wallabies and giant rats. The wallabies (a kind of pademelon, or scrub wallaby, of the genus *Thylogale*) grow to about the size of a collie dog. And the giant rats of the Neon, at almost a metre long, are not that much smaller. Eventually, specimens of both these species were to be of great importance to my research, for both turned out to be unknown to science. As with these animals, it is often the case that species new to science go unrecognised in the field (especially by inexperienced researchers), and that detailed study and comparison is necessary in the lab to untangle their taxonomy. This was particularly true before 1990, when no guide to New Guinea's mammals existed.

Signs of wallabies were abundant in the grasslands of Mt Albert Edward in 1981. Their droppings littered the tussocks. By using dogs to locate them as they rested by day inside the forest, our hunters caught many. Much to my surprise, I later learned that Mt Albert Edward was one of the very few places in New Guinea where one could still see such wallabies. Elsewhere, such as in the highlands of Irian Jaya and on Mt Wilhelm (PNG's tallest mountain), they are long extinct.

As I learned this I began to wonder about the future of the Mt Albert Edward wallaby population. How much hunting would it take to exterminate them? After all, probably the entire population rested by day just inside the fringe of forest surrounding the grassland. Being so concentrated, they are easy targets for a hunter with dogs. Having visited places where they have been exterminated, I suspect they survive on Mt Albert Edward only because the forest is a little denser than elsewhere, and perhaps because hunting pressure is a little less. But with the influx of people to Kosipe, just a day's walk from the Neon, how will they fare in future?

The high-elevation wallabies (such as those of the Neon) differ from those living in the forests lower down. They are smaller, have denser coats and more thickly furred tails, and sport bright stripes over their rump and shoulders. In 1993 I described them as a new species, naming them *Thylogale calabyi* after my old friend John Calaby, who had just retired after devoting a lifetime to scientific studies.

The giant rats were more difficult to deal with. At the time we collected them I assumed that all belonged to a single, well-known species of woolly rat called *Mallomys rothschildi*. Eventually some of the tissues I collected were sent to the South Australian Museum for biochemical analysis. The laboratory wrote back inquiring whether I could possibly have made a mistake in labelling them, for their analysis showed they could not possibly all belong to one species. The critical specimen was a large female rat collected on the margin of the Neon Basin. Its tissues were strikingly different from all the others.

I went to examine the rat. Perversely, this one, of all the specimens collected, had met a dismal fate. It had been located in its burrow by hunting dogs, and was half consumed before we could retrieve it. All that we had been able to rescue were a hand, a foot, a piece of liver (frozen for analysis) and the skull. Faced with such incomplete data, I realised that I needed to examine all of the woolly rat specimens available if I was to resolve the enigma.

Having examined many specimens of woolly rats in museum collections in places as far afield as Canberra, Sydney, London, Hawaii, New York and Berlin, I came to the conclusion that there was not one but four species. The mangled specimen from Mt Albert Edward represented an unnamed species. Thankfully, its pitiful remains had retained enough diagnostic features for me to be able to distinguish it.

Finally, we were able to locate a few other, better preserved examples of this same species. The most complete was collected in 1945 near Mount Hagen by Captain Neptune B. Blood, an Australian kiap who had spent years in New Guinea and was known as the 'King of the Western Highlands'. He had sold the rat to the Australian Museum, where it had lain unrecognised until our study in 1988. I and my co-authors decided to name the new species *Mallomys istapantap*. The rather curious second part of the name came from what our hunters always told us of the species—*dispela i stap antap* (this animal lives on top of the mountain). Its penchant for elevated environments is also reflected in its common name, the Subalpine Woolly-rat.

The collection of tissues for analysis involves some practices which almost anyone except a biologist would find bizarre. Take for example the culture of chromosome preparations. These preparations are best made from cells taken from the testes. Obtaining and stabilising the samples is an involved process, necessitating the culturing of the sample at scrotal temperature.

First, one must slice open a testicle, then place its contents in a small plastic tube full of a culture medium. This must be sealed and placed beside one's own scrotum (or if you lack one, between the breasts) for an hour or so. The liquid is then drained off, some other operations performed, and a preservative added.

My Goilala friends, not surprisingly, found this to be an extraordinary process which commanded their deep attention. I needed to obtain samples from only a few individuals of each species we collected, but the process had become such an important ritual to the Goilala that they were quite disappointed whenever I passed over an animal without performing it. Indeed, whenever anyone new arrived in camp, they invariably requested a repeat performance.

By far the most common of the larger animals we encountered in the Neon were the cuscuses and ringtail possums. These are tree-dwelling marsupials that can weigh several kilograms. They are similar to Australia's brushtail and ringtail possums. During our sojourn there they fed us and our hunters, proving a welcome relief from the canned bully beef and mackerel that were our only other sources of protein.

Of all the possums, the Silky Cuscus (*Phalanger sericeus*) is one of the most attractive. About the size of a cat, its fur is long and luxurious, and as the common name suggests is silky to the touch. The back is a rich, almost blackish brown, which contrasts with the white belly. The creature has the peculiarity of walking around with its tail wound up tightly like a spring, so that it is not visible among the dense fur. This gives the robust animal the appearance of a small bear.

One day our hunters captured a female Silky Cuscus, which they killed. A half-grown, bright-eyed and irresistibly attractive joey in her pouch had, however, survived. Knowing that it was destined for a painful death and the cooking fire, I decided to try to keep it alive until I could place it in a zoo somewhere. It was clear that the bitterly cold nights on the mountain would kill it, so I wrapped it in a sock and slept with it curled snugly on my belly.

The first time we shared a sleeping bag I was awoken in the dead of night by a gentle and not unpleasant nibbling on my inner thigh. Moments later I rose vertically out of my bed with a yell of pain. A pair of red-hot tongs had grasped the end of my penis.

The baby cuscus had managed to thrust its head through one of the several holes in my sock and, seeking either revenge or succour, had bitten mightily into the first thing it encountered.

Inside the hut, all was madness. The Goilala beheld before them a frantic white man screaming unintelligibly, wearing the strange night attire of a single sock oddly attached to the end of his willie. All *I* could see were wild-eyed Goilala, loosing arrows randomly into the night as the imagined enemy closed in. This must be the dread Kukukuku—their traditional enemy whose land bordered the Neon, and whose presence made it a risky place to visit.

Total chaos. Eventually, when I could explain what had

happened, my Goilala companions all went back to their beds, muttering darkly about the *long long* (idiot) white man in their midst.

The trek down from the Neon Basin was not easy. Our group of at least twenty carriers was variously burdened. The two surest-footed were given the task of carrying the liquid nitrogen cylinder. This barrel-sized container is in reality a large vacuum flask. It was by far our most important and fragile item of field equipment, for in it were stored all our frozen tissues, the fruit of much labour.

This unwieldy object was suspended from a pole, to which it was tied tightly with bush vines. At each tilt from the horizontal it let out a puff of white vapour, remarkably similar to the mists which were so feared by the mountaineers.

Other carriers had less awkward but no less important burdens—the prickly Long-beaked Echidna in a sack, a plastic drum full of specimens preserved in formalin, a box of traps. I had my pack, and Percy, as my small cuscus was by then known.

My heart was in my mouth a hundred times on the descent as the flask tilted and the carriers wavered, tempted to drop their precious cargo and run.

But several days later I limped successfully into Woitape with Percy in hand and the cylinder safe.

FIVE

The poet and the python

The day of our departure from the mountains saw us all assembled at Woitape airstrip. Ken, still keen to augment our collections, was doing a little last-minute frog gathering in the nearby bush. I was relaxing, sitting next to our pile of equipment, when my attention was caught by a curious procession crossing the airstrip.

An entire village appeared to be heading our way. At the head of the group were two men carrying a large tea-chest strung on poles. This was placed before me in great excitement. I looked through the fly-wire screen which served as a lid, and understood what all the fuss was about. There, inside, sat curled the largest, blackest and fiercest-looking snake I had ever seen.

I later discovered that it was a Boelan's Python (*Liasis boelani*), a rare snake which is only found in New Guinea's mountains. It was nearly three metres long, and had soaked up the energising warmth of the morning sun.

Suddenly the snake struck. Its head, the size of my fist, rose violently against the fly-wire, shaking the tea-chest. For a moment its fangs—each over a centimetre long—stuck fast in the mesh. The crowd recoiled in horror, children wailing and women screaming.

Clearly, I was expected to deal with this snake.

Seeking inspiration as to how I might proceed, I asked the men how they had got it into the tea-chest in the first place. Well, they said, it had been found in the jungle while it was shedding its skin. It was then cold, and the scales covering its eyes were opaque, making it relatively easy to handle.

All that, alas, had now changed.

I badly wanted to purchase the snake, sensing that it was something special. The trouble was that there was no way that the tea-chest would fit into the Cessna which was to carry us to Port Moresby. The snake would have to be re-housed, preferably in a spare gunny sack, if it was to be transported.

With dread in my heart, I called upon one of the braver locals to distract the monster with a cloth. Gingerly I undid the fly-wire, and with a dash grasped the reptile behind the head. It seemed strangely calm as I withdrew it from the tea-chest. Perhaps it knew who was in control, and it was merely awaiting its opportunity.

In an instant it threw its coils tightly round my forearm and began to pull its enormous head through my hand. In retaliation, I grasped it by the tail with my free hand. This stymied it momentarily, but it soon had another coil on me, this time round my right knee.

I seemed to be losing the battle.

I tried to summon reinforcements. Hobbling from one group of Goilala to another, I begged for help.

What I needed was someone to hold open the gunny sack so I could dispose of this monster inside it. But everyone fled screaming in terror as the snake and its prospective meal approached them.

Then another coil was thrown around the hand which held the tail. I watched in amazement as my hand became miraculously fastened to my knee by the snake's muscular body.

Now I found myself performing a desperate sort of Russian bear dance on one leg, still begging urgently for a volunteer to hold the sack.

I was about to resign myself to a dismal end when Ken appeared, attracted by the screams of the retreating Goilala. He helped untangle the monster, then held the bag open as I flung the snake in. I fastened the mouth of the sack with string. The beast writhed and hissed inside. It would be a better guard of our equipment than I could ever be—by leaving it beside our luggage I could abandon my duties and enjoy the shade of the trees.

The time now came to pay for the snake. As the haggling went on Ken had a brilliant idea—we would pay for it in kind, and by the metre. We took out our remaining canned goods and, by laying the tins of Ox & Palm bully beef end to end, attempted to approximate the snake's length. Some of the locals suddenly believed this must be the mother of all snakes—five metres in length and growing by the minute. When I bluffingly offered to take the reptile from its sack to allow them to obtain a more accurate estimate, however, they quickly settled for a lesser length.

As we finalised our purchase, we heard the aircraft make its approach. It had come from Kosipe where it had picked up Penelope and Alec Hope, and was crammed with the Hopes' luggage and samples. Nonetheless we found sufficient nooks and crannies in the hold to stow most of our cargo.

Finally only the writhing gunny sack remained. The pilot, a florid, overweight Australian who subsequently flew into the side of a mountain, nervously asked what it contained. When told, he expressed great reluctance to have it aboard the aircraft at all. Attracted by the commotion, Alec Hope (bless him) stepped out of the front passenger seat and joined the conversation. It was then that I found out what a gentleman he really was. Without the slightest indication of reluctance, he said, 'Well, if a place can't be found for it elsewhere, it will just have to ride on my knee.'

The pilot looked set to have a heart attack as we took off. The floridness of his complexion increased alarmingly, and he was sweating profusely. Once, when he reached for a lever which lay between himself and A. D. Hope, his hand brushed against the struggling sack, with near-disastrous consequences. A Papuan woman, who had also booked a seat on the flight from Kosipe, actually attempted to open the window and disembark, mid-flight, when she heard what was in the sack.

On touching down in Port Moresby I lost no time taking the snake to the Department of Environment's crocodile farm at Moitaka. There it lived happily for some years, terrifying several generations of Port Moresby school children.

Now I had to take care of Percy the possum. We soon discovered that he suffered greatly from the lowland heat. So (much to the dismay of some of the staff at Burns Philp) he spent several weeks in their cool store, then in an air-conditioned office, before finally arriving safely at Taronga Zoo in Sydney.

The time had come for me to leave Papua New Guinea. Ken and I packed our specimens tightly into drums and obtained the necessary paperwork to export them to Australia.

When we touched down in Sydney, the long trek seemed to be over. On the other side of the customs and quarantine barrier our friends and family were waiting.

I must have looked less than trustworthy in those days. Or perhaps it was our sinister-looking cargo of black drums and steel canisters that alerted the officials. Whatever the case, we

were taken aside by a bunch of severe-looking uniformed officers with sniffer dogs, and given a complete search.

They squeezed out my toothpaste tube, opened each letter
and envelope, and went through each smelly drum. Meanwhile,
we staunchly maintained that every single specimen had been
preserved in formalin and was registered legally on our
import permit, and was thus eligible for entry into Australia.

After a gruelling three hours, our patience was wearing
thin. Finally I was waved on just as the last items from Ken's
pack were being checked. I saw an officer retrieve a roll of zip-
lock plastic bags. Ken said irritably that it was a roll which we
had not even opened.

As the officer unzipped one of the bags, an extraordinary
scene took place. He dropped the bag, recoiling with nose
wrinkled. The sniffer dogs seemed to fall into paroxysms.
Their delicate noses, trained to detect the faintest odour of
any illicit substance, were clearly under violent assault.

Ken, white-faced and horrified, finally remembered where
he had hurriedly put the frogs all those days ago when he
heard the screams which heralded my struggle with the
python.

The serpent now had its final revenge.

PART II

MIYANMIN

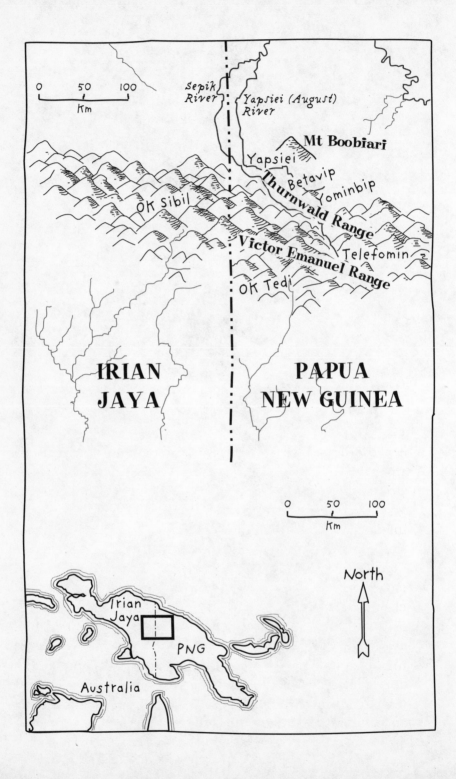

SIX

Spat from the sky

For two long years after my trip to Mt Albert Edward I was compelled to remain in Australia. I had begun a doctoral degree in zoology. My topic was the evolution of kangaroos. It gave little opportunity for more work in New Guinea, but things were not entirely hopeless, since the island is home to one obscure but fascinating genus.

Tree-kangaroos are among the most extraordinary animals ever to have evolved. They are distant relatives of Australia's rock-wallabies but, because of their specialised life in the tree-tops, some have come more to resemble koalas and pandas than kangaroos. Australia has two rather primitive species living in the rainforests of north-east Queensland, but at least a dozen different kinds had been recorded in New Guinea. These are found throughout the mountainous portions of the island, but are elusive and difficult to study.

The evolutionary pathway that led tree-kangaroos into the rainforest canopy is still far from clear. It seems likely, however, that their ground-dwelling ancestors found little to eat on the dark forest floor. Those able to climb into the trees to obtain food were advantaged. Even today, however, tree-kangaroos can look rather clumsy in the tree-tops.

My chances of doing useful work in New Guinea on these shy animals seemed remote, but halfway through my studies I could bear no more. I had to return.

My supervisor, Professor Michael Archer, must have sensed my restlessness. I will always be grateful to him. He was willing to tolerate yet another interruption to my degree that I might roam the Melanesian jungles.

Michael obtained funds from the National Geographic Society to send me back to New Guinea. And so, by January 1984, I was ready to venture into the field once more. This time, my destination was very different, for I had decided to work in the remote Yapsiei and Telefomin areas of Sandaun Province, in far western Papua New Guinea.

By the time the Australian colonial administration of the territories of Papua and New Guinea ended in 1975, most of the country had been brought under government control. Only a few areas were enticingly marked on the map as 'uncontrolled territory'. Access to them was strictly limited before independence, and even by 1984 there was little government influence over the lives of the people inhabiting these last wild areas.

I chose Yapsiei as my study site because it was at the heart of one of the largest pieces of uncontrolled territory marked on the map. It had changed little during the nine years following independence. In 1981 I had seen something of Papua New Guinea as it was in the *taim bilong masta*. I chose Yapsiei now because I wished to experience New Guinea as it was *taim bipo*, that is, before European colonisation had irrevocably altered the ecology of the Melanesian lands and people. Through my studies I hoped to understand that timeless synergy which exists between a highly co-evolved forest people and their environment. Through this study I hoped to perceive the pressures that have shaped an ecosystem as well as a culture.

On this first trip to Yapsiei I was fortunately accompanied by anthropologist Dr Don Gardner of the Australian National University. He had worked with the West Miyanmin since 1975 and is the only outsider I know to have mastered the highly complex Miyanmin language. I owe everything I know of these 'last people' to him and the entrée he gave me into Miyanmin society.

Because we anticipated a long stay at Yapsiei, we had accumulated a vast pile of equipment. This rapidly turned into a major headache for, due to a shortage of aircraft in Port Moresby, we found it impossible to get our equipment on a scheduled air service. The only option was to charter an aircraft. None of the larger airlines had one to spare, but a small, now defunct company called AvDev had a Cessna which could do the job.

The morning of our charter flight saw us cramming every available space aboard the aircraft with equipment and people. Finally it was filled to bursting with our voluminous drums, liquid nitrogen flasks, packs and food. As we sped down the runway at Jackson Airport, our little aircraft strained to take to the air.

Forty minutes into the flight, the Gulf of Papua stretched from horizon to horizon below us. I was casually wondering about the number of crocodiles and sharks inhabiting the murky water when the aircraft yawed violently. I looked out of the window. A stream of oil was issuing from the left-hand engine.

The propeller slowed. The oil turned to smoke—and flickering flame!

The pilot was looking unnaturally pale and shaking as he reached for the button to activate the fire extinguisher. Then he bent down and grabbed a large map, which he spread out right across the windscreen.

He seemed to study the detail of the Gulf area minutely.

I had always been somewhat resigned about the possibility of perishing in an air disaster. In the unlikely event of it happening, I believed that at least everything would be over quickly. As I contemplated the pilot and his map I began to feel that I was very much mistaken in this. I leaned forward and asked him what was wrong.

'Can't maintain altitude on one engine. We have to find an airstrip.'

For forty minutes we gazed at the waters of the Gulf as they loomed ever closer. Forty minutes is a long time to contemplate death by impact, drowning or shark attack.

At last the sight of land below us brought hope. Although the fire was out, the left wing was by this stage streaked black with oil and we were still descending. Nevertheless, it now seemed as if we might make it back to Port Moresby.

This incident remained with me for many years. I have since had countless flights in other small aircraft, a few almost as bad. Somehow the experience seems to have helped me handle them better. But very occasionally (sometimes when travelling on the safest of flights) I panic. I think I can smell noxious fumes in the cabin, or hear that the engines are not running smoothly. The plane seems to skew in the air. It is then that I must use my most potent weapon against panic—one I learned that day over the Gulf of Papua. I close my eyes and sleep.

That day I roused myself just before we landed. I stepped out of the plane quite a different person from the one who had stepped in. My youthful sense of immortality was gone. I now saw the risk in many of the things I did.

We all gathered round as the engineer inspected the damage. The cause was immediately obvious—a tappet cover with a push-rod protruding through it, both drenched with oil. A small piece of the aluminium cover had been dislodged and was lying in a pool of oil. I took this tiny thing and put it in my wallet.

In later years, when I have been in difficult circumstances in aircraft, I have felt for it, drawing comfort from the thought that one can walk away from such crises.

In a few days the engine was repaired and we squeezed back into the aircraft for another attempt. This time, all went well, and after several hours in the air we arrived at Tabubil, then flew on to Telefomin. After a brief stop there, we headed off on the last leg of our aerial journey.

The Telefomin Valley lies nestled in mountains close to the geographic heart of the island of New Guinea. Yapsiei, a lonely government station, lies some eighty kilometres west-north-west, where the August or Yapsiei River leaves the mountains and enters the vast Sepik floodplain. To reach Yapsiei you must take a light aircraft from Telefomin. You soon leave this last frontier settlement behind as the plane tracks along the awesome Sepik Gorge. To the right, the three distinctive peaks of the Drei Zinnen Range tower above the tiny Cessna, while the abrupt, almost vertical face of the Sepik Gorge shuts out all sights to the left. Below surges the mighty Sepik River itself, confined in a narrow cleft cut into lime-stone. The river appears white with the swirl of rapids. In that watery chaos, entire trees can be seen moving along, tumbled end over end by the furious torrent.

Where the Sepik disgorges onto its floodplain, the aircraft banks sharply right, crosses a ridge clothed in primaeval forest and flies into the valley of the August River. Near where the August begins to thread its way over the floodplain, a small, primitive airstrip has been cut out of the forest. It is the first break in the canopy since Telefomin, many kilometres away.

The Yapsiei airstrip is poorly positioned, for its approach end is constantly being eroded away by the August River, which twists and turns restlessly in its bed. With each advance of the river, the shortened strip becomes more dangerous to land on. As a result, the strip (which is also poorly drained) is under constant threat of closure. Staying at Yapsiei, I always dreaded that the strip would be declared closed, leaving me with no way out.

At the top end of the airstrip lie the few buildings that constitute the government station. Yapsiei was established in 1973. It had attracted the Sepik peoples from downstream and the West Miyanmin from the upper reaches of the August River. By 1984 it already had a distinctly derelict look. Grass grew rank along the paths, and mould covered the painted walls of the fibro-cement buildings.

As I stepped out of the plane onto that airstrip for the first time, a blast of hot, suffocatingly humid air enveloped me. I looked at the people crowding around. Most of the men were wearing nothing but a tiny penis gourd, the women a short grass skirt. A few were dressed in the dirty, tattered remnants of western clothes. Almost all were disfigured by disease. Men with swollen scrotums and gross, disfigured legs jostled against me. A disgusting, sweet smell filled the air. I wondered what kind of place I had come to. Did I really intend to spend three months of my life here?

And indeed Yapsiei, I found, was a hell on earth in more ways than one.

Although about 200 kilometres inland, Yapsiei Station stands barely 100 metres above the level of the sea. The days are often made intolerably hot and humid by the baking air which rises off the Sepik floodplain and banks up against the abruptly rising mountains. By afternoon, a rush of cooler air descends the mountains, often bringing with it thunderstorms of titanic proportions. Occasionally these storms are so ferocious that they sound like the approach of jet aircraft screaming down the valley. When such storms hit, the place becomes chaos. Trees writhe in the first gusts of wind. Then, within seconds, nothing can be seen through the pelting rain—not even a hand held in front of your face. The thunder is so loud and continuous that it blocks out all other sound, and it soon seems that the world has become strangely silent. The true silence that develops an hour or two later, as the storm makes its way downriver, is all the more eerie for this effect.

By 1984, problems were beginning to develop at Yapsiei. The station was built primarily to attract and control the West Miyanmin. They originally came from the mountains and have little resistance to malaria, filariasis (elephantiasis) and the many skin diseases that thrive in the lowlands. As a newly contacted people, they have also had to contend with introduced diseases such as influenza, against which they have little immunity.

A generation previously, the Miyanmin had lived in small, fortified villages on the rugged spurs surrounding the upper August River, which they know as the Yapsiei. There, at about 600–1,000 metres elevation, the air is cool and disease had not been such a problem. But both water and gardening land had lain far distant.

When the Australian administration brought a respite from the incessant warfare which existed with neighbouring groups, most West Miyanmin had moved downslope onto the fertile river flats. There they remained scattered and isolated, which at least gave some protection from contagion. But with the founding of Yapsiei station in 1973 they congregated in an environment truly conducive to the transmission of disease. They were also close to sources of contagion such as visiting Europeans and the Sepik people who lived adjacent to and in the station.

In 1984 the mortality rate in the Yapsiei area was truly horrific. In some Miyanmin villages, infant mortality reached 100 per cent. Bloated stomachs, denoting malnutrition and chronic swelling of the spleen due to malaria, were almost universal in the few surviving children, as well as many of the adults. *Grile*, a form of ringworm which makes the skin flake in great concentric circles, was also ubiquitous. It can disfigure every inch of skin on one's body. It was the odour of *grile* which had first greeted me when stepping off the plane at Yapsiei, and I can still recall the sweet, sickly smell today. Throughout my stay at Yapsiei during 1984, the stench was inescapable.

The most disfiguring affliction suffered by the Miyanmin was doubtless filariasis. Many Miyanmin women had one breast grossly swollen, while the majority of the men suffered from swelling of the scrotum (many to enormous size), and swelling and disfigurement of the lower limbs. Kebuge, a West Miyanmin man of about my age who was to become one of my close friends, was already infected when I first met him in 1984. Over the years of visiting, I watched helplessly as his scrotum and left leg swelled, until finally his left foot was nothing but a mass of wart-like growths, his scrotum a bloated mass the size and shape of a football.

SEVEN

The last people

Our arrival at Yapsiei station did not mark the end of our journey. The terrible suffering which disease had brought to the Miyanmin had encouraged many of them to move back upriver, into the small villages which they had so recently left. After some discussion, we decided to base ourselves at Betavip, a village located at the confluence of the Skgonga and Usake Rivers, one and a half day's walk northwest of Yapsiei.

The walk to Betavip was flat, but nonetheless the heat and humidity, muddy track and numerous leeches and mosquitoes made it challenging. I was actually rather pleased about the leeches, for where there are lots of leeches there must also be many mammals for them to live off. This augured well for my work.

We had employed about forty Miyanmin to convey our equipment to Betavip. They straggled out over a distance of several kilometres, meeting only for smoko and lunch. At lunch on the first day we stopped at a little settlement—just a few huts—perched on a high bank of the August River. A man was sitting on the step outside his hut, holding newborn twin boys.

At first the scene seemed delightful. But then I noticed the vacant look on the man's face. One of our carriers whispered that the man's wife had died in childbirth the previous night. With a leaden feeling in my throat, I asked if there was a wet-nurse nearby who could suckle the babies.

An empty gesture was the only response.

Sick at heart, I gave the man our supply of powdered milk—knowing that the milk would be mixed in unmeasured proportions with unboiled water in dirty cups. There was little hope that it would give the babies even the slightest chance of survival. They had looked so untouched by the filthy world they had been born into. They had looked so healthy.

By that afternoon the imposing peak of Mt Boobiari appeared almost straight ahead. The second day's walk took us around its base, then on to Betavip. I was surprised when we entered Betavip on the afternoon of the following day. The village turned out to be a small, pleasant collection of huts inhabited by about eighty people. The square houses were made of poles, neatly thatched over with folded pandanus leaves. All were raised a metre or two off the ground and planted round with brightly coloured shrubs and fruit trees. A vast tract of primary forest, where we would work, lay nearby.

Entering the village, we were surrounded by its inhabitants. After a while, they showed us a hut where we could stay. But we did not have a good introduction to Betavip.

Tired from the walk, we removed our boots and socks, and hung them in the sun to dry. A few hours later one team member went to retrieve his new woollen socks, only to find them well and truly fly-blown.

The first few days of our stay at Betavip were all but unbearable, not because of any physical discomfort, but because of the undying curiosity of the people. Each hour of the day our hut was filled with bodies. When they first arrived, people would stay respectfully near the door, but as the crowd swelled they would edge inside. Finally, a child with a long, green gobbet of snot dangling from its nose would be peering over my notebook, threatening to add to the chaotic marks I was inscribing there. Beside me someone else, with a huge open sore on his leg, would be rubbing up against me. The hot breath and the general stuffiness of the hut would lead me towards a slow implosion. It was all I could do to stifle a scream.

Dinnertime was, if possible, even worse. Then the same crowd, all of whom were hungry, would watch solemnly every mouthful we ate. The air was thick with the smell of *grile*.

At first I simply could not eat under these circumstances. Instead I would hand my dinner to a child in the crowd. But soon, plain, undisguised hunger did away with my scruples, and I ate oblivious to my surroundings.

Worst of all was going to the toilet. The decrepit village pit toilet was something to be avoided at all cost. Indeed, on my one and only visit I got the distinct impression that it was not built to hold the weight of a European. To avoid being plunged headlong into shit, I took to wandering a long way into the bush to relieve myself. During such expeditions, I would invariably be followed by a cloud of small children, eager to see what wonders I might perform in the forest. Louring looks, shouted obscenities and vigorous arm-waving were of no use. It was only when I began to take down my trousers that, my mission becoming obvious, the numbers seemed to diminish at all. Even then I sometimes felt the glare of myriad tiny eyes fixed on me from among the foliage.

This lack of privacy was particularly unfortunate in view of Miyanmin sensibilities regarding waste elimination. I soon learned that the very worst breach of Miyanmin etiquette is to break wind in public. So great is their abhorrence of such a breach that the only equivalent taboo I can think of in our society is masturbating in public. One evening Don, who had been suffering a stomach complaint, did let one fly. Our Miyanmin hosts hung their heads in shame and covered their eyes with their hands. Finally, our translator Kegesep saved the day.

'Well,' he said in Miyanmin, breaking the tension, 'everybody does have an arsehole, after all.'

The curiosity of the Miyanmin did abate somewhat after several weeks, and the moment came when I found myself alone in the hut. After a few minutes of relief though, the silence felt ominous—and I wandered perversely out onto the porch in the hope of engaging someone in conversation!

Our initial stay at Betavip was a formative experience. It was there that I became a competent speaker of Pidgin and made my first close Melanesian friends. It was also there that I gained my first real insights into a Melanesian culture.

The Miyanmin are, by their own reckoning, the 'last people'. That is, they were virtually the last people in Papua New Guinea to live a lifestyle largely unaffected by the European influence. The Miyanmin count this as a misfortune, and are acutely aware that almost everyone else is better off than they are. They bemoan the fact, for instance, that they still do not possess a village council, but instead must make do with a *luluai* (village head-man) and *tultul* (assistant), both of whom are given a badge denoting their rank. In reality, the Miyanmin are not governed so differently from many other remote villages in this regard. In many villages the duties of two men, called the 'council' and the 'committee', conform precisely to those carried out by *luluai* and *tultul*. Despite this, it matters to the Miyanmin that the Government has apparently forgotten to grant them this supposedly more advanced form of administration. This feeling is reinforced by the fact that, owing to their remoteness, the Miyanmin are truly disadvantaged by their minimal health care, educational opportunities and lack of access to western goods.

In pre-contact times, the Miyanmin had one of the most unusual lifestyles in New Guinea. Linguistically and culturally, they show many affinities with the Mountain Ok peoples of central New Guinea, yet they inhabit the lowlands and foothills. It seems likely that their ancestors had migrated from the mountains to the lowlands generations earlier. The impoverished resource base available to them at low elevations, as well as their susceptibility to diseases—especially childhood ones—seem to have forced them into their highly unusual ecological niche.

The Miyanmin used to call themselves the 'road highway men', in reference to their habit of rising before dawn every morning to check the muddy paths leading to their village for the footprints of intruders. If any were found, the village was put on an immediate war alert.

The need for such vigilance stemmed from the reprisals which the Miyanmin invited, for they themselves were among the most avid raiders in New Guinea. Even during the early 1980s they would refer to the neighbouring Atbalmin people as *bokis es bilong mipela* (literally, our refrigerator). While there is a myth among westerners that most New Guineans were cannibals, cannibalism as it was manifested among the Miyanmin is an extremely rare thing among New Guinea cultures.

Before 1973 the West Miyanmin would divide the year into two seasons—the drier time was the pig-hunting season, when they would descend to the floodplain to hunt pigs and other game. The wettest part of the year, when the lowlands were flooded, was the man-hunting season. Then the Miyanmin would travel upwards to the highland valleys, which are densely populated by Telefol, Atbalmin and other peoples. The raids they would stage there had often been years in the planning.

My constant companions at Betavip were Kegesep, a *turnim tok* (translator) who spoke good Pidgin and so could translate from Miyanmin into Pidgin for me, and Anaru, the *luluai* of Betavip village. It was through these people that I learned in a very intimate way about how the Miyanmin once lived, and how their past continues to affect them.

Kegesep was a slight, nervous person, who dressed in dirty shorts and a shirt. He was worried endlessly about *sanguma* (sorcery). Don Gardner told me a story about him which revealed much about how Kegesep saw the world. Don and he had been travelling far up the Skgonga River during an influenza epidemic. It was, perhaps, one of the first such epidemics to hit the area. Their travel was made perilous by the taut social situation resulting from the wildfire-like spread of the disease and its many fatalities. Everyone blamed the epidemic on sorcery by their neighbours, and reprisal raids were expected at any moment.

One morning Don entered Kegesep's hut to find him grey and stricken. It slowly emerged that the previous night Kegesep had gone to the edge of the camp to piss. There he had felt something brush against his leg. It was a snake, he said, which was attempting to climb his leg and enter his anus. Kegesep knew that the snake had been sent by enemies to weaken him. He explained that as a youth he had seen many such snakes taken from the intestines of the victims of his father's raiding parties. Kegesep knew that those snakes had been sent in advance, using witchcraft, in order to weaken their victims.

The 'snakes' Kegesep saw in the bodies of the slain were doubtless the impressive *Ascaris* roundworms which are ubiquitous in human populations in remote areas of Melanesia. These large, active intestinal parasites do indeed superficially resemble white snakes.

Don understood the seriousness of Kegesep's situation, but

was at a loss as to how to help. Finally he gave Kegesep two aspirin, explaining that they were medicine to kill any snakes which may have entered him.

Kegesep made a speedy recovery. I have often been amazed at the beneficial effect simple remedies such as aspirin or vitamin pills have on people such as the Miyanmin. For those with serious vitamin deficiencies there is, perhaps, an almost immediate improvement in general well-being after swallowing a vitamin pill. Likewise, for someone who has never experienced an analgesic, the relief that even a simple aspirin brings can seem tremendous.

I liked Kegesep very much. He was always laughing or smiling, and invariably took the trouble to correct my stumbling Pidgin. It was saddening to think of the numerous fears and obstacles which beset him in his everyday life. I gave him my shirt when I left Yapsiei in 1984. Kegesep died soon after my last visit to Yapsiei in 1986.

Anaru was a powerful man with greying hair, probably in his late forties. He was by far the most healthy man in his generation at Betavip, showing no sign of illness at all except for the usual *grile*. He wore nothing but a short penis gourd, allowing his fine physique to be shown at its best.

I got to know Anaru well when, after spending only a few days at Betavip, I decided to climb Mt Boobiari, the 1,200-metre-high limestone peak which rose abruptly a short distance from the village. The mountain was reputed to be home to one of New Guinea's rarest and most spectacular mammals, Goodfellow's Tree-kangaroo (*Dendrolagus goodfellowi*), which the Miyanmin know as *Timboyok*. This beautiful, chestnut-coloured kangaroo has a long tail mottled with gold, two golden stripes running down its back, and striking blue eyes. It is at home in the tree-tops of New Guinea's oak forests. But almost nothing was then known of it in the wild.

My companions on the trip were Anaru, Deyfu and Imefoop. Anaru and Deyfu were superb hunters. Imefoop, on the other hand, was frail and sickly. His body had been devastated by tuberculosis since childhood, leaving him with little strength. Imefoop had been enlisted as one of our carriers at Yapsiei Station. Don, who knew him quite well, was happy for him to carry our kettle, for which he was paid four kina per day (about six Australian dollars), the same wage as our other carriers. Even with this light burden, Imefoop was often left gasping by the time we called smoko.

Imefoop was extremely pleased to carry for us from Yapsiei to Betavip. The matter was not solely one of money for him. In truth, Imefoop had almost no standing in the community. He was the butt of endless jokes and taunts by the village children, and was largely ignored by the adults. Now he was being paid equal wages to work alongside more able-bodied Miyanmin. For once he was being taken seriously.

By 1986, just two years after we climbed Boobiari, tuberculosis had all but destroyed Imefoop's frame. Fluid accumulated in his abdomen, then flooded into his penis and scrotum, causing immense pain and disfigurement. One day, when the end was near, he approached Don and opened the blanket he had wrapped himself in.

'Look what has happened to me,' he said, in a voice filled with anguish and shame.

In death Imefoop gained a touch of the dignity and influence which had so sadly eluded him in life. As he lay in his hut dying, he shouted out that he was going to punish those little boys who had taunted him for so long. When he died, he said, his spirit would fly to the headwaters of the Skgonga River. There it would cause a landslide which would muddy the water, making it impossible for the children to dive for a quartz stone, their favourite pastime.

Soon, his relatives and friends crowded around him. Each asked for some favour or other which he could bestow on them when he reached the spirit world. Imefoop was at last being treated as a man of consequence.

EIGHT

Boobiari

The climb up Mt Boobiari was short but steep. Mercifully, most of it was through tall primary forest, which got cooler and firmer under foot as we ascended the slope. At about 800 metres elevation we emerged unexpectedly onto a tiny ridge covered in *kunai* (grassland). There, a patch of tall cane grass grew in a small hollow. It was the kind of cane from which arrows are made. Deyfu bent down and gently plucked a few stalks. When I asked him what he was doing, he said quietly, '*Papa bilong mi i stap*' (My father is here). It was a moment before I understood that the cane had been planted atop his father's grave. Suddenly, the symbolism of his gesture overwhelmed me.

The little clearing marked the site of a village which had been abandoned perhaps twenty years earlier. It was a splendid location as far as defence was concerned, for the entire upper reaches of the Usake River could be seen from here. Any enemies would be sighted long before they came near. Despite its defensive advantages, one could not help thinking of the poor women. Every day for countless centuries they had trekked down the mountain to work in their gardens. Each evening they had carried food, bamboo canes full of water, and babies back up the 800-metre ascent.

Another few hundred metres up the mountain we reached a small hut. It was just a roof supported on four sticks a metre or two above the ground. Here, we rested and boiled tea. Deyfu fashioned his canes into arrows, clamping them between his teeth to straighten them.

We were to spend a week at this place.

A few hours later we continued our walk to the summit, which we reached by following a rocky path a kilometre or so on from the hut. As we neared the peak, the vegetation became stunted and wisps of mist lay between the trees. A few more steps and we were at the summit itself, the path ending abruptly at a precipice.

There we had a surprise. A large eagle-like bird was perched in the leafless branches of a stunted tree which overhung the cliff. Although it goes by the ungracious name of the Long-tailed Buzzard (*Henicopernis longicauda*), this is an impressive animal. New Guinea's second-largest forest-dwelling bird of prey, its feathers are shades of soft brown, and it has a long, barred tail. It is rarely seen at close range—this was my only view of it at the distance of just a few metres in all my years in New Guinea.

It glided out over the valley.

Below, through the swirling mist, there were glimpses of the Usake River and the cluster of huts which make up Betavip. I suddenly felt what it meant to be the only European to have scaled Mt Boobiari. I felt a very long way from anywhere.

On the lonely nights we spent together on the mountain, Anaru told me of raids he had taken part in as a young man. The first step towards making a successful raid, he said, was for a big man to 'make ropes'. By this he meant that a warrior who wished to stage a successful raid must create a network of social obligations among the scattered Miyanmin communities, so that enough adult males could be gathered together to undertake a successful raid. 'Ropes' were made by marrying off daughters, distributing piglets and meat, and cementing ties through other gifts. Once the strategic alliances had been forged, the work of planning the raid could begin.

If the raid was directed towards the Atbalmin, then a cane suspension bridge had to be constructed over the Sepik River, which separates the lands of these two people. This might take several weeks. Then, an appropriate village must be located and scouted. It should be a little isolated, containing perhaps forty or fifty people. It was of crucial importance that every one of the inhabitants be killed or captured in the raid, as one escapee could alarm neighbouring villages, who would then descend upon the Miyanmin before they made good their escape.

Anaru described how the village would be surrounded at night. The attack often took place near dawn, when the huts were rushed. The killing had to be quick and total. The men and older women were usually dispatched by being grabbed from behind, and a sharpened cassowary leg bone thrust violently downwards into the gap between collar bone and shoulder blade, so as to pierce the lungs.

Anaru mimed a demonstration using an old blood-stained dagger, with me as a mock victim. The feeling of his sinewy arms around my neck pinning my body to his, and the point of bone biting into my skin, sent a shiver down my spine. It was all done so expertly.

The bodies had then to be butchered, again quickly and efficiently. The head, arms and legs were detached from the torso using bamboo knives. Then the torso would be gutted, and tied, much like a backpack, to the back of the man who was to carry it. The head was carefully wrapped in a package of palm leaves and carried slung from a looped cane handle. A leg and an arm would be thrown over each shoulder, to be grasped in pairs by the wrist and ankle. The bearer would then begin the long trek back to his village. The community would eat well in the next few days. If he was exceptionally lucky, he might also carry away a child strung in a *bilum* (string bag) over his shoulders, or herd a terrified young girl before him.

These raids were vital to the Miyanmin, in both social and physical terms. They gave meaning to the lives of men, who sometimes schemed for years to carry off a successful raid. If they could succeed just once, their names would ring down through the generations. The raids also brought a cornucopia of protein to a malnourished people. Yet even this was not their most important product, for (what mattered most to the Miyanmin) they brought children.

Even in the days before their move to Yapsiei, infant mortality was dreadfully high among the Miyanmin. Once a child had survived its first few years of life, its chances of making it through to adulthood were much improved. Such older children were valued, so that even children adopted after raids were cherished and brought up in loving families.

The full significance of this came to me in 1986, when I visited Yominbip, perhaps the most remote Miyanmin settlement of all. There I met a close family which had been forged in just this way. But that story must wait its turn.

I confess to having spent a few uneasy nights in the shelter on Mt Boobiari after Anaru told me of his earlier life. He clearly loved the 'good old days' and told his story with great relish.

Our days of hunting on Mt Boobiari were a strange mixture of intense pleasure and almost insufferable discomfort. The shelter was so small that it was impossible to stay dry under it during the daily downpour. At night, too, various parts of our anatomy would be exposed to the persistent rain, either by poking out from under the hut, or because of its many holes. Worse, it was so low that I could not stand up in it, and often could not shelter fully from the sun. Despite its disadvantages, there really was no alternative. The ridge it sat on was so narrow that there was literally nowhere else to go.

The worst annoyance on the mountain were the sweat bees. They discovered us very early on. Sweat bees are minute, stingless bees which can swarm by the thousand from dawn until dusk. As their name suggests, they drink sweat. The vast clouds which swarmed about the shelter on Mt Boobiari set up a high-pitched hum which did not cease while there was daylight. They are incredibly tenacious creatures, and will not move from your skin until they are squashed. They climb into your ears, eyes, mouth and nose, under your shirt, pants, socks and hair, by the thousand. The feeling of ten thousand tiny tongues lapping simultaneously at my skin was a torture which soon drove me to distraction.

To make matters worse, one bee in a thousand is in fact another species. This one stings with the ferocity of a high-voltage electric shock. Rest your hand against a tree or pole of the hut, and it strikes. Go to pick up a tool, or brush against the shelter's roof, and it strikes again. Brush bees from your face or arm, and the electrode explodes into action yet again. To sit for a minute in such a cloud of insects is bad enough. Every second is counted. But to spend days on end, with no possible relief, is an absolute nightmare. I even looked forward to the mosquitoes of the dusk, despite the risk of malaria they carried.

For some inexplicable reason, my animal traps caught absolutely nothing the whole time we were camped on Boobiari. The hunters did better, and it was the wondrous beasts located by Anaru and Deyfu that held me there. On our first day Deyfu returned to camp with the body of a large rat in his hand. It was the size of a small cat, and had whiskers which extended more than fifteen centimetres on either side of its face. Its fur was a rich brown above and white below. Remarkably, its balls were larger than those of any of us humans.

At first I could not identify this strange creature. Was it a White-tailed Rat (*Uromys caudimaculatus*, a species common in Australia) with elephantiasis? No, the tail scales were too large. Then I remembered a description I had read some years before of New Guinea's very rarest large rodent. Named *Xenuromys barbatus*, which means 'strange mouse with a beard', it was reported to resemble superficially the common White-tailed Rat. I trembled with the thought that I might be holding one of only five *Xenuromys* ever seen by a European. If so, I would have the privilege to be the first ever to know the weight of this beast, to know where it was sheltering when found, to look into its stomach and learn of its diet, and even to speculate on its need for such titanic genitals. Indeed, I was probably the first European to discover that it was so well endowed.

These thoughts quickly translated into a frenzy of measuring, sampling, preserving—and finally cooking! We were all hungry for meat after a diet of rice and tinned fish, so we stewed the skinned body with forest greens. It was a terrible job preventing Anaru and the others from crunching up the bones as they habitually did with such food. Each time the sound of splintering bone cracked around the darkened campfire I had to seek out the culprit and request the mouthful they were enjoying so much. I felt guilty at depriving them of such evident enjoyment. Still, after it was over, I carefully packed away the bones, and proudly pondered the fact that this would be the first skeleton of a *Xenuromys* ever to grace a museum collection.

The first scientific paper I ever published on a New Guinea mammal was based on the materials I collected from that specimen. To this day I have not solved the mystery of its gigantic testicles.

Each succeeding day on Mt Boobiari brought more surprises. One day Anaru brought in two Ground Cuscusses (*Phalanger gymnotis*). These big possums are relatives of Australia's brushtail possums. Anaru's dogs had located them in their lairs, and when they fled he shot them. The Miyanmin hold this species in special respect. They know it as *Kuyam* and believe that it is a child of their ancestress, Afek.

The greatest surprise of all came near the end of our time on Mt Boobiari. Close to dark one evening, Deyfu arrived in camp carrying a possum which was brilliantly patterned in fiery red, black, sulphur-yellow and white. I had never seen anything like it. It was enormous, for with Deyfu holding its head level with his chest, the animal's tail still trailed on the ground. I felt sure that it must be some undescribed species.

When I returned to Sydney, though, I found that it had been described in the 1930s. The description, just a paragraph, is in German—from it I got little idea of the majestic appearance of the beast. So rare is this animal, which is now known as the Black-spotted Cuscus (*Spilocuscus rufoniger*), that it was thought by many researchers to be nothing but a variant of the Common Spotted Cuscus. Biochemical and other analysis of the specimen collected from Mt Boobiari showed, however, that it is indeed a distinct species.

Disappointingly, the long-desired Goodfellow's Tree-kangaroo remained elusive.

NINE

Rausim laplap bilong kok

The relief of leaving the camp on Mt Boobiari was palpable. My skin was red with bites and welts, my eyes swollen to slits, and I was dirty from being unable to wash for a week. I longed for the comforts of Betavip—a whole floor in a hut to stretch out on, maybe a sweet biscuit and tea, and the pool in the river which was so cool, deep and inviting to swim in.

It was to the river pool that we first headed on reaching the village. We had developed a bit of a routine as far as using the place went. First a Miyanmin friend would go before us, shouting that the women must leave the river and take their pigs and infants with them, for the white men were coming to wash. By the time we reached the place it would be deserted and we could strip off our clothes or penis gourds and bathe for an hour or two.

The village children had found a large piece of milky

quartz which was the focus of a wonderful game. It was our favourite pastime (as it was that of the village boys) to throw it into the depths of the pool, then dive after it. The winner was the first to retrieve it from the green depths. The white quartz shone like a beacon, even in the deepest pot-holes. The pool was so deep that my ears popped and crackled as I approached the bottom, and large fish moved warily off into the green shadows.

On this day, lying stretched out among my Miyanmin companions on the cobble beach, I felt particularly satisfied. I had scaled Mt Boobiari and had come back with great treasure. I was clean and cool again. Encouraged, perhaps, by the camaraderie which had developed between us on Mt Boobiari, our talk soon turned to more intimate matters. My Miyanmin friends said they preferred women with long, pendulous breasts which 'bounced as they walked' (denoting a woman who has breastfed) rather than the pert, pre-lactational mammaries admired by most westerners.

Looks counted for little as far as wives were concerned. A hard worker was what was sought after in that department. By way of explanation one of my friends commented that a man could always try to seduce a girl from a nearby village if he wanted to enjoy a beautiful female.

As this conversation progressed, Deyfu leaned close to me and asked in a whisper why I was so different from them. Startled by the question, I began to grope for explanations about my relatively large size and white skin. Deyfu cut short this tangled speech by pointing between his legs and saying, '*No, hia!*' (Not that, here!)

At once the point of the question became apparent—I was circumcised while they were not. Mustering my finest Pidgin, I expounded, '*Ol tumbuna bilong mi i save rausim laplap bilong kok bilong pikinini man,*' which translates roughly as 'My ancestors developed the habit of cutting off the little skirt of skin that grows at the end of their children's willies'.

Deyfu looked at me solemnly for a moment or two, then

tried to translate this explanation for his eagerly waiting clansmen. After a few words, he fell to the ground, choking and writhing.

He was in paroxysms of laughter!

As he spurted the words out, all our companions fell about helplessly in a similar manner. For a long time, no-one could look at me without becoming hysterical again, and it was at least twenty minutes before the mirth finally subsided.

While all this was going on I began to reflect upon my attitude towards the Miyanmin and their body decoration. At first the Miyanmin's penis gourds, their pierced nasal septums bearing pig's tusks, and their noses perforated to hold the heads of rhinoceros beetles, had seemed the height of bizarre, outrageous and primitive fashion. Until this moment, I never considered that they could conceivably view me in the same way.

But later in Sydney, at the end of this long field trip, I realised just how bizarre European fashion can be. Stepping off the plane, I watched in amazement as two remarkable people glided by. Their eyes were open and bright, their skin impossibly white, and their lips likewise red. For a moment it seemed that they must be visitors from that strange African tribe who paint themselves pale and affect impossibly wide eyes and smiles. But no—they were just young women, acceptably if heavily made up in the current fashion. It took me a few days to view this 'tribal makeup' as normal again. During my long period of fieldwork I had come to accept the human 'norm' as being scantily clad, short and dark-skinned.

The return journey from the swimming hole was always one of apprehension. The path was used every afternoon by an old woman who owned what was surely the largest, most sour-tempered pig in Melanesia. This veritable monster would, almost certainly, have been *mumu*ed (cooked in a stone-lined pit) long ago had it not been for the extraordinary affection that the old woman who cared for it felt for her charge.

At the great rustling noise that signalled the approach of this enormous sow the Miyanmin would leap up trees or into the bush. Often I slipped behind a tree just as the sow ploughed past, clearly enraged at meeting someone who dared to use its path.

Sows are dangerous creatures, for unlike boars (which merely slash with their tusks) they bite fiercely and tenaciously. Many deaths have resulted from such bites.

Everyone in Betavip, with the exception of its 'mother' (as the old woman was known), lived in mortal fear of this pig. When they heard it coming into the village of an afternoon, they would all jump up onto the porches of their houses. Then the great, grunting hog would pass by, followed by a tiny, wizened woman, who weighed just thirty kilograms. (I know this because Don had to weigh her for medical treatment.) She was a quarter the size of the pig, yet kept it firmly under control with a stick. The pig listened to her every word, and obeyed her as a frightened puppy would. This woman had suckled the beast at her breast when it was a piglet. She had fed it the choicest morsels of sweet potato as it grew, and when it was old enough had led it out every day to forage in the forest. In short, it was like a child to her.

The villagers took the occasion of our visit as an opportunity to rid themselves of this monster. Despite the old woman's protests, they argued that it was far too dangerous having the beast around while the white *masta*s were visiting.

The argument went back and forth for days. Eventually, to the old woman's grief, the villagers won.

Doing the beast in turned out to be a complicated process. Before it could be dispatched, the pig's 'real' parents had to be informed. The old lady, apparently, was only the animal's stepmother! She had adopted it when it was a piglet from a couple who lived in a village two days' walk north of Betavip. Making ropes, I thought.

When the pig's parents arrived at Betavip, preparations for the feast got under way. A deep hole was dug on the edge of the village, and a vast pyre of firewood, on which were stacked river stones, was set alight next to it. The pig, meanwhile, was firmly tethered in the middle of the village square, its stepmother sobbing quietly nearby in her hut.

Finally, my friend Kebuge stepped forward and strung his bow. The pig was hit in the chest, but the blow was not mortal and for a moment the squealing, furious creature threatened to break loose from its tether.

Anaru rushed forward in this moment of crisis, carrying a heavy pole. With one mighty blow to the top of its cranium he silenced the animal.

The great sow was converted into pork cutlets in minutes by a horde of Miyanmin wielding bamboo knives, who then wrapped the meat into packages of leaves. Stones which had been heated to glowing were used to line the pit, followed by layers of leaves and herbs. The parcels of meat were placed on top of these, above which was put a layer of banana leaves. On this was plastered a thick paste of taro 'pudding', topped with a layer of the blood-red sauce made from the *marita* (a long, red, spear-like pandanus fruit). The whole was then sealed with a layer of leaves, stones and earth.

The sobbing of the bereaved 'mother' seemed to intensify several hours later when the *mumu* was opened, releasing the delicious aromas of her 'child'. We were moved to pity for her and gave her a few tins of fish (a poor substitute for fresh pork, I'm afraid) for her dinner. But her sorrow was undiminished.

The world underground

Early during our stay in Betavip Don Gardner had treated a woman for septicaemia of the leg. The entire limb had been swollen, red and angry-looking as a result of an infected cut on her foot. She responded splendidly to a course of antibiotics, and after this incident her husband Kaifak, who previously had been rather aloof, became particularly friendly to us. He had heard that my wife was pregnant with our first child and one day he came to me and confidently predicted (correctly as it turned out) that it would be a boy. He insisted that I name the child Oki, which I duly did. He explained that Oki meant 'kick of the cassowary', and that if my child bore this name he would grow up to be strong.

Kaifak had an open, generous face with large, dark eyes and a typically prominent Melanesian nose. In some ways he bore a close resemblance to Harry H. Corbett, the actor who played Harold in 'Steptoe and Son'. Usually smiling, he wore a safety pin through a rather large hole in one ear.

Kaifak had a special link with the spirit world—he was a shaman. His entrée to the spirit realm had occurred one day when he was hunting in the forest and met a ghost. The ghost led him into a part of the forest he did not know. There, it offered him ghostly taro to eat. Kaifak ate it. Normally, consumption of such ghostly taro would result in death. This case was unusual in that the ghost and the human had come to an agreement. Kaifak would tell the (invisible) ghost about events in the world of the living, while the ghost would keep Kaifak informed about how things stood in the land of the dead. The ghost fastened its arms around Kaifak's shoulders, and the two became inseparable.

The dead are a very immediate presence to the Miyanmin. They believe the deceased inhabit a world which in many ways resembles their own, and which is located only a metre or two below the surface of the earth. Most of the activities which occupy the time of the living are also believed to occupy the dead in their subterranean existence.

The Miyanmin sense of space and time is circumscribed. Their knowledge of the world outside their valley is skimpy. Although they have heard of, and possibly even visited places outside, their world is the valley of the Yapsiei River. Regions beyond its bounds take on ever more layers of uncertainty. Even Port Moresby is an almost mythical place.

History, as they see it, stretches back only about three generations. They ascribe the time before the birth of their grandfathers to a remote, shadowy era, perhaps close to the beginning of time itself. As well, Christianity has truncated their vision of the future, for they expect the apocalypse and second coming soon, certainly within their lifetime.

Despite this rather limited view of time and space they accept what seem to me to be extraordinary events with great equanimity.

One clear night some of us were sitting in the village watching the stars. Presently a satellite came into view, appearing as a bright speck travelling slowly across the blackness. I pointed it out, and asked people if they were familiar with such objects. After some discussion a young boy told me that, although they were now seen frequently, they were unknown when his father was a boy. I asked if he knew what they were. When he said no, I tried to give some explanation.

In 1984 Ronald Reagan was president of the USA and his Star Wars program was in full swing. Part of my explanation involved the use of satellites in warfare, and their ability to strike targets in space and on earth. After this revelation, my listeners fell into a long silence and seemed collectively stunned. Then a very young boy approached and asked solemnly, 'Masta, my father is very old. His eyes are dim and he can't hunt any more. Next time you see Mr Reagan, could you ask him if he could get his satellite to shoot some possums for my father?'

One day a striking figure strode into Betavip. It was Ambep, Kaifak's brother. With his arrival, the atmosphere in Betavip suddenly electrified. Ambep had chosen to live in an isolated, traditional village called Kyemana with his extended family. Kyemana was nestled in the hills above Betavip, some half-day's walk away.

Ambep was a slight, older man who wore only a penis gourd, and an object which I at first took to be a strange sort of tea-cosy on his head. His nose was just as prominent as Kaifak's, but his face was narrower and more pinched. His eyes shone with a brightness which Kaifak's lacked.

Despite his whimsical appearance, Ambep was not a person to be trifled with. I asked to photograph him one day, but learned through Kegesep that he angrily refused. Too many people had died after being photographed, he said. In fact, the mortality rate among the Miyanmin was then so high that Ambep was not far wide of the truth in his observation.

Ambep was described, even by his near relatives, as 'cranky'. Over the years he had fallen out with almost everyone except his immediate, controllable family. It was to seek refuge from his own brother that Kaifak had come to Betavip a few months before we arrived—with an arrow lodged in his arm. He had fled Ambep's village after an argument.

The circumstances of this family crisis were highly unusual. Four Miyanmin men, including close relatives of Ambep, had gone hunting. During a storm they had sheltered in a small garden hut, over which towered a giant forest tree. The tree had been left standing (being too laborious to fell) during the making of the garden. And there it had stood, slowly rotting away, for years. At the height of the storm a great gust of wind had broken it, bringing its vast bulk crashing down on the frail hut. All four men had been killed instantly.

There is hardly a rural Melanesian anywhere who would not believe that such an event was the result of sorcery. Such a terrible disaster could only be the work of malicious enemies.

The deaths drove Ambep to madness with anger and grief in a typically Miyanmin way. He had an adopted daughter whom he had captured years before during a raid on the Atbalmin. She was, at about seventeen, just coming to marriageable age, and was both loved and valued by Ambep and his family.

Ambep took his axe and struck her in the neck, then ordered his wife to dismember and cook the body. His little family group was then made to eat it. Kaifak protested—and had been driven off with an arrow in his arm.

I have seen Ambep hunt. He could have killed Kaifak had he wished.

So now we all felt that Ambep's arrival at Betavip foreshadowed further violence. The local pastor was nervous. He threatened to tell the kiap of Ambep's cannibalism. But this would have thrown the village into further panic.

In the midst of all this, I had to deal with Ambep for my own purposes, for he was a highly skilled hunter who brought interesting specimens to me each day.

One afternoon I visited the hut on the edge of the village where Ambep's family was lodged. I wished to explain the nature of my work to Ambep. The single room was filled with smoke and people occupied most of the floor.

One of the young women in the group was suffering severely from tuberculosis. The upper part of her body had been stunted by the disease, and she constantly coughed up frothy, pinkish sputum. Her eyes had that bulging, frightened look of someone who cannot draw sufficient breath. And her repeated coughing made it difficult for Ambep to understand my tangled Pidgin (a language he barely understood in any case).

Suddenly Ambep became enraged. His eyes flashed in anger as he rose to slash her across the head with the back of his fist. She cringed in terror. I stumbled through my explanation, caught between feelings of outrage, disgust and fear.

Ambep's apparent madness in times of grief was not unique. Most West Miyanmin do, on occasion, become crazed with sorrow. This state of temporary insanity caused by calamity is widely accepted in Miyanmin society as legitimate behaviour, despite the fact that mad grief can become an excuse for the most outrageous acts. Gradually, I came to flinch whenever I heard that someone had become 'mad with grief'. It often presaged the most terrible, meaningless and unpredictable violence.

One day Don Gardner had given one of his assistants a brand new mosquito net. The man had treasured the gift, carefully hanging it in his house. Then one of his brother's chickens had entered the hut and defecated on the lily-white net. The first Don knew of it was a furious Miyanmin storming back and forth across the village square, axe in hand. The gist of what he said was this:

'The white man has come to us and has been generous. He

has given me a precious gift—a mosquito net. And what has my brother's chicken done? My *own* brother's chicken has shitted on my new mosquito net. My own brother's chicken!'

At that he swung the axe wildly at some pawpaw trees owned by his brother, which were just coming into fruit. Next, the brother's chickens were slaughtered. These were a highly valuable commodity which had only recently reached the village. Had his brother showed himself then, he may well have suffered the same fate.

The propensity for such events to arise from apparently trivial causes made me perhaps overly nervous. One day the village pastor came to me asking for help to count his money. He needed 140 kina (then about two hundred Australian dollars) to attend the Bible school at Duranmin (two weeks' walk away), and he was excited because he believed that he had 137 kina, almost enough to enrol. I opened his tin and was appalled to see one kina 37 toea (two Australian dollars) lying there. What was I to say? Fearing an outbreak, I could only advise him to keep on saving.

On another occasion, two young boys who were working for me had 'borrowed' Anaru's canoe (a valuable asset) and wrecked it. It was only when a glowering Anaru began to play his *kundu* drum that I saw how the crisis might be dealt with. I went up to his hut and, with a flourish, offered to buy the drum for far more than it was really worth. This brought a smile to Anaru's face, which moments before had been twisted with anger.

In 1986 I almost became a victim myself of the wide-eyed, utterly unpredictable Miyanmin violence. I was sleeping in my hut in the mid-afternoon, after having been up most of the night spotlighting. Suddenly I was aroused by screams and shouts from an adjacent hut. I scrambled to my feet and stood in the doorway. There, in the harsh tropical sunlight, I saw a young man with his bowstring drawn tight. He was attempting to take aim at something through the poles of a hut wall. I knew instantly that he was trying to kill someone. I shouted to catch his attention, saying that if he hurt anyone I would be forced to report him to the police.

When he turned to face me I saw that I had made a terrible mistake. His eyes burned with a madness which showed that he had not heard my words. He wanted to kill, and his bow was already drawn. It was pointing directly at my chest from less than ten metres away.

My shotgun was propped against the door jamb inside the hut, but it would have been utterly useless to reach for it. In the split second I considered this, I saw someone rush from the shelter of an adjacent hut and grasp the young man around the chest from behind, pinning his arms.

He could not loose the arrow.

This man who saved my life was the young man's uncle. He explained to me that the boy had only recently married, and that he suspected his wife of infidelity. It was she he had been trying to kill.

The strangest thing was that later that evening the same young man who had almost killed me came up to my door smiling, proffering a possum he had just shot. He was friendly and relaxed, as if nothing had happened.

He was Ambep's son.

Kaifak's symbiotic relationship with the spirit realm led to an extraordinary bit of politicking on the eve of our departure from Betavip. As we stood in the village square ready to leave, Kaifak began striding up and down in front of the assembled crowd, ranting and raving in Miyanmin. The crowd seemed solemn, indeed disappointed, by what he had to say. Finally we were made privy to the nature of the harangue. What Kaifak had said was this:

'The ghosts are very well treated by the Government in

Port Moresby, you know. Everyone in the spirit world has been given wristwatches and transistor radios. And they already have their own village council'—a sore point with the Miyanmin, who knew that they were almost alone in Papua New Guinea in lacking this form of governance—'And what has the Government done for us? Look at us. We have nothing! Why should they favour the ghosts so, when it is we who vote for them? I'm going to ask these white men to tell Michael Somare'—by then long since out of power—'that this favouritism must stop. The Government must start giving the living people some of the same cargo they are giving to the ghosts.'

I looked at my boots, bit the inside of my cheek to prevent myself from smiling, and solemnly swore that next time I met Michael Somare I would pass on Kaifak's request.

As we left Betavip, I asked everyone to save the jaw-bones of animals they hunted. I promised that when (and if) I returned, I would purchase them so that I could estimate the protein intake which hunting gave each family.

And I did return to Betavip—two years later in 1986, with my friend and colleague, Lester Seri, a biologist with the PNG Department of Environment. Amazingly, only the detestable thug Ambep had carefully saved all his bones. Whatever else he might be, I found him to be a man of his word.

I informed Ambep that I wished to obtain some more samples of the rare giant rat *Xenuromys barbatus* which I had first encountered two years before on Mt Boobiari. He alone, apparently, owned the dog which could reliably track down the beasts he knew as *Boboyomin*. Out of my patrol box I pulled a bush-knife, a small tarpaulin, and a tomahawk. I laid them on the floor of the hut in front of him. Pointing to each in turn, I said, '*Wanpela Boboyomin, wanpela Boboyomin, wanpela Boboyomin*'—Ambep could have his choice of one of these things whenever he produced a *Boboyomin* for me.

That same afternoon Ambep returned triumphant, *Boboyomin* in hand. His dog had detected the lair of the animal amid a great rock pile, the typical roost site for the species. Ambep handed the body over, and with great ceremony requested the tomahawk. He assured me that he would return the next day to obtain the remaining goods.

But then catastrophe struck. That evening, when I visited Ambep's hut, his dog was lying by the fire, twitching and frothing at the mouth. Its eyes rolled in its sockets as it threw fits on the ground. Ambep thought it had eaten or been bitten by a poisonous centipede. Perhaps a jealous rival had sent it to prevent Ambep obtaining the remaining trade goods.

Given Ambep's setback, it was a surprise indeed when he returned the following day, as promised, with yet another *Boboyomin* in hand. After he took the tarpaulin, he explained that he had asked his wife to accompany him in his search. She had thrust her naked hand into innumerable rocky crevices, feeling for the lair of the great rat. Finally she detected one, and by inserting her arm into the lair had managed to throttle it single-handed without being bitten.

No more giant rats, alas, came Ambep's way before we were due to leave Betavip. So the bush-knife remained with us.

Towards the end of our stay we built a series of rafts, as we had done before, to travel down the river, but on the morning of our scheduled departure the Skgonga was in flood and we could not leave. By lunchtime the Miyanmin who were to accompany us had decided that the flood had subsided sufficiently to venture downstream, so our cargo was loaded. At the last minute, our bush-knife was apparently lost in the swollen river. Lester and I set off glumly, suspecting that it had in fact been stolen.

The day after we reached Yapsiei Station, Ambep arrived at our house, unexpected and exhausted. In his hand he held the lost bush-knife. He explained that it had been stolen from us by a young man. Ambep had forced him to reveal its hiding place, and had afterwards beaten him up for his brazen theft. This act of honesty was deeply touching. Ambep could easily have kept the treasured knife, for I had no plans to return to Betavip.

The more I learned of Miyanmin society, the more it seemed that Ambep's violence was simply a more extreme version of the societal norm. Yes, Ambep could be a monster, but he was also a complex human being whose intelligence and honesty outshone that of most of his fellows. How do we judge a person whose culture and attitudes we barely understand? I still think of this strange, contradictory man, and must admit that I came to regard him with affection.

A memory: On the afternoon of Ambep's son's madness, Anaru had come to visit me. We sat on the porch of my hut enjoying a cup of sweet, black coffee, gazing at the lofty summit of Mt Boobiari, lying wreathed in cloud in the distance.

Anaru looked wistfully at the mountain. 'Let me tell you how *Timboyok*'—as the Miyanmin know Goodfellow's Tree-kangaroo—'lives up on that mountain. Every morning, when the sun shines, *Timboyok* climbs into the branches of the highest trees on Boobiari. From his lofty lookout *Timboyok* can see our small village and the goings on of all of the people who live here. From up there, we look like ants to him. *Timboyok* sees us fight, get sick and work very hard clearing forest to make gardens. While we work and suffer, he is watching his children play around him and enjoying the sun on his skin.'

ELEVEN

No greater love

Yominbip: a pinprick of a settlement in the vastness of the Thurnwald Range.

Building a helipad in the Thurnwald Range in 1986 was a difficult task. Don Gardner, wanting to conduct a medical survey there, had sent Kebuge ahead on foot to arrange for construction of the helicopter landing pad. In order to show him the size of the open space required, he had paced out a square fifteen steps long on each side. After Kebuge set off, we waited a month before taking to the air, assuming this would be sufficient time for the job to be completed.

Flying to Yominbip was an extraordinary experience. The helicopter arrived early in the morning from its exploration base in the Green River area. It was a tiny machine with a large glass bubble in front, through which one could see the ground receding as it lifted off. It was my first flight in a helicopter, and the sense of wonder and vertigo as we rose above the canopy and set off towards the distant Thurnwald Range made me almost believe we were about to enter another world. After about forty minutes' travel we came to the rugged ranges themselves and began to search for our landing spot.

The narrow ridge stretched before us, unbroken from high on the mountain summit all the way to the foothills, before dropping abruptly into the valley below. It looked like a great verdant knife blade, encrusted with the verdigris of timeless forest giants. But there was one small brown patch on it—a rust spot—just before the blade tip. Looking closely, I realised that the rust spot was the newly made helipad. In a minute or two we would be ejected onto it. Then the helicopter would swoop noisily away.

It would not return for some time. We had no radio, no way of contacting the outside world.

As the helicopter approached the clearing, a cloud of leaves and twigs rose from the rotor blades. They whirled furiously around us—the pad was obviously too small. The pilot had either to risk his blades in the overhanging canopy or abort the mission.

After a moment's hesitation, he decided to press on and finally made a wonky touch-down. Stepping out of the chopper was tricky, for it was precariously balanced, its skids overhanging the precipice on either side of the knife-edged ridge.

Long after the helicopter departed, the air remained thick with the fragments of falling leaves. Miyanmin, assembled on the promontory, shielded their eyes. Leaf fragments peppered their hair.

Most of the men who had surrounded the equipment and newly ejected human cargo wore only a penis gourd; the women wore a very short grass skirt, although a few of both sexes were embellished with a motley array of decrepit European cast-offs. One older woman, who wandered aimlessly through the small crowd with a dazed look on her face, was dressed in the remains of what had once been a very stylish white and gold silk gown. The effect was made all the more startling by the fact that her nipples, doubtless due to the effects of friction, were poking prominently through the fabric.

Close by, an older man hobbled forward, his penis gourd clearly causing great discomfort under his tight, second-hand football shorts. The people of Yominbip, we discovered, had donned the few European clothes they possessed to honour our arrival. Some, however, were clearly unwilling to undergo the indignity of appearing without their traditional clothing too.

As we moved our equipment from the improvised helipad to the village, a young woman stepped forward to help. She wore a spotless dress, her wavy black hair tied back with a red ribbon in a neat ponytail. After a minute or two, a man in his forties or early fifties also lent a hand.

For a long while after the helicopter left that day, the villagers wandered aimlessly about as if in shock, staring wide-eyed at us and each other as if seeking an explanation. Finally, one came forward in the evening to find out more about us and the purpose of our visit.

When we told them, they found it difficult to comprehend. For they could not believe that outsiders—perhaps the first ever to arrive at their remote village—would come so far to see so little.

True, for a few of the inhabitants of Yominbip our visit was not such a novelty. Some young men had left the village to visit adjacent communities which had airstrips, and had returned with a few trade goods and wonderful tales of the world outside the valley. One had even seen the sea when he worked on a plantation at Madang. And now, on this fine morning in April 1986 (as I, but not they, knew) the outside world had arrived for everyone to see.

It is often quite a task to impart the significance of such seemingly useless work as my own to other people (including many westerners), but here the challenge seemed insurmountable.

Yet on this morning Lester Seri, my dear New Guinean *bras* (brother), was undaunted as he began with a speech to the whole community.

'I am a Papua New Guinean, and I work for our nation. Because this work is so important, the Australian Government has sent a man, a doctor, to help us. He has come all the way from Australia.

'We are here to find out about your animals. The Government is worried that in many places all of the food animals have been killed out. They want to find out what animals survive here, and how you look after them. We're interested not only in your food animals, but your pests too. Your snakes, worms, rats and even frogs. Yes, everything. We want to see at least one of every kind of animal that lives here, and we will preserve some in this medicine [formalin], and take them back to the Government to show them. We need your help with this work. When you come across an animal in your everyday activities, such as gardening and collecting wood, we would like you to tell us about it, and bring it back to the village. We will pay you for your help, and if you have no use for money then we have food and some other things that you might want.'

Everyone appeared rather stunned by this news, and it seemed that Lester, even though he was a fellow countryman, was just as strange a being to the inhabitants of Yominbip as I was. He was subject to the same number of stares and surreptitious touches—including a rather spectacular below-the-belt lunge by one female senior citizen, who I suppose was uncertain about his sex. But it was only with the passing of the weeks that I began to understand just how foreign we were to this small community, and what our arrival had meant to its members.

The village head-man was already greying. He did not know his age, and when I first asked he replied that he might be seven. On being asked to reconsider, he ventured an age of four. This man was a great font of traditional knowledge, as was his aged uncle, although the uncle was past relating much of it.

The head-man's uncle was quite the oldest Miyanmin I had ever seen. Probably in his seventies, he was already an elder when the great raids of the 1950s took place. Although deaf as a post and with rapidly fading eyesight, the old man was not quite helpless, for he remained active and each day he crawled through his small garden to weed it.

One afternoon, as Lester and I worked away measuring, skinning and recording data from our specimens, we saw the old man squatting in the shade of a hut, seemingly lost and indifferent to the world. A woman had located the burrow of a Water Rat (*Hydromys chrysogaster*) in her garden and had dug the animal out and brought it to us. Water Rats have the most deliciously soft and sleek fur. Inspired by its touch, I carried it over to the old man and put it into his hands. He got up, at first not understanding what I meant. He felt the animal I handed him with the gentleness one might reserve for a child. *Ayam*, he whispered (the Miyanmin name for the creature), as the hardened look of indifference which characterised his face melted away. It was replaced by the most beatific smile.

We all felt sorry for the uncle. Each evening he would chop his own firewood. It seemed too strenuous a task for his decrepit frame. One afternoon Don Gardner cajoled a young boy into chopping the wood for him. A few minutes later the old fellow began jabbering away. There was the sound of wood thumping against a wall. Then the boy came racing past, followed a short time later by a well-aimed faggot. It seemed that the old man valued his independence above firewood.

I must admit that the old uncle got in the way a bit. Whenever we cooked rice he seemed to be on hand, staring into the pot, mumbling to himself in amazement. He was wondering aloud where we had found so many ant-eggs. Often, while I was out on my daily rounds checking traps and nets, I would almost trip over him. There he would be, on all fours, weeding and mumbling to himself. Sometimes he would be in his garden, sometimes not.

One night he nearly caused our expedition to end in disaster. Lester had gone off spotlighting on the ridge above the village. The old man had decided to camp out that night and was sitting in a humpy on the edge of his garden a few minutes' walk away.

Late in the evening, on his way home, Lester unexpectedly encountered the old fellow. He was awake, sitting beside his fire, by then reduced to glowing coals. He saw Lester's torch, and quickly reached for his bow and arrows. Lester called out cheerfully to reassure the old man—and then remembered that he was stone deaf.

Cursing himself for his stupidity, Lester also realised that the old man might not know what a torch was. He turned it off just in time. The old fellow was already gliding through the undergrowth, bow-string taut under the burden of a man-killing arrow. Lester retreated quickly into the forest, and came back to the village.

When we returned a little while later to check on the old man, we found that he had lit the mother of all bonfires. It was so vast that it was scorching the tree-tops above the shelter. Sitting uncomfortably close to the conflagration, he was chanting loudly, in a frantic effort no doubt to drive off the malefic spirit who had disturbed his solitude.

The village favourite was Oblankep, the head-man's son. He was one of the few active young men in Yominbip and a great hunter. Although there were perhaps thirty other adults in the community, my life soon began to revolve around Oblankep's family.

Oblankep's father was highly respected—a natural leader with a commanding presence—and without his friendship our stay may well have been untenable. It was he who organised for vegetables to be cooked for us daily, for our washing to be done, and a multitude of other small hospitalities that made life enjoyable. He would often sit by us as we worked, always curious, and occasionally solicitous of the eventual fate of our goods, wishing to know if any would be left behind when we departed.

His eyes lit up whenever my steel file appeared. It was a simple five-dollar file that we used to maintain our bush-knives and traps, but he regarded it as the most desirable of objects. Finally, one afternoon, he brought forth his own ageing bush-knife. I felt its edge. It was almost as blunt as the rear of the blade. He explained that it no longer cut properly—just *chewim daun diwai* (tree). It seemed the smallest of courtesies to sharpen his blade for him. Within minutes, every knife in the village was before me, awaiting resharpening.

It was only an hour's work. But I did not realise the full burden of my labour until a young man came hobbling towards me later that afternoon.

He had tied his leg above the knee with bush vine. When he released his hold on it, blood spurted out from an artery which had been severed just above the knee. The size of the cut was horrifying, and there seemed no way to staunch the blood. I used up a considerable proportion of my bandage supply simply covering the wound.

I had only just finished dealing with this emergency and was wondering how people normally coped with such ghastly accidents, when a group of women came rushing forward, wailing terribly. A young mother had been cutting firewood, her child playing by her side, when the bush-knife unexpectedly glanced off the timber. It had almost severed a toe from her child's foot.

I had never had to deal with anything more serious than a minor cut. Rapidly slipping into shock, I dressed the wound as best I could.

The list of walking wounded increased. Oblankep neatly sliced off the top of his left thumb; others bore sundry cuts

and wounds. Clearly, sharpened bush-knives behave in unpredictable ways in the hands of those who are used to blunt ones.

The large and horrible gashes I treated over the coming days
became symbolic to me. They were as palpable as the gulf in
understanding between myself and my new-found friends.

Oblankep knew the habits of all of the larger marsupial species
intimately, and just where and when to find them. Working
with him was one of the greatest privileges I have ever had. In
his company, Lester and I ranged from the mossy forests
perched on the very summit of the Thurnwald Range down to
the steamy jungle in the river valleys below. For days Lester
camped with Oblankep in the forest of the upper reaches of
the Thurnwald Range, which are uninhabited and rarely visited. It is one of the most glorious places on earth. From there,
the surrounding lowlands seem eternally covered in cloud, the
high peaks jutting from them like islands. Unfortunately Lester
was overcome with malaria while there and returned to
Yominbip more dead than alive.

While Lester was recovering I hunted the middle slopes,
between about 1,000 and 1,700 metres elevation. I did much
work by night.

Conditions were dreadful, as the slopes were steep and slippery, and nettles formed most of the understorey. One night,
after scrambling for several hours through the forest, I spotted
the dull red-eye shine of a possum in a tree far above. As we
had not yet obtained any possums at this locality, I decided to
take it as a specimen.

I was standing on an extremely steep slope, and it had
begun to rain. Rain filled my eyes as I slipped the safety catch
off the gun and raised it to take aim. Almost immediately, and
without warning, the ground gave way under me. I went tum-
bling down the slope into a dense patch of nettles some ten
metres below. The gun landed beside me, but by some miracle

it did not go off. What I would have done had I shot myself at this remote place I know not.

There are at least two kinds of nettles at Yominbip. One has a painful but not dangerous sting. This the Miyanmin use when they are tiring during a long walk. They pull it up by the handful and flagellate their bodies with it, claiming it refreshes them. I tried it once, but came out in a rather painful red rash which re-activated itself every time I washed. It felt like being rubbed all over with highly potent liniment.

The second nettle species, while superficially similar, is much more potent and is said by the Miyanmin to be dangerous. It was into this that I had fallen. My long-sleeved shirt and long pants saved me from serious injury, but my hands, ankles and face swelled with an angry red rash for days afterwards.

I came to appreciate Oblankep's friendship and trust all the more when I heard some of his life story. He had endured terrible experiences, the worst of which occurred while he was working as a labourer on a plantation near Madang.

He had 'signed up' while visiting the nearest big government station at Telefomin. The recruiter told him of the adventures to be had in the big city and conscripted him for two years. Conditions were appalling, with long days of exhausting labour, and bashings for those who complained. Much of his pay went on the necessities of life, with only a few small luxuries.

Things came to a head when Oblankep received news of his elder brother's death. To complete the traditional funeral rites he needed to return home, but his request to do so was flatly refused by the plantation manager. That evening Oblankep and a few of the other men, finding the manager alone, assaulted him and fled the plantation, leaving behind most of their goods and pay.

For almost a year Oblankep lived the life of an itinerant in Madang. It was there that he met Maria, his wife. He arranged for the traditional marriage payments and requested a one-way airfare from his relatives and friends for he and his new wife to fly from Madang to remote Telefomin. From there they walked for the best part of a week to reach Yominbip. It was she who had helped us with our cargo on that first day.

The head-man and his wife were very fond of Oblankep. We often sat together and talked. One day the head-man announced, to my great surprise, that he would tell me the story of how he had found his son.

It was, he thought, in the late 1950s or early 1960s, the year of the last great raid in the Yominbip area. The Yominbip people had planned this raid for years. They secretly built a cane suspension bridge across the Sepik. A large party of warriors crossed the bridge by night and surrounded an Atbalmin village.

On a signal, they descended and slaughtered every one of the fifty-odd inhabitants of the place, sparing only a few young girls and children. The party was kept busy dismembering the bodies and making the pieces into convenient packages until the following morning. The head-man, who was then young, set off with the gutted torso of a male victim tied to his back, a severed arm and a leg slung over each shoulder and a head wrapped in a palm-leaf package hanging by his side.

On the outskirts of the village he was stopped by a faint, persistent sound. It was a crying baby, less than a year old, hanging in a *bilum*, or net bag, on a tree by the path. Its mother must have rushed from her hut when she heard the raiders and, in a desperate attempt to save her child, had hidden it there before being cut down. He took the string bag and slung it over his shoulders. After a few steps the child, comforted by the warmth and rhythmic step of its new step-father, quieted and fell asleep. It did not know that it was being carried between the severed limbs of its real parents.

While relating this extraordinary story, the old man took Oblankep's hand in his own with great tenderness. When he finished he added, in Pidgin, in a quiet voice, 'I knew then that my son would be a good man. He did not cry, but was good and quiet when I carried him.'

Oblankep was looking into his father's face, smiling. I was still shocked and confused by this account of familial love, when the head-man's wife joined in.

'We ate his Atbalmin parents. They were fat. They gave me all the milk I needed to nourish two children. Oblankep grew strong on them.'

Histories such as Oblankep's were perfectly acceptable in Yominbip. Indeed, they were the norm, and telling the story of a person's origins in this way seemed to reinforce their sense of belonging in Yominbip society.

Since the early seventies, the inhabitants of Yominbip had fallen on hard times. The Australian administration effectively stopped raids by protecting surrounding communities. Because of the appalling infant mortality, there were relatively few children in Yominbip, and the village was slowly becoming depopulated.

With the passing of the old ways, an odd amalgam of western religious and Melanesian beliefs was taking root. A Christian *rebaibal* (revival movement) had swept through Yominbip some years before we arrived, despite the fact that, at that time, the community had not yet been converted to Christianity. These 'revivals' are a unique Melanesian response to evangelical Christianity. They are fanatical affirmations of faith, aimed at obliterating the pagan ways which still persist in most societies.

*Rebaibal*s have apocalyptic overtones. When a *rebaibal* reaches fever pitch, people often cease making gardens and undertaking other useful work because they believe that the second coming is imminent. In the 1970s and 1980s, *rebaibal*s spread like wildfire throughout the remote areas of Papua New Guinea, passing from one inspired village to the next. At Yominbip the spirit house was burned to the ground when the movement gained hold, and the ancestral skulls were thrown into the river.

In a place like Yominbip one loses track of time. Suddenly there were only a few days left before the helicopter would return to collect us. I began to think about dividing up the goods that would be left behind, and we worked on improving the helicopter pad to facilitate our evacuation.

Oblankep and his family were dismayed that we were leaving them. Oblankep wore a long face, and redoubled his efforts to find the few rare species that we had not yet obtained, spending most of each night out hunting.

On our last evening in Yominbip we were working restlessly in our hut, packing and repacking the equipment, when Maria, Oblankep's wife, paid an unexpected visit. As she spoke her voice was low and desperate, and hatred and fear mingled as she told her story in Pidgin.

She had grown up in a small village just outside of Madang; although her family was poor, she was used to the city life and loved it. She met Oblankep in the market at Madang while he was living there. She thought him handsome and took him home to meet her family. He told stories about Yominbip—describing it as a large village not far from a great town and the coast.

Maria's parents accepted the marriage offer. Knowing that she was unlikely to see her parents again, she bade them a tearful farewell.

Oblankep's manner changed when they arrived at Telefomin. He assaulted her and forced her to walk, pregnant, to Yominbip. The journey almost killed her. Since then, alone among strangers, she had borne him a child. She worked daily in the remote gardens. She had grown to hate Yominbip. Those stories about this place—he had told her lies.

She whispered hoarsely, 'Please take me with you. When the helicopter comes, please take me with you.'

'But what about your child?'

'Leave it,' she said savagely.

When she slipped away I felt a great sense of unease. Should we steal Maria from Yominbip (for that is how

Oblankep would doubtless see it), or should we refuse her request? I dared not mention her visit, for she might be severely beaten for what she had done thus far. A failed escape attempt might even result in death.

Most murders in Papua New Guinea result from the theft of women, pigs or land. We would be compromising our own safety were we to attempt to help her escape. And there were other more complex issues to consider. Virtually the entire community of Yominbip had come together as a result of kidnappings. Oblankep had kidnapped his wife, but he himself had been taken by force from his original family. In such a situation it would be useless to try to explain the rights and wrongs of Maria's case. Morality as I knew it would simply not be understood.

I worried at the problem all morning until a faint mechanical sound announced the imminent arrival of the helicopter. I ran to Oblankep's hut, and found Maria seated firmly in a corner, her father-in-law standing near her. I could not see her face. With forced jocularity I asked if there were any messages I could take out for anyone. No response. I filled the awkward silence by asking Oblankep to come to my hut so that I could give him some gifts. Everything I was leaving behind I then put in his and his father's care, to be used by the entire community.

The chopper drew nearer. When it had almost touched down on the new pad I saw Maria crying at the door of Oblankep's hut. In the din of the rotor blades Lester began loading our specimens and equipment into the cargo hold, unaware of what was going on. I turned back to Maria, her face contorted with tears.

Behind her Oblankep watched, his eyes hard and angry.

TWELVE

The refugees

In the mid-1980s a group of refugees from Irian Jaya moved into Yapsiei.

Irianese refugees had already been arriving in increasing numbers at the border villages of Papua New Guinea. They had fled from a brutal Indonesian army intent on 'pacifying' the province. The refugees received assistance in the form of food, clothing and equipment from an international aid agency.

When all of this 'cargo' was flown into Yapsiei, the Miyanmin were aghast. Relationships between them and the refugees were none too cordial. The Miyanmin felt that their Government had betrayed them—yet again. They, citizens of Papua New Guinea, had virtually nothing, yet the Government had provided all of this cargo to these newcomers! Miyanmin big men strode up and down the airstrip, shouting their abuse at one and all in Port Moresby. It was, as far as they were concerned, just one more indication that they were the 'last' people. It made no difference whatever when Don explained that the aid had come not from Port Moresby, but from international agencies, for such niceties concerning the higher levels of government were impenetrable to them.

The refugees must have arrived sometime between February 1984 and April 1986. It seemed that they had not been in Papua New Guinea for long when I met them, for they spoke hardly a word of Pidgin. Fortunately, there was a Bahasa–Pidgin *turnim tok* living in Yapsiei at the time, and through him they told their story.

I have no way of knowing whether this story is true or not. What I do know, however, is that the people I interviewed were, as they had stated, Amungme from south-central Irian Jaya. I took down many animal names in their language, the accuracy of which I later verified.

The Amungme live near the Freeport gold and copper, mine in central Irian Jaya, some 500 kilometres west of Yapsiei. To get to Papua New Guinea by foot, these people would have had to traverse some of the most rugged terrain found anywhere on earth. It is a miracle that any of them survived their journey.

The Amungme refugees said that their plight began when an Indonesian official was sent to their village to oversee the reorganisation of their lives. The official (probably a Muslim army officer) said that, according to the Indonesian Government, it was unacceptable for them to live in their traditional manner. Amungme men and boys live together in a men's house, while the women live in smaller houses with the younger children and pigs. The official insisted that—in good Muslim fashion—the men move into houses with their wives and children. The pigs were to live separately.

Such a suggestion was bound to be looked on unfavourably by the Amungme. Many Melanesian men believe that too

much contact with women is debilitating. Were the Amungme
to do as commanded, they believed that they would become
ensorcelled and rapidly sicken, or fall in the next battle.
Furthermore, the new arrangement would leave the family
wealth (in the form of pigs) vulnerable to theft. Pig theft is
endemic in many areas, and the loss of a family's pigs could
have catastrophic repercussions. Marriages would have to be
postponed, and traditional compensation would go unpaid,
leading to more tribal wars.

At least partly as a result of such beliefs, the Amungme
were unwilling to do as the official suggested. When the
matter was pushed by the official, he was assaulted and
forcibly ejected from the village.

A few days later, helicopters were heard flying above the village. They landed, disgorging a large number of Indonesian
troops. These soldiers separated the men from the women
and children, and led them into two hastily constructed
barbed-wire compounds. Then they began asking the men
whether any of them would like to see Irian Jaya become independent of Indonesia. Many of these simple bush people
replied that they most certainly would. A man was then taken
aside and decapitated in full view of the others.

A fire was lit in a forty-four gallon drum, and lengths of
wire were heated to a white heat over it. Other men were then
taken aside, and one by one had heated wires thrust right
through their abdomens.

That night the remaining men decided to break out of the
compound and flee into the jungle, leaving their families to
the mercy of the soldiers. The refugees said that 300 men fled
into the jungle that night, but it seems unlikely that such
large numbers were involved, as even the largest highland villages have fewer people than this.

Whatever the case, the group fled eastward through the
jungle. Many died of starvation while others fell victim to
hostile tribes.

As they were crossing the southern foothills of the

Carstensz Range (which lies to the east of the Freeport mine) they encountered a tribe which lived in houses built in the tree-tops. These people lowered rope ladders when they saw the Amungme, then climbed down and attacked them.

My informants thought that the bodies of about thirty Amungme were carried up into the tree-houses by their attackers.

After several months' hard travel, the survivors reached the village of Ok Sibil, adjacent to the Papua New Guinea border. There they made contact with Ok Sibil tribesmen and were at first welcomed and fed by them.

This was a deception, for that night as the Amungme slept their hosts turned upon the refugees, killing many. The Amungme believed that this happened because the Ok Sibil people were being paid a bounty of 50,000 rupiah (then about thirty-five Australian dollars) for each border-crosser whose head was presented at the local military post.

The Amungme are a tough people and a few days later they regrouped and raided Ok Sibil. They killed several people and forcibly abducted a number of young women. At the time that I interviewed the refugees, they were keeping these women as their wives. Neither could speak the first language of the other, so doubtless the relationships were not altogether happy ones.

The refugees crowded close around me. They had heard that I had a shotgun. Could they borrow it, they asked, so that they could return to Indonesia and 'pay back' for the injuries they had suffered?

Horrified at the thought of being at the centre of an international incident, I ensured that the gun did not leave my side until I saw it safely on board the Cessna which would take me to Port Moresby.

PART III

TELEFOMIN

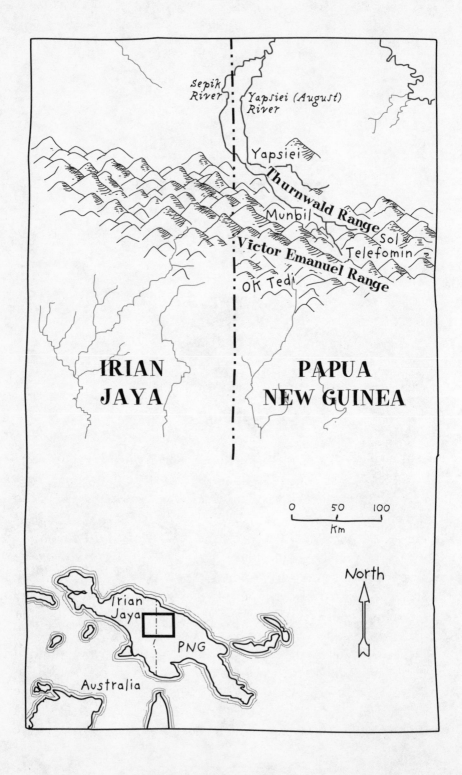

THIRTEEN

Exit by airbed

I first went to Telefomin in 1984. My arrival was a disaster which began during the last few days I spent at Yapsiei. Don Gardner and the rest of our party had decided to travel from Betavip to Yapsiei on rafts. I had never done this before. So it was an exciting prospect which I looked forward to mightily.

The morning of our departure was glorious, still and warm, and the river was flowing smoothly, reflecting the surrounding forest on its surface. It appeared to be a perfect day for travel by water. No more painful footslogging through swamps for us, I thought gleefully!

The raft I was travelling on was crowded and the constant babbling of my companions soon became an annoyance, as the noise was scaring off any wildlife well before we got close enough to view it. It was also a frustration to have to float past so many things I wished to get a closer look at, simply because the raft was not manoeuvrable enough. Finding these lost opportunities intolerable, I decided to inflate my airbed and float alongside. That way I could act a little independently, and get a close look at anything I particularly wanted to.

The head of a Soft-shelled Tortoise broke the smooth surface of the river not far from the raft. I set out to glide close to it. I soon became totally absorbed by the creature, which I had never previously observed in the wild.

The tortoise dived. Then I spotted a Brahminy Kite perched on a branch overhanging the river. The stately brown and white raptor just stood there as I approached it—a regal sight. Somehow, the creatures of the river did not view me as a threat as I glided past on my airbed. Perhaps they thought I was dead, or just another floating log.

Alone on the river, the raft out of sight, I seemed to have found paradise. Now that the noisy human caravan had passed by, the sounds of riverbank life were extraordinary. Birds and other animals seemed to emerge from nowhere.

All day I floated alone down that enchanted river, observing at close quarters wildlife which I had never encountered before. In the afternoon I passed a great circular eddy which must have been at least fifty metres across. I swirled slowly around in company with the great logs and other debris held in its grip. Lying face up, I watched the crowns of enormous trees outlined against the sky as they seemed to rotate around my head. It was one of the most magical days of my life.

In one place a great log jam all but blocked the river. Travelling ahead of me, a member of our expedition had been surprised to find the remains of a wallaby, half-rotten, lodged in it. He had clambered from the raft over the slippery logs and gingerly retrieved the skull for the museum collection. Months later, when our specimens were being cleaned and prepared at the museum, my attention would be drawn to some curious holes in the skull of this wallaby. It slowly dawned on me that they were puncture holes made by a crocodile bite. The wallaby had not drowned as I had assumed. It had been killed and stowed in the log jam by a crocodile when the water level was higher, probably just a few days before we had floated past.

Meanwhile, I drifted blissfully alone and unaware, down the river.

But by late afternoon I realised that I had no idea how far I was from Yapsiei station. It even seemed possible that I had passed it without realising—and was now headed for the mighty Sepik.

If I had missed the station I was in severe trouble, for there was no human habitation before me for many, many kilometres.

Alarmed at my disorientation, I now paddled on with purpose, looking for some sign of human settlement. As the last rays of the sun streaked across the sky I began to panic. Then I spotted the Papua New Guinea flag atop a pole high above the riverbank.

It was the flagpole at Yapsiei station.

As I clambered up the bank, I was met by Deyfu, who had arrived by raft an hour or so before. He looked at me sternly and led me towards the edge of the forest. There, on a pole, sat one of the largest crocodile skulls I have ever seen. Pointing to it, he said that the creature had been killed a few weeks before in the river, just by the station. I felt incredibly stupid.

The worst, however, was yet to come.

The night I arrived at Yapsiei, I awoke in the small hours of the morning gripped with the most terrible stomach cramps. A visit to the toilet was clearly imperative, yet I dreaded it. The dunny outside our fibro cottage was of the pit variety with a dirty wooden seat: a far less salubrious option than squatting in the bush. Worse, at least to me, was the fact that it provided an ideal habitat for a considerable population of large, hairy spiders. I left my roll of toilet paper there between visits and next time found a particularly ugly specimen secreted in the cardboard tube. By day most of them hid in nooks and crannies, but by night they were everywhere.

Large, hairy spiders, I am ashamed to admit, are the one thing I fear above all else. That night, I had to face my fear countless times as the pains became worse and worse.

By morning I was nauseous and began vomiting. I no longer had the strength to crawl to the toilet, and lay instead inside the crude, metal shower cubicle in the fibro house. Each time something emerged from either end of me, I turned on the cold shower and was cleansed under its cool flow. This unfortunate condition persisted for several days, during which time I ate nothing. By the time the little Cessna arrived to take us to Telefomin, I felt weak, but had recovered enough to carry on with my research.

FOURTEEN

The navel of the universe

While staying at Yapsiei in 1984 I heard much about Telefomin. Some Miyanmin represented the place to me much as some Australians still regard London: a remote, yet central, ancestral homeland.

Before I climbed aboard the Cessna at Yapsiei airstrip I asked Anaru what he knew of the Telefol. 'Their language sounds like the croaking of frogs,' he said. He told me that all of the Mountain Ok, the Miyanmin included, had originally come from Telefomin. He mentioned an old Telefol man called Femsep, who had the power to blight the taro of the Miyanmin. He spoke with great respect of this powerful sorcerer. I got the feeling from Anaru that I should watch out for this old fellow and his magic.

And Don Gardner had told me a little of the history of European contact at Telefomin. It was unique, he said, in being the only place in the Australian colonial territories where an organised insurrection against the administration had taken place.

In 1953 the Telefol cut off and murdered two young Australian kiaps and four Papuan police. Telefol warriors then massed at the station and attempted to kill the remaining Australians. Among them was Norm Draper, a quick-witted Baptist missionary. Draper grabbed Femsep's son, who was playing near the radio shack, and held him hostage until relief arrived.

The Telefol cut logs to roll onto the airstrip in order to prevent other Australians landing. But Draper radioed for help before they could be deployed. The uprising was over almost before it began. The principal rebels were sentenced to death, along with a number of other Telefol men, but the sentences were later commuted to terms of imprisonment.

Telefomin truly is remote from the other major centres of human population in New Guinea. The densely populated central highlands of Papua New Guinea lie hundreds of kilometres to the east, while Irian Jaya's Baliem Valley lies even further to the west. As a result of this isolation, Telefomin is a bit of a backwater, albeit with a very distinctive culture.

Sweet potato (introduced to New Guinea about 400 years ago) is the backbone of agriculture in most other areas, but at Telefomin it plays a very minor role. There, taro (a much older indigenous crop) still reigns supreme. Curiously, the Pacific Rat (*Rattus exulans*), which was introduced to New Guinea about 3,000 years ago and is a great pest in houses and gardens throughout most of the country, is absent from Telefomin. Again, this probably reflects the region's remoteness.

The material culture of the Telefol is also distinctive. The Mountain Ok (all of whom trace descent from Telefomin) are the only mountain people in New Guinea with an elaborate carving tradition. Their shields and house-boards (boards with a small oval opening which acts as a door) are beautifully carved in abstract designs which are often coloured in ochre, black and white.

The dress of the Mountain Ok also differs from that found in most parts of Papua New Guinea, but is similar to that worn by many mountain tribes in Irian Jaya. Women wear a skirt made of grass and are rarely seen without a laden *bilum* slung from their foreheads. These beautifully looped string bags are made from the bark of a particular tree. When new they are snowy white and soft, but incredibly durable and elastic. They are used to carry taro, other food, firewood and even children. It was a *bilum* which had saved Oblankep's life. Telefol *bilum*s are renowned throughout Papua New Guinea for their strength, durability and artistry.

The dress of the men is rather elaborate. It consists of a long gourd which is worn over the penis and tied at its base to the scrotum. A few loops of cane are worn around the waist, and a bone or boar's tusk through the pierced septum of the nose. The heads of rhinoceros beetles are worn through holes at the nose tip, and the stiff, cylindrical spine-like feathers from cassowary wings go through holes at the sides of the nose. These cross above the nose, imparting a boar-like fierceness to the face. The *bilum*s of men are often elaborately decorated with feathers or other objects. In times past, an intricate head-dress of cane and ochre was also worn. The nature of both head-dress and *bilum* denoted the stage of initiation that a man had reached.

For a while, traditional dress mixed rather oddly with new influences in the Telefomin area. One man was famous for wearing the pink, pudgy leg of a plastic doll in place of the yellow gourd usually affixed to the penis. The pink plastic baby flesh and cute baby foot looked somehow obscene in its new role. Another was known for wearing a cigar case.

By the time of my first visit to Telefomin in 1984 there were still a few old men who wore the penis gourd and cane bands, but by 1990 even they were gone. By then, almost everyone was clothed in dirty European cast-offs. These clothes are donated by Australians to the Baptist mission, which ships them to Papua New Guinea to sell to the Telefol.

On this first visit to Telefomin I flew from Yapsiei via the Sepik Gorge. Approaching the valley on this route, one sees that its entrance is marked by a precipice of titanic proportions. This cliff of white limestone, perhaps 1,500 metres high, stands guard on its southern side. On the very lip of the cliff is a tiny village. It looks like the work of ants in proportion to the scale of the massive white scarp below.

The small government station and mission post at Telefomin are nestled in the base of the steep but flat-bottomed valley. The Sepik River flows near its southern margin, but at a level several hundred metres below the main valley floor. My best guess as to how the valley formed is that long ago a landslide blocked the Sepik River, damming its waters to form a lake which filled the entire Telefomin Valley. Perhaps the towering white cliff is the scar left by this huge prehistoric landslide. Whatever the case, sediment must have been deposited in the ancient lake for a long time, finally building up to a thickness of several hundred metres.

When the dam wall broke, the lake drained and the river began to cut down through the sediment accumulated in the lake. Today the river has cut so far that it runs well below the level of the old lake bed.

In 1987, when a road was being constructed in the valley near Telefomin, workers unearthed fascinating evidence of the ancient life that once lived around the old lake system. The bull-dozer cutting the track came across a layer of fossilised leaves and stems preserved in a bluish clay. Near them was most of the skeleton of an extinct marsupial. The animal, a distant relative of the wombat, was like a panda in size and shape. It must have inhabited the forest surrounding the lake. The fossil plants remain unstudied, but when they are examined they should give an intriguing glimpse of what those forests were like aeons ago.

The old lake surface is now all grassland, having being cleared in prehistoric times, but small remnants of forest have survived in gullies. The southern wall of the valley is also grassland. There, the mountain wall rises abruptly to over 2,500 metres elevation. It is so steep that fires lit at its base during dry periods carry right to the top, killing the forest as they go.

When I first saw the Telefomin Valley it seemed to be a dull, forbidding place. Cloud closed it off like a blanket over a basin. Below, through the constant drizzle, a maze of muddy tracks skirted swamps and led to sombre-looking buildings. Moss and lichen growing on every exposed fence-post and dead tree testified that rain and cloud were life's constants here.

Dan Jorgensen, a Canadian anthropologist who had already spent several years with the Telefol, was then living in a village called Telefolip. Telefolip lay about forty minutes' walk south of the airstrip along a slippery, muddy path which wound its way through grassland. I was anxious to meet Dan, for my experience with Don Gardner had shown me just how valuable contacts provided by anthropologists can be.

A small cluster of huts lies near the place where the turn-off to Telefolip leaves the main track. I inquired after Dan at one of these, and an old man led me down the side path through long *kunai* grass. Soon, we dropped off the plateau into a steep gully, and the environment suddenly changed. We were walking through a grove of magnificent *Araucaria* trees. Around the edge of the grove they were saplings but, further in, the pines were soaring giants, mist swirling through their crowns. Their straight, clean boles carried patches of bright green moss, which contrasted with their walnut-coloured bark. At one point the path dipped under the trunk of a fallen giant, giving me a chance to measure myself against the diameter of one of these magnificent trees. It was about a metre thick.

The most striking thing about the grove was the quality of the sound. It seemed as if, in an instant, we had left the noisy, muddy world of drizzle and people and entered a large, open-air cathedral. The villages with their slippery paths and clamour of pigs and children were left behind. Even the sound of the rain had vanished—high above the drizzle was caught in the canopy. One could not feel or hear it below. The path itself had also become more pleasant, for it now passed over a soft carpet of leaves and moss, muffling our footfalls.

Suddenly, a bird flitted between the lower branches of one of the *Araucarias*. I held my breath as I recognised it as a male Splendid Astrapia (*Astrapia splendidissima*). With their long tails and curved beaks, these magnificent birds of paradise are imposing creatures. From a distance they appear to be all black, but when viewed more closely you can see the iridescent patches on their chest and head, which are beautiful beyond description. Their glorious tail plumes are highly valued every-where. As a result, they are avidly hunted and are usually shy. I looked at my companion for signs of interest in the bird. I was astounded that he took almost no notice of it as it flitted about in the branches just above his head. He simply trudged by, head down, along the path.

Too soon light showed through the trees ahead of us, signalling the end of the *Araucaria* grove. We came to a fence, and before us stood the wall of a building the likes of which I had never seen before in New Guinea. It was a barn-like structure about as tall as a two-storey house, and as we walked around to the front of it I could see that the only egress lay via a tiny oval door halfway up its front wall.

Stretched out before this remarkable structure lay the village of Telefolip. It consisted of a dozen or so houses, arranged in two rows facing a path leading to the barn-like building. The houses all stood on pedestals of soil about a metre high. The pedestals had been created, apparently, by the soil between and around them being worn away by count-less generations of feet. This never happens in most of New Guinea because the village site changes regularly.

What struck me most about Telefolip was that everything was traditional. Not a nail or iron tool, not a plastic bag or piece of nylon rope gave any hint that this village belonged to the end of the twentieth century.

Dan Jorgensen was sitting in one of the huts, surrounded by senior Telefol men. He was in deep discussion with them, but he welcomed me warmly. I was breathless with the excitement of seeing a bird of paradise at such close range, and blurted out my tale of the sighting.

But that particular bird, it seemed, had been displaying for several weeks now in the sacred grove.

The grove of *Araucaria* trees, Dan explained, belongs to Afek, the ancestress of the Telefol. The large building at the end of the sacred grove was her cult house, where young Telefol men are taken so that the secrets of the ancestress can be passed on to them. No woman is ever allowed to enter it. Indeed, no woman is allowed even to enter the sacred grove of *Araucaria* trees through which I had just passed. Instead, they had to take a steep, muddy path that passed into the village via another route.

Dan explained that literally everything about the grove was sacred. Not a single leaf, not even an annoying mosquito, could be disturbed in it. Over generations the birds had learned about this, and even normally shy creatures such as the birds of paradise sometimes display fearlessly within easy reach of an arrow. Open displays by valuable birds such as the Splendid Astrapia chagrin the Telefol—which explained the glum look on the face of my guide. It must be a bit like seeing a jewel on the ground, but not being allowed to pick it up.

Telefol believe that human life itself began in the sacred grove and cult house at Telefolip. For them, this is where the first human being lived, and it is the place from which all Mountain Ok people originated. To Telefol, Telefolip literally is the navel of the universe. I think I became enchanted with Telefomin on hearing this. The Telefol are the Melanesian people I feel most happy and at home with to this day.

After chatting for some hours with Dan, I entered the Telefolip cult house for the first time. The tiny doorway is perched high on the side of the building, at the top of a rickety ladder. From this insecure perch, one must somehow squeeze through the small oval hole to gain access to the interior. The squeeze is so tight and the venture so perilous that the experience is somewhat akin to being born. The symbolism of this is doubtless not missed by Telefol boys when they enter the cult house for the first time, soon to emerge as men.

I led with one leg and my head, and had to double my leading leg up under my chin to get it in. My back was meanwhile bent double and followed only with considerable persuasion and the helpful positioning of two Telefol acting as midwives.

After entering the house and unbending, I could at first see nothing. As my eyes adjusted to the gloom I perceived that the four walls of the building were decorated with tens of thousands of pig jaw-bones and skulls. Between them hung *bilum*s containing human skulls and limb bones, while a few old Telefol shields, clubs and other implements were propped against the walls.

Two hearths were present on the floor. Dan had told me that the one on the left was the taro hearth, the other the arrow hearth. A few implements relating to the respective activities of agriculture and war were scattered near or above the hearths, and some firewood lay nearby.

Dan explained the significance of the two hearths in the cult house. Rituals associated with the taro hearth were performed for the benefit of agriculture, pig husbandry and related matters. Those of the arrow side were responsible for warfare and hunting. The people of Telefolip were divided into two major groups which corresponded with these hearths. The arrow clan had been in decline since the arrival of the Europeans. This was due to the fact that warfare and hunting became less important after the Europeans brought peace and western goods.

The room was not very tall, as most of the height of the

building consisted of a vast area enclosed below the floor. This space underneath had no entrance. I had difficulty learning anything about it, but some years later an old man intimated to me that it was actually inhabited by Afek.

Dan Jorgensen did me an invaluable service by providing introductions to two senior men from Telefolip. Amunsep and Tinamnok were both arrow men. I was fortunate, he said, that in Amunsep I would meet one of the last of the old arrow clan. His knowledge of the mammals of the region was unequalled.

On leaving the cult house, I was led directly to Amunsep's house, which lay to the left, just a few doors down. It was, if anything, even darker than the cult house itself and the roof and walls were blackened with soot. The space was divided into two chambers. The one at the rear was presumably used for sleeping and cooking, while the larger antechamber at the front of the house seemed to serve in part to entertain visitors.

A group of Telefol men sat in waiting for me. They grasped my hand and greeted me with the click handshake so characteristic of west New Guinea. This is done by placing the knuckle of your forefinger between two knuckles of your friend's fingers. The friend then pulls away rapidly, producing a loud clicking sound. After performing this ritual, one man announced that he was Tinamnok, Amunsep's nephew, but that Amunsep, unfortunately, was away hunting.

The decorations in the antechamber of Amunsep's house were extraordinary. Some beautiful *bilum*s, bows and arrows, and other items hung or leaned against the walls, but the centrepiece of the display was suspended over the entrance. There, in row after row, were the jaw-bones which the great hunter had collected over a lifetime. There were hundreds, nay thousands of them, and they were all arranged according to size and species. Even I, as curator of mammals at the Australian Museum, could not have done a better job at classification and display. Curiously, no rat jaws were present, and a few other species were notable by their absence. I learned the

significance of this only as I began to understand Telefol culture—Amunsep had caught and collected only the jaws of
animals which were considered suitable food to senior men.

Tinamnok and his family more or less adopted me while I
stayed at Telefolip. They decided that the best place by far for
me to carry out my research was in an area of garden land
near the headwaters of the Sol River. This area was adjacent to
some rugged limestone country which was inhabited by tree-
kangaroos.

Tinamnok was a gentle man in his forties and a superb
hunter. He was someone whose company I enjoyed
immensely. He owned an aged blunderbuss of a shotgun, the
accuracy and reliability of which were extremely questionable.
He was deeply attached to it, however, and steadfastly refused
to use the more modern weapon I carried. Each time I suggested he borrow it his eyes would widen and he would bite on
the knuckle of one finger as he displayed mistrust, even fear,
of my shiny new gun.

Despite his abilities as a hunter of medium-sized marsupials, Tinamnok professed no skill in catching *D'bol*, as the
Telefol know Doria's Tree-kangaroo (*Dendrolagus dorianus*).
For that I would need to consult Amunsep, and he was still
away up-country hunting. I was dismayed, but decided, instead
of just waiting, to accompany Tinamnok and a young man
called Willok on a journey to a high valley on the Sol River,
half a day's walk away. This was Tinamnok's country.

FIFTEEN

Journey to the Sol

The trek up to the Sol is a steep one. Most of the way lies through primary forest and is relatively easy going despite the ascent, except for a constant succession of slippery logs which would test the balance of a tightrope walker. The only substantial barrier to be crossed is the Sol River itself, which one encounters about halfway along the track.

The Sol is a major tributary of the Sepik. It is a considerable, tempestuous river which floods frequently. On this first trek we reached it at about lunchtime.

I knew well before I saw it that we were in for a difficult crossing, for I could hear the roar of the water from a great distance. As we drew closer I could distinguish dull booms above the roar, as of distant cannon. These sounds were made by great boulders which were being picked up and dashed against the stream bed by the current. As we neared the riverbank, the gunpowder-like smell of crushed rock filled my nose. The stream was grey, like a furious flow of liquid mud. Although unpolluted, it looked and smelled like a river filled with mine tailings.

Heavy rain must have fallen in the catchment of the Sol to cause such a torrent. The old log bridge which previously spanned the river at this point had been swept away and I was certain that we would have to turn back. Tinamnok, however, had no such doubts. He strode into a clump of casuarina trees growing by the stream and began felling the tallest.

After a few minutes the trunk fell in a graceful arc over the torrent, its top just reaching the opposite bank. Tinamnok's dog was the first across. It strolled over, winding its way around obstructing upright branches as if it were negotiating a broad pathway between villages.

Tinamnok himself was in the middle, walking just as casually, when he realised that I had misgivings about making the crossing. He came back and cut me a long stick with which to stabilise myself, then led me by the hand across the impromptu bridge. By keeping my eyes fixed firmly on the opposite bank I found the first part of the crossing relatively easy. The casuarina bole was clean and covered with rough bark, which gave a good grip.

It was only when I came to the centre of the stream, where some large branches blocked my way, that I struck trouble. There I made the mistake of looking down. The water was moving with such frightening speed just half a metre below me that it was dizzying to behold. I could not focus my eyes fast enough to see anything but a vicious, rushing blur which threatened to pull me in.

I began to lose my balance. But the thought that to fall off the log meant instant death snapped the hypnotic hold the torrent had on me. Trembling and holding Tinamnok's hand more firmly than ever, I negotiated the obstructing branches, and in a few moments was on the opposite bank.

After this perilous crossing, it was difficult for me to relax for the remainder of the trip. The thought of the Sol, ready to rise at my back and cut off my retreat at any time, preoccupied me. I was not sure that I had the courage to cross it in flood again.

Almost immediately on arriving at the little lean-to that Tinamnok used as a shelter when hunting, I fell ill once again with symptoms similar to those that I had experienced at Yapsiei. I later learned that I was suffering from giardia, contracted from the dirty water of the Yapsiei River. The return of this illness on the Sol left me helpless. I had not eaten properly for more than a week, and it took all my strength just to crawl around my trapline each morning and to weigh, measure and skin the specimens I caught, as well as those which Tinamnok brought to me.

While I stayed around the lean-to, Tinamnok would go out hunting, often for two or three days at a time. He would sleep in a hollow tree or nap on a sunny riverbank, returning only when he had met with success. In this he was accompanied by Willok, the youth whom Tinamnok had adopted. Willok, an Atbalmin (whose territory abuts the Telefol to the west), was a clean-shaven, open-faced lad who seemed to attach himself to me with genuine affection. He was not a good hunter, but like many Atbalmin had endless patience when searching tree-hollows and potential nest sites for the smaller arboreal animals. He collected some of the rarest and most interesting mammals I encountered during my work at Telefomin.

Willok, though, had a most unfortunate habit, which turned everyone's stomach, even his stepfather's. Whenever Tinamnok returned with a Coppery Ringtail, and this was a very common species, Willok would eagerly offer to help me skin and gut it. His assistance consisted of removing the intestines and feeling excitedly along them. On detecting a small lump, he would carefully pierce the bowel wall with his fingernail and victoriously pull out a large, yellow tapeworm. Next, by way of culinary preparation, he would run it between his fingers to remove some of the adherent fecal matter—then he would drop the writhing parasite straight into his mouth!

My Telefol friends informed me that Willok's habit was an Atbalmin foible which was quite as abhorrent to them as it was to me. As a biologist I was intrigued by the possibility that this apparently edible parasite might infect its human consumer. So I beat Willok to several of the worms and, when I returned to Australia, sent them to a parasitologist for study. The parasitologist was intrigued too, for edible parasites are rare indeed in nature. He doubted, however, that harm would come to Willok from his dietary predilection, for the guts of ringtail possums are highly specialised. Anything which could live in them would find the human intestine a hostile environment.

Some years later I received a copy of a scientific paper in the mail, in which the parasitologist had described the worms I had collected. As it was a species previously unknown to science, he coined a new name for it—*Burtiella flanneryi,* apparently in my honour! To this day I feel somewhat ambivalent about being associated with this culinary wonder.

One night, as I was lying sick and alone under my shelter and feeling rather sorry for myself, a dog walked casually into camp. Presently, it was followed by another, then another. Some minutes later a man arrived.

It was Amunsep. He had arrived back at Telefolip and, hearing of me, had come to help me find tree-kangaroos.

Amunsep appeared to be in his fifties. He had a broad face with a typically large Melanesian nose and frizzy hair which was greying at the temples. Over one eye was a boil the size of a hen's egg. He wore ex-army shorts and a military beret, but had doubtless spent his early years dressed in *kamen* and *autil,* the traditional Telefol penis gourd and cane waistband. Over his shoulder he wore an exquisite *bilum* made with the care and eye to utility that only Telefol women possess. It was decorated like no other I had ever seen, for the tail tips of at least twenty *D'bol* tree-kangaroos adorned its outer surface. Around Amunsep's neck hung a miniature *bilum* which was even more beautiful than the first. It looked impossibly small to be of any use.

Amunsep was doubtless surprised to find anyone at the camp. Perhaps he thought me too lazy or incompetent to follow Tinamnok as he hunted. Whatever the case, it was difficult to disabuse him of his opinions, for Amunsep was a traditional man who spoke neither English nor Pidgin. After less than a week at Telefomin I had picked up precious little Telefol. Still, I greeted him with the customary phrase, '*Ngum saro*,' which he returned before sitting by the fire. After an awkward silence I fished a cooked sweet potato out of the ashes (these formed our principal food at the camp) and passed it to him. As he ate, I began to read aloud the list of Telefol animal names which I had laboriously collected from Tinamnok.

With each name correctly pronounced, Amunsep would mime the animal's behaviour, imitate its call and indicate, by pointing either up, down or around, its elevational distribution. First there was *Bogol*, as the Telefol know the New Guinea Harpy Eagle (*Harpyopsis novaeguineae*). So powerful is this bird that it is reputed to carry off young tree-kangaroos, and even human infants neglected momentarily by their mothers. The call of the male sounds like the release of a tense bowstring. This is followed by the low clucking call of the female. Amunsep imitated the calls perfectly. His mime of *Bogol*'s terrifying descending talons and the fierceness of its eye had my heart in my throat.

Finally, I came to the tree-kangaroo, *D'bol*. Instantly, the animal came to life before me. Its immensely powerful forearms, its fearfully sharp claws, its imperious stare as it looks down at its assailants from high in the canopy—all were conjured true to life. The snuffling sounds and grinding of its teeth to signify annoyance were there, as were its peculiar posture and hop.

When I finally looked up from my list of animal names it was nearly 2 a.m. A starry night promised good hunting on the morrow.

The first grey strands of dawn brought acrid smoke to my

face. Amunsep was already up, kindling the fire to warm himself. As I watched from my wet sleeping bag, feeling sicker than ever, Amunsep took the tiny *bilum* from around his neck. From it he extracted what appeared to be some native tobacco. He rolled the leaves into a mini cigar, lit it and inhaled deeply. Grabbing the nearest dog by the foreleg, he roused it from slumber by blowing the smoke straight into its nostrils. The whimpering animal was released and the process repeated on the others.

Amunsep next took the pale bark of a plant known to Telefol as *tabap kal.* He chewed this scented bark until it was pulp. Again he took up the dogs and blew the white fragments straight into each one's face. Finally, he took from the *bilum* a pebble of beautiful, deep red agate, rolled smooth and pellet-like by a stream. With this stone he rubbed each dog gently on the forehead, all the while chanting under his breath. Then Amunsep was gone, and I was left alone for another two days in that beautiful forest.

One afternoon Amunsep and Tinamnok returned together to camp. They had the usual cuscuses and ringtail possums, but *D'bol* had eluded them.

By now I felt well enough to walk. The expedition was over without a glimpse of a tree-kangaroo, and together we descended from the world of *D'bol* into the world of people.

The raging Sol River of my nightmares had been tamed by rainless skies. I walked over it by stepping from stone to stone, even finding time to enjoy the sun on its bank, where I sat listening to the tinkling of its flow.

SIXTEEN

The cuscus has four fingers

The nights and days on the Sol with Tinamnok, Willok and their family were enchanted times. Between 1984 and 1990 I returned again and again to the valley to trek up to the forests growing at its head. Each time I shared their garden lodge, but over the years it was enlarged to shelter our party. Sometimes there were as many as four or five other Europeans with me, so these extensions were necessary.

I think that Tinamnok's family looked forward to our visits. They took great interest in the strange things we brought. On one visit I carried a gunny sack full of live mud crabs, which were then to be had very cheap at Koki Market in Port Moresby. The Telefol are entirely land-locked and had never seen such things. Their eyes widened in amazement as they examined them. I asked for a large pot which I filled with water. I placed some mud crabs inside and began to heat it.

The kitchen was absolutely crowded with people who had come to see the marvel, but as the pot began to heat one of the crabs loosed the bonds which held its pincers down, and pushed off the lid of the pot. The sight of the great nipper waving above the steam sent the assembled multitudes screaming into the night. Most had returned by the time the crabs were cooked but few could be induced to taste them. Despite this reluctance, virtually every inhabitant of Telefolip went around for weeks afterwards adorned with bits of crab carapace or claw.

With each visit I got to know the area better. Once, the most extraordinary growth of luminescent fungus was evident throughout the region. Hundreds of small, slender toadstools, light brown by day, were transformed each night into bright green parasols. Other luminous fungi infected dead wood. A forest giant, which had fallen years before, seemed to have every fibre of its rotting frame impregnated with the hyphae of one variety which shone less powerfully than the green toadstools. You had to turn your torch off for a time before it took on its full glory. When your eyes adjusted to the darkness, a most amazing sight appeared, for there, running off through the forest, were segments of trunk and branches up to a metre thick, which had been shattered and separated during their fall. They shone with a silver light and one could play mental jigsaw with the glowing pieces. The astonishing thing about the scene was that no other plant matter was infected with the luminous growth. Yet, by day, you could not discern the huge broken tree, so smothered was it by other debris.

Although these were spectacular fungi indeed, the most remarkable glow came from a bank of senescent grass growing by a garden. The fallen stems spilled down the bank for about five metres, and every one of them was infected with a species which gave off a silvery, sparkling luminescence. By night, this transformed the mundane bank into a shining, frozen waterfall.

On the whole, the mammal fauna of the Sol region contained few surprises. Cuscusses were the most common species
caught, and our hunters must have brought in over a hundred
of them during the time I worked there. We kept only a few for
the museum, for the vast majority belonged to just one
species, the Silky Cuscus (*Phalanger sericeus*). Then, towards
the end of an expedition in 1986, a hunter brought in a young
cuscus which looked different from all the others. When I
returned to Australia I found that it resembled an adult which
I had captured a year before on the Nong River to the south of
Telefomin. At the time, I assumed that this animal was a
hybrid.

With two specimens I began to rethink my ideas. Then
Lester Seri showed me a female he had caught near Tifalmin
years before. Here was a third. Biochemical and morpholog-
ical studies subsequently made it clear that these specimens
represented a distinct, very rare and primitive kind of cuscus
which was found only in the Telefomin area. I named it
Phalanger matanim, the last name being that which the Telefol
know it by. Even today, this curious creature is known from
only six specimens.

As I continued work on the Sol, I learned a little about what it
means to be Telefol. At the centre of the Telefol world-view is
the story of Afek—Afek of the *Araucaria* grove—the ancestress
of all the Mountain Ok. There are many versions of her story
and doubtless the one told to me is not precisely the same as
that told to others. Indeed, because of my interest in animals,
I probably learned more of the parts of the story relating to
wildlife than of other aspects. Despite the difficulty of learning
the whole tale, one needs to know the story of Afek in order to
appreciate the Telefol world-view.

According to the Telefol, Afek was the first person to exist.
She lived in the cult house at Telefolip with her children. At

least one of her children was a man, while the others included the Long-beaked Echidna (which Telefol know as *Egil*), the rat (*Senok*) and the Ground Cuscus (*Quoyam*). For a long time, they all lived happily together in the house with their mother.

Egil was the first of Afek's children to leave home. He complained to his mother that the smoke from the cooking fire hurt his small and weak eyes. Afek said it was best that he go and live in the high, mossy forest surrounding the Telefomin valley. She told her human son that Egil was his brother, on no account to be harmed in any way.

Because of this injunction, Telefol never until recently hunted this rarest of New Guinea animals. In the 1950s echidnas were so common at Telefomin they could be met with even in the immediate vicinity of Telefolip. This taboo against hunting Long-beaked Echidnas was unique in all of New Guinea, making Telefomin at that time the last stronghold of this now endangered species.

So powerful was the taboo against harming *Egil* that Telefol believed that to walk into Telefolip with echidna blood on one's hands would be to bring disaster upon all Mountain Ok people. Even today, when all Telefol are nominally Christian, many older men refuse to touch, eat, or even look upon a dead *Egil*. Despite this, the Long-beaked Echidna is no longer seen in the Telefomin area. Younger men, who have been Christian since adolescence, capture the animals and sell them alive for fabulous prices to non-Telefol living at Telefomin, or carry them for sale to neighbouring tribes.

It is with a heavy heart that I must relate that in all my time at Telefomin (1984–92) I never saw a living Long-beaked Echidna.

The story of Afek continues in this way. Senok, the rat, was the child who never left home. Instead it stayed in Afek's house and became a pest to humans. The rat which infests Telefol houses is the Small Spiny Rat (*Rattus steini*). Despite its name, this is a sizeable and smelly rodent, which does considerable damage to crops. In traditional times, the species did have a use; before store-bought food became widely available, *Senok* was a major protein source for Telefol women.

The story of *Quoyam* (the Ground Cuscus) is perhaps the strangest of all those told about Afek's children. The Ground Cuscus is a large and powerful animal which is respected by many Mountain Ok groups. This is doubtless because it is a child of Afek, and indeed is regarded as a most human-like animal. Telefol say that *Quoyam* steals food from their gardens. It places taro pieces in its pouch just as a human thief would hide stolen taro in his *bilum*. Even the story of how Quoyam came to leave his ancestral home has distinctly human overtones.

Quoyam lived happily with his mother until he reached adolescence, when he became interested in the opposite sex and curious about female anatomy. One day, driven by carnal curiosity, he inserted one of his digits into his mother's vagina. Angered, she chopped off the offending digit with a stone axe. As a result, Telefol believe to this day that *Quoyam* has but four digits on its forepaw.

Biologists have a problem with this story, for we know that, like all species of cuscus, *Quoyam* has five digits on each forepaw. When I first drew this anomaly to the attention of a Telefol youth who had caught a specimen, he looked uncomprehendingly at the paw with its five robust digits. Shaking his head, he said that it *must* have four fingers and that, despite its appearance, the animal he had caught was perhaps not *Quoyam* at all!

How to account for the persistence of this Telefol belief in the face of such glaring contradictory evidence? The answer may lie in the fact that Ground Cuscusses are pugnacious creatures. Old males can be terribly scarred, with eyes torn through, ears missing, and claws and digits bitten off. Perhaps a sufficient number of large males have sacrificed a digit on the field of battle to keep the myth alive in the minds of the Telefol.

To return to the central theme of the Afek story, Telefol believe that, because of the association of the ancestress with Telefolip, the village has a special place in the Mountain Ok cosmology. They believe, indeed, that they occupy a physically and spiritually central position in the region. As a result, the rituals they conduct at Telefolip are thought to have repercussions throughout the Mountain Ok world.

This special sense of responsibility has perhaps led to the rather stolid and serious demeanour of Telefol. They are sometimes slow to laugh, and the Telefol ideal is to appear to disdain frivolity. Indeed, Telefol characterise themselves as sober, responsible people, qualities they find lacking in their neighbours. The Miyanmin, they say, are fiery and violent and—like children—prone to temper tantrums. The Atbalmin, they suggest, are also like children, without a real sense of responsibility or a worry about the future.

It is this sense of social gravity, perhaps, which accounts for the survival of the Telefolip cult house when so many lesser cult houses in the region have been abandoned. Since European contact, Telefol culture has been under immense pressure, both deliberate and inadvertent.

Perhaps the most mortifying discovery the Europeans brought the Telefol was that the world is a much larger place than they suspected, and that its centre does not necessarily lie at Telefolip.

Christianity came to Telefomin after the Second World War, and a Baptist mission has been established just a few kilometres from Telefolip since the early 1950s. Young Telefol have discovered that there are other ways to gain status than their tradition offers. By becoming pastors, or gaining power and influence in some other way within the church, they have learned to circumvent the social control of clan elders, and to bring traditional authority structures into question. It is all too easy for these aspiring young leaders to label ancient rituals as the work of the devil in an attempt to discredit the old power structure. This has led to the decline of many traditional beliefs.

As a result of these influences, the most important initiations occur today not at Telefolip, but at other cult houses in areas to the south which are peopled by the Wopkaimin and which are under Roman Catholic influence.

Some of the young Telefol men who became pastors have moved to other Mountain Ok communities to spread the good word. In 1986, I met one such man at the Atbalmin settlement of Munbil, some fifty kilometres west of Telefomin.

The Munbil airstrip had been opened just three weeks before my visit, and was still being lengthened and smoothed out as our Cessna came to a screeching halt metres from the jungle at the end of the clearing.

The Atbalmin working on the strip appeared to have had little contact with the outside world, for they were dressed in grass skirts or penis gourds, and most spoke little if any Pidgin. Moses, the Telefol pastor, introduced himself to us, and invited us to stay in the newly completed medical clinic by the strip. He told us that after he had heard the gospel message as a youth at Telefomin twenty years previously, he had decided to live among the Atbalmin at Munbil as a missionary.

Moses had long promised the Atbalmin that, if they prayed earnestly and followed gospel teachings, the day would come when Europeans would arrive and bring wonderful things with them. Our visit, he said, was the fulfilment of a dream which had been twenty years in the making. He begged us to buy the tomatoes and carrots which the village women grew. He explained that the Atbalmin would not yet eat such strange food and were growing them only for sale to the expected influx of tourists. If they saw us eat them, he reasoned, they might be encouraged to consume them themselves, or at least grow more for trade.

Despite his high expectations of us, we got on quite well with Moses—until one morning when our small group (myself and four members of the Australian Museum Society) went down to the river to bathe.

The river ran at the base of a steep cliff about fifty metres below the village. We all (including two women) stripped to our briefs and enjoyed a thorough wash. I was aware that all the while we were being observed from the cliff top by Moses and about two hundred Atbalmin.

When we climbed back to the village, Moses was almost in tears.

'For twenty years,' he lamented, 'I have tried to teach these women to hide their breasts modestly, as the Bible says we should. Now you come and display yourselves shamelessly in front of my whole congregation. What will they think of me?'

I have often wondered how I should judge Moses. He had devoted his life to doing good as he saw it. Yet what had he achieved? He might, perhaps, have introduced a more varied diet and thus improved nutrition among the Atbalmin. But would this be counterbalanced by the diseases introduced as people started to wear dirty European cast-offs? Perhaps it is true that a little knowledge is a dangerous thing.

The Baptist missionaries at Telefomin have worked hard to wean the Telefol from what they see as their pagan ways. More than once I was told they had offered to purchase timber cut from Afek's sacred grove at Telefolip. They had also apparently discouraged people from participating in the renewal of the cult house itself, a job which must be undertaken every twenty years or so, as the construction materials used deteriorate rapidly.

During the latter part of the 1980s it was sad to see clear signs that the old Telefol culture was falling away. The last people to dress traditionally were rapidly fading. Telefolip was falling into disrepair, and even the sacred grove of *Araucaria* trees was no longer sacrosanct. I remember walking through the grove in 1984 in the company of a young Telefol man, when he saw that a branch had fallen from one of the larger trees. He was greatly alarmed by this, and looked intensely at the fallen limb as if trying to extract meaning from it.

When I last visited the grove in 1992, a great *Araucaria* lay by the path—its trunk hewn into segments with a chainsaw.

Had the tree fallen before it was cut up? Yet a decade before, the cutting of even a fallen tree would have been unthinkable.

Although the Telefol experienced dramatic social change between about 1950 (when government influence began to be felt) and 1990, they had yet to suffer the breakdown in law and order which so often accompanies such changes in Papua New Guinea. Robberies were all but unknown at Telefomin while I was there, and the tight-knit and isolated community seemed to retain relatively powerful control over the worst excesses of its young men. Telefol do not easily give themselves over to lawlessness. They are too responsible for that.

Nevertheless, by May 1992 the houses of Telefolip had a neglected look and were clearly no longer inhabited. Weeds grew up around them, and creepers twined around door-covers which would, perhaps, never again be opened. The cult house itself was entirely dilapidated. Great holes in the roof had allowed the rain in, and precious Telefol shields (worth thousands of dollars on the international art market) and *bilum*s full of ancestral bones were mouldering away on the floor. It seemed as if the modern world had finally won. Telefomin was no longer the centre of the universe. It had been converted into just another remote, grey, government station.

SEVENTEEN

Femsep—a Telefol big man

The arrival of the Europeans at Telefomin has left many people confused, groping for explanations of the phenomena which have so transformed their lives. This change has indeed been so rapid, yet so uneven, that extraordinary misunderstandings are inevitable.

I was intrigued to find Tinamnok show enormous interest in a candle, having never seen one before—yet battery operated torches were passé for him. Likewise, light aircraft are completely accepted at Telefomin as everyday means of transport, yet how would its people respond to a bicycle?

The coming of western technology is a favourite theme of Telefol stories. Several times I was told the story of the first torch to arrive in the valley. It had been brought by a young man who had visited a trade store. Everyone considered it a wonder—too valuable indeed to remain the property of such a young, irresponsible fellow. His aged and respected uncle, therefore, took possession of it. One night the uncle set out hunting. Using the torch, he was so successful that he became mightily burdened under the mountain of possums he had killed.

He had wandered far from home and in the middle of the night it began to rain. Unconcerned, the old man stopped under a tree and gathered some kindling. He applied the torch closely to the twigs, looking for the expected flame. After some time, his fire remained unlit and frustration was rising in the old fellow, who was by now wet and freezing. Finally he was roused to a fury and threw the torch to the ground. It broke and he spent the night in darkness, huddled under his pile of possums. When he returned to the village in the morning he threw the torch at the feet of his nephew, cursing the useless item along with the lad who had acquired it.

One can sympathise with the sense of disorientation at the intrusion of the modern world which is felt so keenly by Telefol. The effect of intrusions on their isolation became apparent to me during a visit in 1986. I was staying on the Sol River when several people arrived in a state of high excitement, saying that the Third World War had begun. They claimed to have heard on the radio that the Americans had attacked the Russians and that many cities were already destroyed. Some reports were quite precise, stating the number of MiGs and other aircraft lost on both sides.

As it was the Reagan era and the Cold War was still alive and well, this terrifying news had an aura of plausibility about it. I spent several days in a highly anxious state, questioning people closely about where they had got their information, and exactly what they had heard. They were so consistent and adamant in their stories that I really did come to believe them. The thought then occurred to me that perhaps all that remained of the world was this tiny valley high in the mountains of central New Guinea.

Returning to Telefolip several days later, I found that everyone there laboured under the same apprehensions.

No-one knew where the news had come from, but it did seem as if America and Russia were at war, and that terrible destruction had been occasioned by nuclear weapons.

It was only when I got to Port Moresby some weeks later that I learned the full truth. The nuclear reactor at Chernobyl had blown up. Chinese whispers had transformed this event into a world war by the time word reached Telefomin.

Often on the Sol, I would be approached by a Telefol elder in the dead of night. He would whisper to me: 'This evening I told you everything of the secrets of Afek. Now tell me, friend, where does money come from?'

At first I did not understand the nature of these questions, and would respond by saying that money represents accumulated wealth and that my ancestors had worked and saved hard. They had invested their money in banks or companies, creating even more wealth.

On hearing this my listener would typically become irritable and say, 'Money does not come from work. You come here and pay us to work for you. We carry your equipment and feed you. You do not work, yet it is you who have the money. Now tell me really, as a friend who will keep your secret, where does money come from?'

What the Telefol wanted to hear was the magic formula whereby money could be literally made.

One night I was asked, in a similar vein, how aircraft were created. Many Telefol had by this time visited the newly opened Ok Tedi mine, so I decided to begin by explaining the basics of where raw materials such as metals came from. I said that aeroplanes were made of metal, much like the copper and gold being dug up at Ok Tedi. This was taken to a factory, where a great number of people with different skills fashioned it into an aeroplane. I added that probably no one person knew how to make an aeroplane, but that it was a joint effort which took many people.

Again, my Telefol friends listened with patience, but finally, and rather plaintively asked, 'Just tell me how to make them.'

It was as if I knew the secret of magically creating aeroplanes, but refused through selfishness to share it with him.

Before I left Telefomin in the 1985 field season, I decided that I should try to meet Femsep, a man of whom I had heard much. He had lived through all the changes I have described and had played a vital role in some of them. As a result of what Anaru and Don Gardner had told me, and an article I had read by Tom Gilliard of the American Museum of Natural History, I felt that I already knew quite a lot about this most famous of all Telefol, and that my meeting would bring few surprises. How wrong I was.

Tom Gilliard was an ornithologist who worked with Femsep in the 1950s. Ironically, Gilliard arrived in Port Moresby from New York on the very day that the two Australian kiaps and four native police were dying at the hands of enraged Telefol and Elip warriors. Gilliard had planned to work at Telefomin, but because of the massacre his plans had to be delayed. By the time he finally did reach Telefomin over a year later, Femsep had been arrested for his leading role in the murders, tried, and sentenced to death. His sentence had been commuted to life imprisonment, but he had been released from jail in Wewak and returned to Telefomin when his death through sickness seemed imminent.

As Gilliard records it, he found Femsep 'sitting in the round entrance to his dwelling. He was a tiny man, emaciated by dysentery and fever...totally naked and the holes in his nose lacked the slender decorative cassowary quills other men wore. His hair was shorn in a prison cut—the strands that had once intertwined in a great horn of carefully wrapped cane shafts were gone ...'*

---

* Alan Ternes, *Ants, Indians & Little Dinosaurs*, Scribner, New York, 1975, p. 102.

As he questioned this rather pathetic figure, Gilliard discovered that Femsep had travelled throughout most of the territory of the Mountain Ok, and that he knew more about wildlife than any Telefol living.

This same impression was conveyed to me whenever I asked about a particularly obscure animal, or piece of traditional knowledge. The answer was always '*Femsep i save*' (Femsep would know).

On that morning in 1985 when I set out to meet Femsep, I walked along the track leading to Telefolip. I had armed myself with a few cans of tinned fish and sticks of Paradise Twist tobacco by way of a gift, such things being de rigueur on meeting such an eminent person. As I went I saw an old man walking in front of me. I soon caught up with him and greeted him in Pidgin, '*Apinun wanpela, Femsep i stap we?*' (Good afternoon sir, do you know where Femsep is?) To my amazement he replied that he himself was Femsep. My surprise came in part from his physical appearance which, despite Gilliard's description, did not match my mental image of the great man. Femsep was *tiny*. In height he reached somewhere near my middle. Furthermore, dressed in the ubiquitous European cast-offs, he was quite unexceptional looking.

Somewhat embarrassed by the unexpected meeting, I explained that I hoped to talk a little about his life. I handed the tins and tobacco over. Femsep stopped and after looking slyly around to make sure that there was no-one watching, hid them in the long grass beside the airstrip. He said that if he took them home they would only be eaten by his family. Better to hide them where he could return and enjoy them himself.

As we walked along, I felt that I should let Femsep know that I was not a complete tenderfoot, but had worked for some time in the Telefomin area studying mammals. By way of introducing myself I said that I had worked with Amunsep and his family. On hearing this, Femsep pulled a mournful face and said, '*Amunsep i dai pinis!*' (Amunsep is dead.) I was deeply shocked, for I had met Amunsep just the day before, and had enjoyed a cup of tea with him. When he had enjoyed my discomfort for a few moments Femsep burst forth with peals of laughter, clearly delighted that he had tricked me so thoroughly.

After some more preliminary banter I questioned Femsep a little concerning his role in the uprising of 1953, but he claimed to have little knowledge of it, and denied emphatically that he had played a leading role in the massacre. This denial, I knew from contemporary accounts, was entirely untrue.

When we reached his destination, I parted from the strange old fellow with a renewed respect for his cunning. To the end of his life he remained adventurous and ever game to try new experiences, and I heard that a few days after we met he had flown by helicopter to Green River to visit his son, who was working there.

Two years later Femsep died. Telefol envisage the death of a big man as being like the fall of a great *Araucaria* tree. 'The *drii* has fallen,' they would say when speaking of such a death. Femsep must have been well into his eighties when he died. So highly regarded was he that the local community obtained some bags of cement and built a monument to him. It is, as far as I know, the first and only such monument ever built by Telefol to honour a Telefol.

But did Femsep end up buried beneath the concrete monument, or was it only a splendid ruse to trick the *tablasep* (white people) once again? Secretly I hoped that, in the best Telefol tradition, Femsep's body was exposed in a secret place in the forest, and his bones collected for display in a *bilum* in the Telefolip cult house. Exposed burials are now illegal in Papua New Guinea, yet it would not be the first time that Femsep had stood against the rest of the world and won. The Baptist missionaries and public health officers at Telefomin would be appalled.

Much later, in 1995, during one of my visits to the mining town of Tabubil, I ran into my old Telefol friend Trondesep. We spent a morning gossiping and talking about friends and places we knew. I heard, to my great sorrow, of the death of Amunsep about 1993 as well as that of Tinamnok a year later. This last was truly shocking news, for Tinamnok was by no means old or infirm and had always enjoyed good health. Apparently a lung infection, either influenza or pneumonia, killed him. Perhaps a handful of antibiotics could have saved him.

I learned that Willok had married and his wife had already given birth to their first child. Then Trondesep told me something which seemed difficult to believe. The Telefolip cult house had been rebuilt, and some young initiates had begun the six stages of ritual instruction that would carry them through to manhood. This was heartening news, but even now I am not sure whether it is true, or whether Trondesep was simply telling me something he thought might cheer me up.

At lunchtime I took Trondesep to the Cloudlands Hotel where he had a T-bone steak. He fumbled with the knife and fork until finally, in frustration, he grabbed the steak with both hands and began to chomp away happily on it. A group of mining people, both black and white, sent louring looks our way as Trondesep enjoyed his meal. I had quite forgotten that Trondesep was a short, barefoot Telefol with a pierced nasal septum, who was dressed in dirty clothes. I had thought of him as a tribal leader, a man of knowledge whose dignity and generosity of spirit should be obvious to everyone. How, I wondered, could people be made to see beyond the external, and into the greatness of character that can grace a person, regardless of appearance, language or culture?

And meanwhile, the *drii* are falling everywhere. In their place are coming men who have not needed traditional skills and knowledge to become big men. Instead, they have cast their lot with religion or western learning. The land, and the balance between it and its people, will be irrevocably changed by this.

I am glad I have met great traditional leaders like Femsep, but their passing fills me with apprehension for the future.

PART IV

OK TEDI AND BEYOND

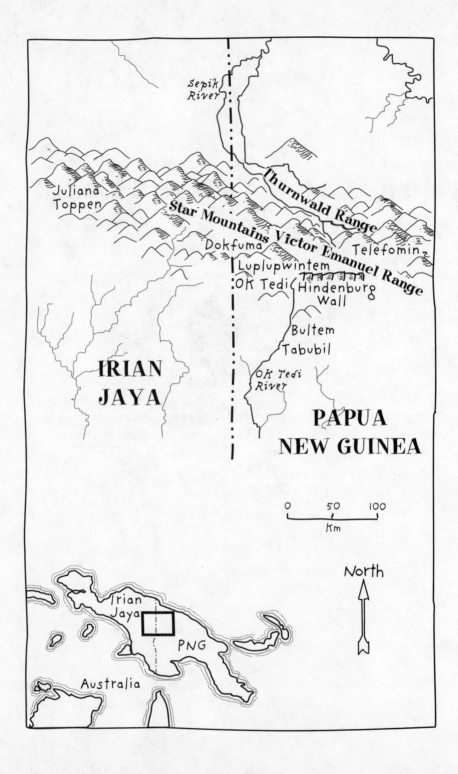

EIGHTEEN

Bat from the ice age

If social disruption had come rapidly to the Telefol, the pace of change they experienced was snail-like in comparison with that forced upon the Wopkaimin, another Mountain Ok group who live on the southern slopes of the Star Mountains.

The Wopkaimin live in some of the most difficult terrain in New Guinea. Rainfall is over nine metres per year at the village of Bultem (their main settlement), and is only slightly less elsewhere in their territory. A sunny day is a rarity, and a week without rain is virtually unknown. To make matters worse, the topography of the area is breathtakingly vertical. Relatively flat spots suitable for agriculture and village sites are almost as rare as sunny days, and where they do occur are usually small. Such places are known as *bil* to the Mountain Ok, explaining the number of airstrips which bear the term as a suffix (Tabubil, Tumolbil, Defakbil, etc.).

These factors have dictated that the Wopkaimin live in tiny, scattered family groups in a few favourable localities in their vast territory. Until the 1970s they spent their lives isolated not only from the outside world, but also isolated, most of the time, from their neighbours. They remained in this state, and virtually uncontacted by the colonial administration, until exploration for the Ok Tedi copper mine commenced. Then, within a few years of the discovery of commercially exploitable deposits of copper and gold, the outside world arrived *en masse* in their little villages and forests. The impact was as enormous as its results were unexpected.

My association with the Wopkaimin people has largely come about because of a very unusual bat. In 1975, Jim Menzies, a biology professor at the University of Papua New Guinea, described an extraordinary, newly discovered species of bat. The description was based on some bones found in cave deposits in Chimbu Province, some 400 kilometres east of the Wopkaimin. The bones dated to the end of the ice age, some 12,000 years ago. Similar caves in the area had produced the remains of Tasmanian Tigers, giant wombat-like creatures and large extinct wallabies. The bat bones themselves seemed to belong to a big, cave-dwelling species which was unique in the bat world in entirely lacking foreteeth (incisors).

The creature, it seemed, was now extinct.

So unusual was the find, though, that it created international interest (and much later still was reported on briefly by Michael Crichton in his novel *Jurassic Park*). Menzies named his new bat *Aproteles bulmerae*. The first name means 'incomplete at the front', the second is in recognition of Susan Bulmer, the archaeologist who recovered the remains. The new species soon became known to biologists (and indeed the wider public) as Bulmer's Fruit-bat.

Just two years after its discovery the anthropologist David Hyndman, who was living with the Wopkaimin, accompanied some friends on a bat hunt. The cash economy and western goods had just arrived in the area, due to employment opportunities with exploration teams working for Ok Tedi. As a result, Wopkaimin hunters possessed, for the first time ever, a shotgun and some nylon rope.

The hunters walked to a cave called Luplupwintem, a name which means 'gathering place cave', in reference to the enormous number of bats which used to congregate there. This cave is so huge, and its entrance so formidable, that it had been inaccessible for millennia. The shaft is a vertical doline at least 300 metres deep, which opens below into a cavern the size of a cathedral. Even if people could have got in, the vast chamber the bats roost in is so high that mere arrows could not reach the bats clinging to its roof.

The bats themselves added to the majesty of the place. The Wopkaimin say that when the bats ventured forth each evening in their tens of thousands the ground shook with the thunder of their wingbeats. Men had to cover their ears to avoid being deafened by the sound.

Whatever the case, one particularly brave man climbed down the rope into the massive doline, and expended five whole boxes of shotgun cartridges shooting bats. Thousands of bats were obtained and that night there was a grand feast. Hyndman saved a skull and a couple of jaw-bones, as well as a skin which he stuffed, to allow him to identify the unusual bats which had been served up to him at dinner.

To Hyndman's chagrin, however, village dogs ate the stuffed bat skin before it could be taken to Port Moresby for identification. The skull and jaw-bones, though, did arrive safely at the Zoology Department of the University of Papua New Guinea.

Imagine Jim Menzies' surprise when he opened the package and saw a complete skull and jaw-bones of a bat which lacked incisor teeth, and which just a few weeks before had been someone's dinner. At that moment he knew Bulmer's Fruit-bat was not extinct, but had somehow survived near the Ok Tedi mine in far western Papua New Guinea.

The two scientists returned to Luplupwintem as soon as

they could, but found to their dismay that the great colony had vanished. During the intervening period, other groups of hunters had visited the roost (the Wopkaimin say they were from Tifalmin), and they utterly devastated the colony. The scientists saw only two bats circling the roost, and subsequent visits revealed none at all. It seemed as if Bulmer's Fruit-bat had become extinct again—virtually at the moment of its rediscovery, without so much as a skin surviving so that researchers could know what it looked like. Indeed, it remained almost as mysterious as when it was known only from ancient fossils.

Not surprisingly, the people of Bultem (the village closest to the cave) regard Luplupwintem as a sacred place, and normally will not harm any bats which roost there. The story of the cave and its special significance was told to me by Noken, village leader in the late 1980s. He was old then and ill with what appeared to be tuberculosis. He whispered the tale to me in jumbled Pidgin, after first making sure that no-one was eavesdropping.

I was sworn to secrecy by Noken, who said that the story was known only to fully initiated Bultem men and were it to become known to the enemies of the Bultem people, it could be used against them. Consequently, I cannot repeat it here. Suffice to say that the villagers believe that any injury visited upon the bats will be inflicted upon them in turn.

In the explosion of change which contact with the outside world brought in the late 1970s, these beliefs were temporarily disregarded by some. Indeed it seems possible that people from other villages (who do not hold such beliefs) had been drawn to Bultem by news of the exploration teams, and had done most of the killing in 1977, while the Bultem people merely looked on.

Because of my work at nearby Telefomin I had become fascinated by Bulmer's Fruit-bat. During a survey of the mammals of the Telefomin area which Lester Seri and I conducted over the eight years from 1984 to 1992, we searched every cave in the region without finding a trace of the species. Our search was made difficult, to say the least, because we had no idea of what the bat looked like. Indeed, all we knew of it was that it was large, lived in caves, and had no foreteeth.

A few of the caves we investigated were exciting places. I am somewhat claustrophobic and Lester has a morbid fear of snakes (which are common inhabitants of caves in New Guinea), so we were hardly the most suitable pair to carry out cave exploration work. Despite these shortcomings we crawled, slithered and clambered into just about every cave and crevice we could manage around Telefomin, in the process recording the occurrence of dozens of species of bats, frogs, enormous spider-like pseudo-scorpions—and snakes.

There is one cave I shall never forget. Located on the Nong River, it lies one and a half days' walk south of Telefomin near the Hindenburg Wall, an extraordinary cliff-face I had heard much about. The river itself flows through a beautifully forested valley almost entirely undisturbed by human activity. The cave lies in the valley bottom, far from help were any needed. Its entrance is a narrow slit. After a crawl of a few metres, it opens into a cathedral-sized chamber which is lit through a hole in the roof. A few insectivorous bats roost in the twilight near the entrance, but I saw little else of interest in this first great chamber.

Because of the lack of bats, I began to investigate some water-filled pot-holes in the floor of the cave. The water was so still and clear it was impossible to judge its depth, or even to see it in some instances. There were beautiful, rounded stones in the bottom of some pools, while in others lay bones. Looking closely, I saw that they were human, and not very old bones at that. I hid this discovery from our Mountain Ok companions, for they are nervous of the spirits which are thought to inhabit caves, and they seemed to be more on edge than usual.

As Lester and I walked deeper into the darkness, we left the Mountain Ok near the entrance. They seemed unwilling to go further, and kept talking of the *masalai* that inhabited the cavern.

After going some distance I became aware of a low, rumbling sound. At first it seemed to be so bass that I felt rather than heard it. At the same time, the atmosphere was rapidly becoming opaque, thickened by a strange mist. This was quite unnerving, for the cave was so large that one could easily be standing in the middle of it and see nothing but white-out in all directions.

Rounding a corner, I lost sight of Lester's torch-beam.

I moved forward slowly, hardly able to see the cave floor, feeling instead for a wall to guide myself by. The rumbling became a deafening roar, which seemed to shake the very sides of the chamber.

With relief, I finally made contact with the wall. Feeling upwards, I detected a large, wooden object in front of me. It was an enormous tree-trunk, jammed high up in the cave.

Abruptly, I understood the nature of the place. The sound and mist were coming from a subterranean waterfall of immense proportions. Its reverberations filled the chamber and shook the floor. When the volume of water going over the fall increased, the chamber in which I stood was flooded. Trees carried by the floodwaters were lodged in the walls and roof.

The bodies of people, it seemed, were also carried in. They decomposed and their bones settled in the still pools of water near the cave mouth.

Suddenly I felt disoriented. How did I know that I was crawling away from, rather than towards, the waterfall? The mist was now so dense I could hardly see my hand in front of my face. Suppressing my growing panic and flattening myself against the cave wall, I kept moving slowly on.

Gradually the mist began to clear and the rumbling sound receded. In my confusion I had begun to retrace my steps. I walked past the bones in the pot-hole with a feeling of terror not unlike, I imagine, the feelings that this cave aroused in my Mountain Ok companions.

As a result of this investigation and many others like it,

Lester and I became confident that there was no major roost site occupied by Bulmer's Fruit-bat in the area. Had there been, the chances are we would have found it.

Although we never located the species during our survey, it turned out, through a most bizarre twist of fate, that we held a partial solution to the mystery of Bulmer's Fruit-bat in our grasp all along. For over all the years during which we searched for the species in remote New Guinea, a specimen was gathering dust within two hundred metres of where I worked daily in Sydney!

Almost a decade later, that piece in the puzzle was to fall into place.

Partly due to lack of funding for collection management, since the 1950s about two thousand 'problem specimens' had built up in the mammal collection of the Australian Museum. These specimens lay uncurated and unstudied in various drawers and cabinets. In 1990 I obtained funding to examine, register and curate this material.

Late one afternoon, the curatorial assistant who had been employed to carry out this difficult task knocked on my door. In her hand she held a box of unregistered bat skulls. As I casually picked one up, searching for some means to trace its identity, my breath caught and my heart began to beat wildly. The well-preserved skull had no foreteeth.

Impossible as it seemed, I was holding in my hand a skull of the almost mythical Bulmer's Fruit-bat.

The skull was accompanied by a tag which bore a single number '24/85'. This we recognised as being a preparation number, allocated to a specimen when it is sent to the taxidermist for mounting or cleaning. The assistant quickly checked the catalogue and brought me a skin from the collection with a number which matched the one on the skull. The skin was labelled as that of a common Bare-backed Fruit-bat (*Dobsonia magna*), which it superficially resembled. A brief glance at its fur, feet and wings, however, convinced me that the label was wrong. A band began to tighten around my forehead and I felt a queasiness in my stomach. At that moment, I realised, I was the only scientist on earth who knew what Bulmer's Fruit-bat looked like.

Afterwards I examined the skin in a more systematic manner and began to see that it was quite different from that of the common Bare-backed Fruit-bat. Its fur was finer, its facial features more square and the claws were brown rather than ivory. There was also an extra claw on the wing. Furthermore, although it was the size of a Bare-backed Fruit-bat, this was still a juvenile. The adult must be much larger. If so, it would be the largest cave-dwelling bat on the planet.

When my heartbeat slowed a little and my dazed brain began to think more clearly, I began to wonder whether this might all be a bizarre dream. After all, how could a specimen of the world's rarest bat have got into our museum collection unnoticed? Who could have collected it, and where?

The answers, it turned out, lay in the label attached to the skin.

The bat had been collected in 1984 by Steven Van Dyck of the Queensland Museum. He had accompanied me to Telefomin and Yapsiei on my first expedition there. Steve is an expert on the taxonomy of marsupial mice. He had decided to work at a place called Afektaman, which lies at an elevation of 1,400 metres in the Telefomin Valley—while I had gone to the Sol River—because he felt he had a better chance of encountering marsupial mice at that elevation.

He must have been exceedingly busy on the day he collected Bulmer's Fruit-bat, for the entry in his field notebook gives only the barest details: the animal's sex, weight and forearm length. Alongside was scrawled the mysterious word, *Woflayo*.

On our return, Steve and I had divided our specimens between the Queensland and Australian Museums. Among the material acquired by the Australian Museum was the bat. It had gone to the taxidermy department where the skin had been stuffed, but through an accident in curation or preparation the skull had become separated from the skin. The skin had been identified in the field as that of the common Bare-backed Fruit-bat, and had been labelled as such in the collection. The skull had been placed in a box of problem specimens lacking data. Neither time nor money had ever allowed for the mistake to be rectified.

By now I knew a little Telefol and suspected that *Woflayo* was the name of a person. And so, with some help from Ok Tedi Mining, Lester Seri and I were soon on our way to Afektaman, on the trail of Bulmer's Fruit-bat. Our ace card was *Woflayo*.

Afektaman is a pretty little village overlooking the range which lies to the south of Telefomin. It is situated at the entrance to the Sepik Gorge, and is only about thirty kilometres in a straight line from Luplupwintem, which had been, until 1977, the sole roosting place of Bulmer's Fruit-bat.

On our arrival at Afektaman we immediately asked whether anyone called Woflayo lived there—and were led straight away, so easily, to a man of late middle-age who lived in a tiny collection of huts a kilometre or so from the village itself.

Woflayo invited us into his house, and offered us a cup of tea. As we talked, it became clear that Woflayo's Pidgin was rather limited. He was a conservative Telefol who clung fiercely to his traditions. He did not deign to learn the new lingua franca.

After we had explained the purpose of our visit, Woflayo commented that it was a good thing we had arrived that day, for later in the week he was leaving for Batalona. I was at first nonplussed as to where exactly Woflayo might be going. Batalona did not sound like any Telefol place name I had heard. After some more discussion it became apparent that Woflayo was off on a very long trip indeed. He was headed for Barcelona, where he would lead a Telefol dance troupe as part of the 1992 Olympic Games celebrations!

Woflayo's careful observance of tradition had clearly paid

off. Of all Telefol, he was renowned as the one who knew the ancient dances best, and was thus the natural choice as leader of the troupe. What, I often wonder, did the good citizens of Barcelona make of Woflayo, bedecked in penis gourd, cane waistband and feathered head-dress, chanting and swaying to his Telefol rhythms?

After we drank our tea, Woflayo took us to a garden at the back of his hut. There, he showed us the stump of a small fig tree. It was in this *tiup* tree, he said, that he had shot the bat which he had sold to 'Masta Steve' in 1984.

I was flattened.

What an anticlimactic end to a journey which had begun with such excitement months ago and thousands of kilometres away!

A bat which Woflayo had shot in his back yard and thought nothing of had brought strangers to his door from another continent… And in a few days, he would dance to a crowd of tens of thousands on a continent as foreign to him as the far side of the moon.

Our work on this trip would not have been complete without one final check of Luplupwintem. This was now doubly important for we felt that Woflayo's bat may well have flown from there on the night of its demise. If young bats were in the area in 1984, there was just a chance that an undetected breeding colony might yet survive in the great cave.

Lester and I had flown over Luplupwintem on a previous occasion when journeying from Telefomin to Tabubil, so we knew how rugged the region was. On that occasion we had flown down the Sepik Gorge early in the morning in a tiny Cessna.

It was a hair-raising journey from the start, for the gorge twists and turns, and the aircraft often appears to be headed directly towards a vertical wall with no means of escape, when it suddenly twists to follow the gorge on its tortuous course.

We turned south-west as we followed the Ilam River, a tributary of the Sepik. Then the plane climbed until we were flying
just a hundred metres or so above the vast, flat limestone
plateau known as Finimterr. That morning a thin mist veiled
the plateau, but through it could be seen occasional patches
of brown grassland as well as the green of alpine scrub.

Below there somewhere was Luplupwintem.

Absorbed in trying to read the topography and locate the
cave, I was caught completely unawares. The little plane suddenly began a precipitous dive towards the curtain of mist.
Before the full impact of my terror was upon me, we had dived
completely through the mist. We were flying straight down
beside an enormous rock-face. Vast caverns and splashes of
water-stained cliff zoomed past us.

Then the plane began to pull out of its dive.

The pilot turned to me and said, 'What do you make of the
Hindenburg Wall?'

The Hindenburg Wall is often dubbed the eighth natural
wonder of the world. It is a huge limestone cliff which runs for
tens of kilometres across south-central New Guinea.

I had seen, I was tempted to say, quite enough of this 1,500-
metre vertical drop to last me a lifetime.

The day after we said farewell to Woflayo, Lester Seri and I
climbed aboard a helicopter at Tabubil airport and headed
back to the Finimterr plateau.

We landed in an area of grassland where the chopper could
touch down, approximately three hours' walk from the cave
entrance. Then we set out on the long and difficult track over
limestone pinnacles and sink-holes to the cave mouth itself.

For hours we picked our way over small pinnacles and through
dense, mossy, upper montane scrub. It was a closed, almost claustrophobic world which seemed to engulf us. Then, after we
turned one last corner, the path opened into empty space.

At last we had arrived at the rim of Luplupwintem.

Luplupwintem is the most spectacular cave I have ever seen. Its entrance is as unexpected as it is grand. We found ourselves standing on the very lip of a vast, roughly circular shaft, perhaps four hundred metres across, its walls plunging vertically for hundreds of metres. Looking across the chasm to its southern face, I saw that we stood at the lowest point of the entrance. All round, the cliff-like sides of the doline soared hundreds of metres overhead, as well as below. It was by now early afternoon, and a shaft of sunlight pierced down into the gloomy depths. I could see that the doline opened into a cathedral-sized cavern, across the mouth of which flowed a fine, almost mist-like waterfall. The height of the south wall appeared to be the best part of a kilometre, if not more.

As we rested, exhausted, at the edge of this grandeur, we heard a strange, twittering noise coming from far below, inside the cave. It sounded like the calls of parakeets, but no self-respecting parrot would roost in that gloomy place. Instead, we saw a large fruit-bat sally out from the cavern below and fly through the shaft of light.

This was exciting indeed. But had we rediscovered Bulmer's Fruit-bat, or had a colony of common Bare-backed Fruit-bats settled in the cave in their place? We waited anxiously for dark in order to find out.

About half an hour before dusk the bats began to circle ever higher in the doline, then to fly out over our heads as they left the roost to forage. They were very large fruit-bats, and by the time the last had left the cave we had counted 137 of them.

By observing their flight path we developed a strategy for netting one. But it was not going to be an easy job, for the area offered little scope for mist-net setting.

Unfortunately, there was nowhere to camp at Luplupwintem, and we had left the bulk of our equipment at the grassland patch where the chopper had dropped us. By 9 p.m. we had to begin our long walk back, arriving at camp about midnight.

For each of the next three days we walked back to Luplupwintem, and each evening tried a new technique to capture a bat. Our efforts met without the least success. The bats would fly too high, or to one side, and the small hours of the morning saw us returning to camp exhausted, wet and lacerated.

With only a single day remaining before the helicopter arrived to pick us up, it was time for desperate measures. Considering the flight path taken by the majority of bats, and the topography of the entrance, Lester and I concluded that we would have to set a mist-net high above the canopy, in a position where it virtually overhung the great precipice itself, if we were to stand a chance of catching one of the bats.

This was a perilous operation, and it was critical that the net tension be right, otherwise it would not work.

Executing this dangerous manoeuvre took an entire afternoon. We finished just as the bats began to stir below. Exhausted, we waited for them to begin to stream out from their roost. This is what I later wrote:

> The previous three hours had been pure terror. In order to set the net we had to climb two large moss-covered trees that overhung the rim of this enormous cave, which plunges down vertically for several hundred metres. It was a fifteen-metre climb to the canopy, and we first had to cut a clearing for the net with bush-knives. Then we each had to manipulate a seven-metre pole, with mist-net attached, into place, and fasten it to the trees. All the while the light was fading, and the vines I had used to ascend the tree were becoming smooth with wear.
>
> We finished—and darkness descended.
>
> Clouds of mosquitoes surrounded us as we sat there, crawling into our ears, nose and eyes. We were unable to slap them for fear of disturbing the bats. Then at last we heard the distinctive 'pok pok pok' wingbeat as they left the roost. The noise of one bat after another colliding with the net high above our heads sounded encouraging, until we realised they were bouncing off again. The

net had been set too tight, and we would have to climb high into the canopy of trees above the cave to loosen it. And it had to be done quickly. In ten minutes the skies would be empty of bats.

The thought of climbing the tree again filled me with dismay; then I realised from the sounds overhead that Lester was already halfway up his tree.

The climb seemed easier in the darkness, for I could not see the yawning chasm below, nor could I see the tree sway as I reached the thinner branches of the crown. Almost immediately upon loosening the net, a bat struck and became firmly entangled. I held onto the tree with a crooked elbow, stuck the torch in the fork of a branch, and began to haul in the net. The bat was understandably furious, attempting to bite everything around it. It was much larger than I had expected. When I reached the animal I realised I'd have to cut the net and carry down the section containing the violently struggling bat.

Cutting done, I began my descent in darkness, for in the struggle to pull in the net my torch had fallen. Suddenly I began to feel my centre of gravity shift, and I realised I was supporting myself by the mist-net pole, which I had tied loosely to the tree. I grabbed wildly for further support and caught a liana vine. I climbed down the last few metres shaking, the furious fruit-bat struggling to be free.

Lester was waiting with a calico bag. Carefully he placed the bat inside, then took up his torch and peered in. We looked in amazement at the indignant face of this bat. Its incisors were missing. In our grasp was an animal once thought to have become extinct at the end of the last ice age, some 12,000 years ago. We hugged each other with joy—after eight years of field work together in rugged western Papua New Guinea we had rediscovered Bulmer's Fruit-bat!

Lester and I now think that Bulmer's Fruit-bat may have survived all through the 1970s and 1980s at Luplupwintem. Given what we now know of the rate of population increase at the roost, it seems likely that perhaps as few as ten to twenty bats escaped the massacre in 1977. The tiny population which remained had probably gone un-noticed in the vastness of the main cavern for over a decade, until numbers had built up sufficiently that they could again be detected at the cave entrance by their noise.

Over the past few years we have learned much about this intriguing bat. It really is the world's largest cave-dwelling bat, it breeds once a year, and females do not breed until their third year of life. Its numbers are growing slowly (there were about 160 individuals in 1993), more slowly indeed than its reproductive rate would suggest they should. We suspect that it is still being hunted somewhere, probably at one or more of its feeding sites.

Most hearteningly, the local Wopkaimin owners of Luplupwintem have agreed to ban hunting at the cave. They were never happy with the transgression of the taboo which protected the cave and its bats, but were uncertain of its relevance in the face of the modern world they found themselves engulfed in.

The Wopkaimin are slowly regaining their own sense of balance. By 1993, six young men had agreed to undergo traditional initiation. They looked magnificent in their red clay body paint and extraordinary, taro-shaped head-dresses.

The return of the cave to a traditional form of protection gives Bulmer's Fruit-bat its best chance yet to recover. If this is successful, perhaps the day will again come when the ground will shake to the wingbeats of tens of thousands of Bulmer's Fruit-bats.

NINETEEN

Expedition to the Stars

The western world was well into the space age, and the first moon landing only four years away when, in 1965, the first European explorers ascended to the summits of the Star Mountains.

Jammed up against the border with Irian Jaya, the Star Mountains are Papua New Guinea's most mysterious range. Their peaks were named from afar by the Dutch explorers who first saw them in 1910. Perhaps they chose the names of stars and constellations because the jumbled peaks seemed as profuse and remote as the heavens themselves.

By the time I began work at Telefomin, the Star Mountains were still biologically unexplored. They beckoned irresistibly. When the opportunity arose in the late 1980s to undertake some biological survey work there (courtesy of the Environment Section of Ok Tedi Mining), Lester Seri and I jumped at the chance.

The mining town of Tabubil lies at approximately 600 metres elevation on the southern slopes of the central range. It is, like most mining towns in New Guinea, a conglomeration of fibro cottages, offices and new roads, all constructed in a fresh gash in the forest. The town is noisy, and one feels more distant than ever from the real bush.

What makes Tabubil different from other mining communities is its remoteness and the appalling weather conditions in the area. It is always exciting to fly into Tabubil. The area receives rain on 300 days each year, and cloud can hang over the foothills for weeks at a time. Inward-bound flights are frequently diverted to Kiunga (from where there is road access to Tabubil), and those that are not often have to make several attempts at finding an opening in the clouds so that they can locate the airstrip. On the ground the atmosphere is warm, humid and sticky. You can feel the fungus growing on your skin from the moment you step out of the plane.

The first wildlife I noticed in Tabubil were its spiders. The great orb weavers are everywhere, their strong yellow webs covering metres of bushes and trees. One could hardly miss them, for the webs were festooned with ejecta which whimsical Melanesians have tossed into them. Those near the hotel supported a tasteful array of beer cans. A monstrous web near the mess held plastic plates, cutlery and yet more cans, while one near the town centre had election posters and even a few thongs. One poster promoted 'Pius Fred', candidate for the seat of North Fly Open. His mug shot did little to inspire confidence, and we hoped that, if he won, the Speaker of the House never requested the 'Member for North Fly Open to be upstanding'.

In the middle of each web lies a great silvery spider with an abdomen the size of a grape—its legs a handspan in width. Although first horrified by them, I soon became fascinated. Watching them trim their webs as the wind increased, add guy ropes when it changed direction, and put on extra strands when conditions were favourable, I began to view them as tiny, diligent sailors on the breeze.

But these sailors are all females. If you look closely, you can see another, much smaller spider (often more than one) near the female. This is the male, and his life is perilous. Amorous intent forces him to keep company with his potential mate, who is at least a hundred times his size. She, however, is much more interested in him as an entrée than a paramour, so he must be circumspect.

Whenever I disturbed one of the webs, the female would freeze momentarily in fear. The males invariably chose this moment to have their way with her. They looked like naughty boys as they nimbly approached the female, manoeuvring their large black copulatory organs over her genital pore, then thrusting briefly before cautiously retreating.

When I looked very closely I discovered yet other, even smaller spiders in the webs. These belonged to a different species entirely. They lived as thieves, taking insects trapped in the webs, which were presumably too small to interest the builder. The eyesight of the orb weavers must be too weak to detect these little opportunists.

The Mountain Ok people have a special use for the webs. They fashion fish traps out of them. They search for a four-pronged stick, which they whisk into web after web with a circular motion. Soon it becomes a container of sticky web and trapped spiders. They place this in a river or stream, cup upward. There, miniature fish adhere to the sticky fibres.

Our access to the Star Mountains lay through Tabubil, for the Ok Tedi Mining helicopter base was there, near Bultem—home of the traditional Wopkaimin owners of the mountains. Indeed, they had built Bultem on its present site in order to be closer to Tabubil. As a result, it has an untidy appearance when compared with most traditional villages, for the architecture is a mixture of traditional and modern styles, and a number of motor vehicles in various stages of disrepair are parked around the central square.

I had been given the name of a man called Griem by David Hyndman, the anthropologist who had worked with the Wopkaimin in the 1970s. So, arriving at Bultem that first time, I sought him out and was surprised to be led to an elfin man of about my own age, dressed in the ubiquitous dirty western cast-offs. Griem informed me that his name was now Freddy, and that he worked for the mine driving the titanic trucks which hauled ore from the pit to the crusher. When I mentioned a possible trip to the Stars, his eyes lit up and he said that, with my help, perhaps he could get a week or two off work to accompany us.

Freddy has led one of most extraordinary lives of anyone I have ever met. He was a youth when Ok Tedi Mining began exploring for minerals in the Wopkaimin area. He still remembers the day a helicopter tried to land at the bottom of his father's taro garden. Freddy and his mother were terrified, but his father, in a remarkable act of bravery, rushed into the garden and began loosing arrows at the monster which was threatening his family.

Less than two decades had passed since this signal event, yet by the time I met Freddy he was a contented man with a family of his own, and was more familiar with trucks, helicopters and aircraft than I. Freddy taught me that Alvin Toffler's ideas about future shock are not always right.

Freddy and I talked at length about the impact of the Ok Tedi mine on Wopkaimin life. On the whole, he said, things had been improved remarkably by the presence of the mine. This view is widely held among the Wopkaimin, who have received many direct benefits from developments brought by mining. This is not to say that they have entirely escaped the traumas associated with rapid change. But they have been more in control of its pace and impact than many indigenous people in a similar situation.

Over time, this was evidenced, for example, in the continuance of men's initiation at the Bultem cult house. In 1987 I met two initiates in the Tabubil supermarket. The young men, dressed in penis gourds and elaborate ochre head-dresses, pushed a trolley loaded with rice and tinned fish along the aisles. There, they mingled with the wives of company employees and other customers, without causing the slightest commotion. Then, in 1993, I met more young initiates in Bultem village itself. One—an earnest young man by the name of Tarapi—had accompanied us to Luplupwintem to help perform a census of Bulmer's Fruit-bat. Tarapi displayed a sense of social responsibility rare in someone his age. One day, perhaps, Tarapi will be a great traditional leader.

Not all New Guineans, though, are happy with the developments at Ok Tedi. The tribal groups living further downriver from Tabubil, for example, are angered at the damage done to the ecosystem of the upper Ok Tedi River. The river provides them with important food sources, and this is being affected through the disposal of tailings. Until recently, these people received relatively little by way of compensation.

Freddy told me that in his eyes the most substantial benefit provided by the mine is the health service, which is now readily available to all. Many Wopkaimin (himself included, Freddy said) would have died long ago were it not for the medical assistance available there.

Freddy perceived that his quality of life had also improved as he gained access to western food and goods. Things have gone so well for him that he now owns a Toyota Landcruiser, and has been able to plan several trips overseas. By 1992 he was planning to go to the Vatican to see the Pope (Bultem is now a Catholic village), but when I returned a little later that year he informed me that he had changed his mind. He had met a Filipino mechanic in Tabubil who spoke of the delights of the flesh awaiting the traveller in the nightclubs of Manila. As a result, Freddy had decided on a more secular holiday.

At the end of one long conversation, I asked Freddy if there was anything else the mine could do for him. He sat deep in thought for a while, then said that he would like a kerosene heater.

My knowledge of Wopkaimin culture, and the changes that contact with the west have wrought, was rudimentary on the day in 1987 when I first met Freddy and asked him to accompany me to the Stars. He suggested that we bring along his uncle Serapnok, who owned a good hunting dog. I was rather wary of Serapnok at first. He had a hawkish nose and narrow, hatchet face which gave him a rather sinister appearance—rather like the vampire in *Nosferatu*—and because of this, and our lack of a common language, it took me some time to overcome an instinctive distrust of him.

Freddy told me that he knew a good place for a helicopter drop and base camp. It was a patch of subalpine grassland known as Dokfuma, located at 3,200 metres elevation, and deep in the Star Mountains. There was a problem, however, for discussions with the helicopter pilot revealed that his machine could carry only 160 kilograms at this elevation. This meant that we would have to run several trips in. Furthermore, because of the extreme changeability of the weather in the mountains, we had to think carefully about what would be taken up on the first journey, as whoever and whatever went could be trapped there for an extended period.

After some consideration, it was decided that the first load should consist of myself, a tent and sleeping bag, some clothes and food sufficient for a week. That way, if bad weather trapped me alone at Dokfuma, I could sit it out in comfort.

By 6 a.m. on the morning of our departure, the weather at Tabubil looked fine, allowing us a trouble-free take-off. This was a relief, for the weather around town is frequently foul. On approaching the Star Mountains, however, it was clear that a dense fog over the peaks would prevent us from landing.

We returned to base, and I sat at Tabubil airport for several hours while the helicopter ran errands in the lowlands. All the while, I watched the clouds thicken above me.

At about 9 a.m. the opportunity came to try again. This time we found that conditions had improved slightly in the mountains, but they were rapidly deteriorating around Tabubil. The pilot asked me whether I wanted to land, explaining that the poor weather at Tabubil might well prohibit a second trip. I was anxious to begin work, and asked him to try to drop me in the alpine herbfield we could vaguely make out below. It looked like the place Freddy had described a few days earlier as Dokfuma. The pilot made a note of his position and began to descend.

Below was a bowl-shaped patch of grassland, surrounded by lightly wooded ridges. Frosty air accumulates in a place like this, preventing the growth of trees. On this morning, dense cloud hung over the hills that formed the bowl margin, but the cloud was thinner in the middle, so that the centre of the herbfield could occasionally be glimpsed from above.

The helicopter began to lower itself gingerly into a gap in the cloud hanging close to the ground. A sudden bump told me we had landed. It was time to get out and unload the chopper.

In a minute I had my pack and a drum beside me, and the helicopter was receding into the break in the mist above.

After hours amid the crowd and bustle of Tabubil airport, then a trip aboard a noisy helicopter, Dokfuma seemed to be preternaturally quiet. It was also extraordinarily cold. The chill air caught my breath and nipped at my fingers.

It took me a few minutes to tear myself away from the sound of the departing chopper and to stop wondering whether I would hear it again that day, or even that week. I roused myself to activity. Dragging my equipment to higher ground to keep it from getting too wet, I was dismayed to find myself breathless. It seemed that my old foe, altitude sickness, was going to be a feature of this trip too.

Work completed, I sat on a mossy tussock, my breath rasping noisily. I tried to take in Dokfuma.

All around, every tussock of moss and bunched herb was covered in a gossamer of spiders' webs. The webs were brilliantly apparent because the sun had not yet burned off the beads of water which adorned them like pearls on a string. Nearby, a pincushion-sized rhododendron flowered, its long, trumpet-like red blooms the only brightness in a sea of mossy gold and silver green. Somewhere close, a toadlet emitted its short, creaky call from under a miniature tussock.

The mist-shrouded *Dacrycarpus* trees surrounding Dokfuma formed an open woodland. These relatives of Tasmania's Huon Pine are stately, rather sparse, pyramidal trees five to seven metres high, with tiny, dark green leaves and lichen-covered bark. They lent a sombre beauty to the scene. The almost impenetrable tangle of upper montane rainforest which surrounded the Neon Basin was largely absent here—it was only in limited areas that one found such thick scrub.

From beyond the veil of mist came a strange, rustling, tinkling sound: the wings of a large bird in a grove of trees. Birds of paradise and pigeons are the only species which make such a sound.

Now the distant thud-thud-thud of the returning helicopter could be heard. The weather was kind to us and on trip after trip it brought in Lester, Freddy, Serapnok and his dog (tightly trussed up and tied into a *bilum*), and Hal Cogger, herpetologist and final member of our expedition.

I soon found that even though Dokfuma lay at a similar elevation to the Neon Basin, it was a very different kind of subalpine habitat. The Neon had been relatively dry underfoot and tussock grasses tended to predominate. Here at Dokfuma a dense and prickly mass of moss, lichens and herbs grew atop a swamp. The ground, even on the slopes, was sodden, and we found our campsite actually moving gradually downslope as our tracks cut the raft of moss free from its surrounds.

When the mist lifted from Dokfuma and the sun warmed my skin, I began to see more of the beauty and less of the discomfort of the place. To the north lay the white limestone pinnacles of Mt Capella, while to the north-west lay the peaks of Scorpion and Antares—the very highest of the Star Mountains. Far away to the west, in Irian Jaya, a single reflective point sparkled like a diamond in the sunshine. It was Juliana Toppen, dusted by a fresh fall of snow.

A small creek running to the west drained Dokfuma, and at the end of the valley formed a picturesque waterfall. Beyond this small drop and across the lightly wooded valley edge stood a vast and imposing mountain. The great pyramid-like monolith was called Deng by the Wopkaimin people. There was no other name to be found for it on our maps. This mountain dominated the nearer scenery of the valley in a rather sinister way.

I sometimes watched Deng for hours on end, for it was high atop Deng that the weather of Dokfuma was made. Some afternoons, warm currents would rise up its abrupt southern face. Within seconds, great swirling clouds, forming the most fantastical shapes, would materialise out of clear air. Often they would disappear just as suddenly, as the warm air crossed the summit, but at other times they would grow and engulf Dokfuma—sometimes for days—making work and helicopter landings impossible. Deng ruled our lives. At times, especially when it spawned fierce storms, it seemed as if Deng might even decide whether we lived or died.

One of the special delights of Dokfuma was its birds, for they were more abundant, fearless and glorious than I had ever seen before. The mountain *Schefflera* (relatives of the umbrella tree) were in flower and their fruit and nectar-filled flowers attracted birds in their hundreds.

Each morning, a male Splendid Astrapia in full plumage would display in an isolated *Dacrycarpus* tree behind our tent. While it sat still with the sun behind it, it looked like nothing more than a large, black, crow-like bird with a long tail and bill. But when it moved about, the brilliant iridescence of its feathers flashed red, blue and yellow in the sunshine.

One morning, in the upper montane forest, a male King of Saxony Bird of Paradise (*Pteridophora alberti*) flitted onto a thin branch hardly a metre above my head. Although only about the size of a mynah, the King of Saxony is one of the most bedazzling birds I have ever seen. Its yellow breast was the first thing to attract my eye, but its most striking feature is doubtless a pair of bright blue, enamel-like feathers, each at least forty centimetres long. These extraordinary structures sprout from each side of its brow. They are highly modified feathers and appear to consist of a series of small, enamel-blue flags strung on a pole.

I had only ever seen these striking feathers adorning a highlander's head-dress. There, they often form the centrepiece of a stunning feathered array, but on the living bird they are used to create an even more sublime effect. When at rest, the feathers lie along the bird's back, rather like a pair of long, curved pencils stuck behind the ears of a bank clerk. As the feathers are far longer than the body of the bird, they trail out behind when it flies.

This magnificent creature now let out a curiously insect-like call, rather like a malfunctioning piece of electrical equipment. I had heard this call countless times before, without catching sight of the creature which made it. Now I watched in astonishment as the bird began to bounce on its perch, spluttering and rattling as it went. Next it moved its long, antennae-like brow feathers forward over its head. Hesitatingly at first, it moved as if it were performing an acrobatic feat of extraordinary difficulty. The feathers waved gracefully forward, shimmering in the sunlight. Quickly they were retracted and the motion began again. This time the arc through which the feathers moved was wider, until the bird finally pointed them straight out in front of its body. In this posture the creature resembled nothing more than an impossibly large longicorn beetle with bright blue antennae.

I was, I am sure, as attentive to this wonderful display as any lovelorn female bird of paradise. Then, suddenly and all too soon, the most magical twenty seconds of my life were over. The bird flitted off through the moss-covered branches and was lost from view.

Obeying the call of nature often brings unexpected rewards in New Guinea. I have, for example, directed a golden arc onto a mossy mound, only to have an undescribed species of toadlet leap from the greenery. One morning during this trip I carried my shovel a considerable distance from the camp to the back of a small rise, around which grew a grove of gnarled *Dacrycarpus* trees. There I could contemplate nature in privacy.

I was fully absorbed in the beauty of my surroundings when I heard, near at hand, the same distinctive tinkling wingbeat I'd heard on the morning of arrival. Now, two large, velvet-black birds glided into the lower branches of a tree quite close to me. Slowly, they began to pick their way upward through the branches, eating small fruit as they went. When they reached the top they took off in a short, downward flight and landed in the tree adjacent to me. With the exception of the distinctive sound of their wings, they were largely silent.

Large orange patches were visible under their wings as they flew. Then they were so close that I could see clearly the fleshy, bright orange wattles the size of dollar coins wobbling comically behind their eyes. Here before me, unbelievably, was a pair of Macgregor's Bird of Paradise (*Macgregoria pulchra*), the rarest of all.

Macgregor's Bird of Paradise lives only on the summits of three of New Guinea's highest mountain ranges. There is a small population on the summit of Mt Albert Edward (although I failed to see them during my visit there). There is another in the Snow Mountains of Irian Jaya, while the third is found here in the Star Mountains. Each is clearly a relic population whose distribution has dwindled as habitat has shrunk since the last ice age.

As I watched these magnificent birds I was amazed they had survived at all, for they were so large and fearless that surely all of them should have ended up in a cooking pot long ago. Doubtless the remoteness of their remaining habitat has protected them from this fate.

I squatted far longer than necessary, watching these wonderful birds. It seemed that the pair liked being together, for they followed one another closely as they picked their way through the thin foliage. At last they passed from view. I reached down for a handful of wet moss, followed by a handful of a drier variety—so much more comfortable and ecologically friendly than paper!

The business of my trip was mammalogy. But I was disappointed to find the mammals of Dokfuma less obvious and interesting than the birds. As in the Neon Basin, the tiny faces of the Moss-forest Rats and Mountain Melomys were those encountered most commonly when emptying the trapline in the morning. There were clearly other mammal species about, but it was difficult to trap them.

One particular track near our camp fascinated me. Still very fresh and broad, it clearly belonged to a largish mammal. Every evening I placed a trap either on or near it. But I never did discover what the animal was—every morning I returned to find the trap knocked out of the way by some unknown, yet clearly very muscular beastie. My best guess was that it was a giant rat of some kind. My failure was unfortunate, for the identity of the giant rats inhabiting the Star Mountains remains mysterious.

Freddy and Serapnok would depart from the camp each morning with dog in tow. By afternoon they would return, more often empty-handed than otherwise and we would sit by the fire chatting. During these intervals I learned much about both of them. Freddy was one of those generous people who is always delighted to see his friends happy. Serapnok is happy-go-lucky and good-natured. He delights in nothing as much as playing the village clown.

After discovering the lighter side of Serapnok, I was amazed to learn one afternoon that it was he who had single-handedly almost exterminated Bulmer's Fruit-bat. He had dangled on a rope hundreds of metres above the ground inside Luplupwintem in order to reach the bat colony and had, he said, taken Bultem's very first shotgun with him, along with his five boxes of cartridges.

It was a tricky descent. As he went over the edge he shouted back to his wife that she had better get a move on and marry someone else, for he was sure to slip on the way down!

When he reached the bottom of the cave, Serapnok took up his gun and shot directly into the thickest part of the bat colony. He was nearly knocked unconscious by the rain of stricken bats falling on his head. After that, he shot at an oblique angle to avoid the falling bodies. Time after time the shots rang out and Serapnok gathered at first hundreds, then thousands, of bats. He filled *bilum* after *bilum* with them, tying each load to the rope to be hoisted aloft. Finally there were no more bats to be seen and Serapnok tied himself to the rope and yelled to be pulled up. That night, the Wopkaimin ate bats till they were farcarted.

Serapnok and Freddy's hunting forays here at Dokfuma, however, were proving so unsuccessful that at length I began to suspect that they were walking only just far enough to sit down and light up a Paradise Twist undetected, before returning to be fed in the afternoon. But all scepticism was dispelled one day when they did return triumphant. Freddy came in the lead, carrying a large brownish bundle of fur, while Serapnok followed, burdened only with a *bilum*, the mouth of which had been fastened. The pair had caught a tree-kangaroo. As I examined the dead female carried by Freddy, Serapnok unfastened his *bilum* and a tiny joey poked its head out. Dokfuma, as he became known, soon became the camp favourite.

The adult tree-kangaroo looked rather unusual, and I suspected that it may have represented an undescribed subspecies of Doria's Tree-kangaroo. This eventually turned out to be the case, and we gave it the name *stellarum*, meaning 'of the stars'. As events turned out, this was not an entirely appropriate name, for later survey work showed that it is distributed right across the mountains of western New Guinea, from the Irian Jaya border to the mountains just east of the Paniai Lakes. Recently I bestowed the common name of Seri's Tree-kangaroo upon it, in recognition of the lifetime of effort which *lewa bilong mi* (my close friend) Lester Seri has put into documenting the fauna of his country.

As the time passed here at Dokfuma there proved to be no wallabies, and neither was there evidence of Long-beaked Echidnas or pigs—again in contrast with the Neon Basin. Just why these species should be absent at one place yet common at another I have never discovered. As if in compensation, Dokfuma had plenty of New Guinea singing dogs. These diminutive, dingo-like creatures are descended from the dogs brought to New Guinea about 2,000 years ago from islands to the west. Like dingoes, they howl in chorus. The haunting call is usually heard at day's start and end. For me, it is always evocative of the mountains of New Guinea.

New Guinea singing dogs are extraordinarily shy. Although I heard them often at Dokfuma, I saw them only once, and then almost by accident. One morning everyone except me had left camp to hunt or hike to the west. Hal had gone in search of further specimens of an undescribed frog he had found. I had to stay behind to maintain the trapline, and I spent the first few hours after the party departed relaxing in my tent. Suddenly I heard the chorused yodel-like howl of the dogs much closer than ever before. They had clearly been watching us and had seen the departure of the party earlier that morning. Although they are almost preternaturally canny animals, they are unable to count. On seeing the bulk of the group depart, they assumed the camp was deserted. Lying motionless in the tent, I watched the dogs approach. When they came within a few hundred metres they became alarmed and turned back. They must have somehow detected my presence.

The time finally came to leave Dokfuma.

Looking forward to being warm and having something underfoot except slush, I was not unhappy when we heard the sound of the returning helicopter. Deng was kind to us, and we enjoyed pleasant weather all the way home.

PART V

NORTH COAST RANGES

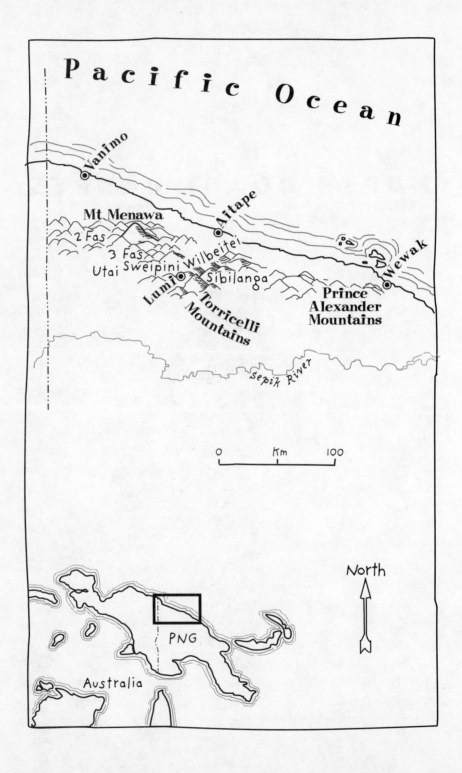

Pacific Ocean

Vanimo

Mt Menawa

2 Fas

Aitape

3 Fas

Utai Sweipini Wilbeitei

Wewak

Lumi Sibilanga

Torricelli
Mountains

Prince
Alexander
Mountains

Sepik River

0   Km   100

North

PNG

Australia

TWENTY

Torricelli Mountains

Back in July 1985, after a stint at Telefomin, I decided to travel to the Torricelli Mountains to assess their suitability as a site for a faunal survey. The Torricellis form part of the eastern end of Papua New Guinea's North Coast Ranges. They run roughly parallel to the north coast between the Irian Jaya border and Wewak, a distance of about 200 kilometres. Only a narrow coastal plain separates the mountains from the sea, while the vast floodplain of the Sepik separates them from the taller central ranges. Long ago the Sepik floodplain was occupied by the sea, and the North Coast Ranges would have formed islands lying many kilometres off the coast.

The Torricellis are a low mountain range, reaching only 1,500 metres in elevation. They had been largely ignored by previous researchers. My interest in them was piqued by a scientific article, published a few years earlier, describing a

new species of large gliding possum, which was apparently
unique to the Torricellis. Given the long isolation of the
ranges, it seemed possible that the gliding possum was not the
only mammal unique to the region. A whole undescribed
fauna might be awaiting the patient researcher.

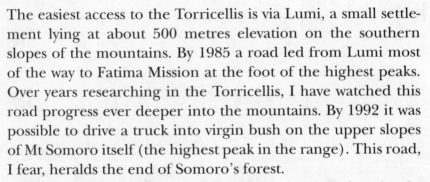

The easiest access to the Torricellis is via Lumi, a small settlement lying at about 500 metres elevation on the southern
slopes of the mountains. By 1985 a road led from Lumi most
of the way to Fatima Mission at the foot of the highest peaks.
Over years researching in the Torricellis, I have watched this
road progress ever deeper into the mountains. By 1992 it was
possible to drive a truck into virgin bush on the upper slopes
of Mt Somoro itself (the highest peak in the range). This road,
I fear, heralds the end of Somoro's forest.

It is always slightly unnerving arriving at a new location in
Papua New Guinea. You have no idea what the locals will be
like or how you will be received. Stepping out of the Cessna at
Lumi that first time I would have been met by a small, wizened
fellow known to one and all as Lumi Man. Lumi Man looks
official. He wears a clean white shirt and blue shorts.
Sometimes he carries a clipboard and pen. Lumi Man greets
each stranger as they step from their aircraft with a long,
detailed harangue. This harangue can be disconcerting, for
Lumi Man delivers it in a language which no-one else can
understand.

On subsequent visits to Lumi I have seen Europeans stand
puzzled and embarrassed for long minutes as they strain to
understand Lumi Man and his function. Meanwhile, everyone
else in Lumi enjoys the joke enormously. The best response,
apparently, is to shake Lumi Man's hand rather formally, an
honour which he delightedly returns with a crisp salute.

My first reaction to Lumi Man must have been the same
sort of embarrassed immobility I have witnessed so often in

others—but I have no memory of it, or indeed anything else much about Lumi in 1985. As for the rest of the expedition, my recollections of it are few and dream-like.

On that first exploratory trip I decided to stay in the village of Wigotei, about half a day's walk from the Catholic mission centre at Fatima. I was feeling slightly unwell when I arrived. This, I thought, probably heralded an incipient bout of malaria. Malaria is the constant companion of mammalogists working in lowland New Guinea, for our work leaves us very vulnerable to infection with the malarial parasite.

Most New Guinea mammals are nocturnal. To observe them, one must be in the forest at night, which is when the *Anopheles* mosquitoes are active. Mammalogists are often occupied for hours at a time at a mist-net, attempting to disentangle bats without hurting them. All the while you are surrounded by a buzzing cloud of mosquitoes. Because both hands are fully occupied coping with live bats, you cannot even wave them away. No matter how well protected you are by clothing and insecticide, there always seems to be a dozen proboscises inserted into your bloodstream at once.

Anti-malarial drugs offer only partial protection. Malaria, it seems, mutates so rapidly that it becomes resistant to each new drug soon after it is developed.

As a result of these problems, I have learned to live with *vivax* malaria (the most common and least dangerous strain) while in New Guinea. Indeed, malaria often seems to cause my worst troubles in Australia. One attack in Woolloomooloo was particularly dangerous. I was enjoying a pub lunch with some friends when the first symptoms came on. The attack developed rapidly and my friends went off to find a cab to take me to a doctor. I began to feel cold and decided to take a stroll in the weak winter sun.

As I paced up and down the street, a police car cruised by. The police seemed to take a great deal more interest in me than they usually do. My first impulse was to stop and ask them for help, but something in their expressions made me stop. Then I realised how I must look: pale and sweating, shaking violently, with my arms clasped around my chest. And I was walking along a street notorious as a shooting gallery for heroin users.

I could just see myself in King's Cross police station, trying to explain that I was not a junkie, but was in fact suffering from malaria. The enlarged liver and spleen that develop with malaria are exquisitely vulnerable to physical damage. A vision floated before me of my untimely demise from a ruptured spleen inflicted by a constable's boot, its owner having decided I was an obnoxious, smart-arse junkie. With these thoughts swirling around my head, I rushed into the pub and hid in the toilet, to await escape, some minutes later, in the cab.

I have had to take a philosophical view of this inevitable infection with malaria because I simply could not do my field-work otherwise. The 1985 expedition was so expensive, time-consuming and difficult to organise that to pull out just after arriving in this remote and fascinating region was not something which, in all conscience, I could do.

So—just a few days work, I told myself now, would repay all the trouble. I swallowed a couple of quinine tablets (still the most effective if oldest anti-malarial) and resolved to stick things out at Wigotei.

The next afternoon I went out to set up a mist-net. On the way back to the village I was struck down with a ferocious bout of fever. It was as if someone had delivered a blow to the base of my skull with an axe. I had a blinding headache and could not walk nor focus my eyes properly. With the help of some villagers, I struggled back to my hut and took more quinine, certain that I was suffering the mother of all malarial attacks.

From what I can remember, time passed strangely at Wigotei. Nights were an absolute torture, for sleep was banished and I lay soaked in sweat in a fevered state. The seconds ticked by through the hours of darkness as I longed for a sip of water and the balm of sleep. In place of sheep, I counted the pandanus leaves which made up the roof. I never got to the end of a row, for my disordered brain lost track, even among the neatly arranged fronds.

The days were little better. I lay in the insufferably hot hut, parched and aching for water. A stream of people passed by, each one sticking their head in the door as they muttered '*tarangu*' (a term of sympathy in Pidgin, roughly translating as 'commiserations'). Somehow, I failed in my efforts to communicate to them my need for water. Thankfully, every now and then a kind woman would come by with a bamboo cane full of the precious stuff and I would drink it and down a few more quinine tablets.

My thinking was not clear enough to ask the people of the village to carry me to the mission hospital and they did not take the initiative themselves. Perhaps they were waiting for my European bulk to reduce itself before they were willing to shoulder me for hours over the rough terrain. I continued to take quinine. Worse, I became confused as to how many tablets I had taken. This is highly dangerous, as quinine is not a drug to fool with.

Death from quinine overdose is horrible. It is impossible to reverse the effects of the drug, so death is inevitable. As time went by, what began as a slight ringing in my ears increased in volume until it resembled church bells. Soon, the bells turned to cannons. This is a common side-effect of quinine and it finally alerted me to the fact that I had probably already taken far too much.

I sometimes seemed to have a lucid period around midday, which lasted about twenty minutes. During one of these intervals I arranged to be carried by stretcher to the mission clinic. I remember very little of the journey, but do recollect a series of semi-hallucinatory visions, including one which featured an extraordinarily large snail sitting on the trunk of a tree. From my unusual orientation, I also recall being intrigued by a black claw which one of my bearers was wearing on a string around his neck. When we arrived at the mission, I somehow managed to buy the necklace from him.

This, it eventuated, was the most important specimen I acquired during the short expedition.

At the mission hospital, the Catholic nursing sister in charge took one look at me and said, 'You have the worst case of malaria I have seen for some time. Have some quinine.'

I was beyond debating the point with her, indeed almost beyond caring, and swallowed the bitter pills once more.

That evening, lying in a mission hospital cot, an extraordinary sense of calm came over me. The torture of the thirst and fever, the terrible tension that pain creates, all left me. I was at peace, simply lying there in utter tranquility, experiencing a level of relaxation deeper than I had ever felt before.

At one stage I was aware of a nun coming in and undressing me. Her hands and eyes searched every part of my body. I grew up a Catholic and spent my primary school years being taught by nuns. It did not occur to me to wonder why she was touching me like this. Normally, I would have been embarrassed beyond words by such intimate contact, but that night I merely lay there, blissfully peaceful. It was as if it were all happening to someone else.

I don't remember anything at all of the following few days. My next memory is of lying in a bed in Boram Hospital in the coastal town of Wewak. The ward was full of dying people. It was primitive and dirty. A large and menacing male nurse, ears and nose pierced in traditional fashion, advanced towards me bearing a hypodermic syringe. I swear that he wiped it on his grubby shirt sleeve before jabbing it into my arm, saying, 'I'm sure you have the worst case of malaria…'

After he had taken the blood sample, I crawled out of bed and kept moving until I saw a friendly face. It was the hospital dentist. He took me home with him, where I stayed until I was fit enough to travel back to Australia.

I had been suffering from scrub typhus. Victims of this disease who go untreated for six or more days have a frighteningly high fatality rate. Years later, when I again met the nun who first treated me, she told me that she only thought I had another twelve hours to live if I did not receive treatment.

Her search of my body, she later told me, had yielded the bite mark of a scrub typhus tick. This tick is not stupid. It tries to bite on the genitals, knowing that this part of one's anatomy is likely to come in contact with another animal, which may harbour a partner for it too.

Fortunately, the nun had a supply of the appropriate drugs on hand and after administering them she evacuated me to Wewak. I owe her my life.

It took me a long time to recover. For several months I did not experience an uninterrupted night's sleep. My short-term memory was devastated. It was impossible to remember a new face or name, or use a telephone, simply because I could not retain a string of digits for long enough in my mind to dial the number. Eventually I found a way around this particular difficulty—by writing the number I wished to dial on a piece of paper and sticking it to the telephone. Other problems persisted, however, and my inability to remember faces and names provoked a million embarrassments and inconveniences.

Eventually I was able to examine the small collection of mammals I had made at Wigotei. Of all the specimens I had gathered, it was the claw I purchased from my stretcher-bearer which proved most difficult to identify. I felt it must be from a tree-kangaroo—yet it differed in detail from anything I knew about. The fur at its base was black and it was larger than any tree-kangaroo claw I had ever seen.

Only one species, the Grizzled Tree-kangaroo (*Dendrolagus inustus*), had previously been reported from the Torricelli Mountains, but this was not its claw. It seemed that at least one other species of tree-kangaroo was present in the mountains, but what was it?

TWENTY-ONE

The wildlife clan

Three years were to pass before I could return to the Torricelli Mountains to investigate this mystery further. It is difficult enough even at the best of times to raise funds to do research in New Guinea—but when I told people about the large, black claw and my feeling that it might be from an undescribed species of tree-kangaroo, their scepticism made it clear that it would be all but impossible for me to attract funding on such flimsy evidence.

I decided to 'stretch' some existing research money. In 1988 I received a grant to investigate the mammals of New Ireland in the Bismarck Archipelago to the north of New Guinea. A side-trip to the Torricellis would only cost a few hundred dollars extra. I somehow justified to myself this redirection of funding and hoped the granting body would never hear about it.

At Fatima mission I made the acquaintance of Father Patrick McGeaver. I must have met Pat in 1985 (although I cannot remember it) because when we met again in 1988 he greeted me like a long-lost relative.

Pat leads a rather Spartan life. His house lacks windows and is made of tin. His furniture is basic and he has none of the amenities most people in the west take for granted. His daily fare consists principally of boiled potatoes. When I visited his kitchen to drop off a few delicacies I had brought from Australia, the cook thanked me and grumbled that Father ate far worse than his parishioners. While this situation scandalised the cook, it did not seem to worry Pat, who has a fondness for the pratie that only the Irish can muster. On the night we met in 1988 he sat me down to a simple yet delightful meal of boiled potatoes and an egg.

After we had eaten, Pat produced an unlabelled bottle filled with a clear liquid and, his eyes sparkling, asked me if I was familiar with poteen. It was the real stuff, doubtless brewed in some illicit still on the west coast of Ireland—and it was wonderful. Glasses were filled and we settled in for a long evening.

We talked about the state of hockey, rugby, Australian and Gaelic football and a number of other sporting topics. The room began filling with moths. It was drizzling outside and the weather was mild. These are perfect conditions for flying insects of all kinds. Pat got up to close the wooden shutters. I begged him not to, as I needed live insects to bait my traps and this represented a windfall. As we sat there speaking long into the night, moths flew around us like a great living snowstorm. The room filled with them. Some were large and black, like great swallowtail butterflies. Others were smaller and every colour of the rainbow. Some, indeed, were exquisitely transparent. I have never seen such a cornucopia of gorgeous creatures. At the close of the evening I scooped them by the hundreds into my cloth bags while Pat went out to turn off the generator.

Father Pat is an Irishman for whom Gaelic is a first language. He is one of the new style of Roman Catholic missionaries and is a vital force in the lives of the people of the Torricelli Mountains. As we got to know each other, I began to see what motivated Pat. He told me that his own language and culture had been banned and belittled at the hands of the invading English and that he was certainly not going to see that happen to his Papua New Guinea parishioners. They had, unfortunately, been converted in the 1930s by Catholic missionaries of German extraction who had suppressed the local culture. Pat was determined to redress that.

Under Father Pat, the region had experienced a dramatic cultural revival. The Mass was now said in Olo (the local language) by this Irish priest dressed to a turn in Melanesian finery. His cuscus-fur head-dress and bird-of-paradise plume armlets shook gloriously as he sang. Indeed, hearing Mass said by Father Pat dressed in his full regalia was one of the most moving experiences I have ever had in a church.

It was with some pride that Pat told me that the revival of old traditions had gone so far that, as a special favour to the visiting Bishop of Vanimo, parish women had danced bare-breasted in procession through the church while singing hymns.

But the revival had gone much deeper than ceremonial formalities. Pat had questioned the old men closely concerning their pre-Christian customs and had incorporated traditional elements, where appropriate, into the celebration of the sacraments. Thus, traditional words from birth and initiation ceremonies, many long forgotten by the community, were now said at baptisms and confirmations. Pat also bought ochre for decorative purposes and sponsored festivals on these occasions.

For the first time in decades a *haus tambaran* (ancestral

spirit house) had been built in Wilbeitei village and in it were stored the spirit masks, all newly made, for which the area was formerly famous. But the house now had a double purpose. Though great spirit masks, some five metres tall, were hung around its walls, at its centre was parked the new community truck, the result of an investment and savings scheme instituted by Father Pat.

Pat's revival of the village traditions had come at a critical moment. The Olo had been influenced by Christianity for the best part of sixty years. They were a lot further down the road to westernisation than even the Telefol. It was dismaying to find that Pidgin was commonly used, even in conversations between the Olo themselves, and that only the very oldest members of the community remembered what traditional clothing looked like. Had Father Pat arrived just a decade later, he may have found precious little to preserve.

Father Pat suggested that I base my research at the village of Wilbeitei. Here was a community which had been revitalised by this new brand of Catholicism. On our arrival, the village store was opened and a present of food was made to us. We were accepted with open hearts into the bosom of the people. Partly as a result of the goodwill of the villagers, I began a most wonderful period of study.

My most important contact at Wilbeitei soon became Kaspar Seiko. Kaspar is a traditional village leader who is old enough to remember the earthquake of 1934. This earthquake was one of the most severe ever felt in New Guinea. It devastated villages, gardens and forests throughout the Torricellis.

Kaspar knew about the tree-kangaroo which possessed black claws. He called it *Tenkile*, and he, Kaspar Seiko, was custodian of a *ples masalai* (forbidden place) called Sweipini, commonly referred to as *as ples bilong Tenkile* (the centre of

Tenkile's world, its original place). Sweipini is located at the very summit of the Torricelli Mountains, in an area of dwarfed, mossy trees and eternal mists.

When I explained the reason for my visit and my desire to see a more complete specimen of the tree-kangaroo, Kaspar agreed to try to obtain one for me. He decided to search for *Tenkile* in his hunting ground near Sweipini but, because of the sacred nature of the locality, neither I nor anyone else was allowed to accompany him.

Kaspar explained that at the heart of Sweipini lies a small lake. The Olo believe that this lake is the home of gigantic eels. On the approach of anyone except Kaspar himself, the frogs inhabiting the lake take fright at seeing a strange face and begin to croak loudly. The noise awakens the giant eels, which can cause terrible weather, blighting crops and bringing widespread famine. Hundreds of people would die of hunger were this to happen.

Kaspar returned a few days later bearing a small bundle of fur. It was a tiny *Tenkile* joey. The little creature had been killed by Kaspar's dogs. Although saddened at its death, I was also elated and surprised at my first sight of a whole *Tenkile*. It was black all over—a condition then unknown among tree-kangaroos. Here, surely, was an animal which was unknown to the outside world. It was a major discovery, for it is rare for such a large mammal to have remained undescribed until the late twentieth century.

So in 1989, armed with funds gained on the basis of this more substantial find, I began an extended period of fieldwork in the Torricellis. My first move was to undertake a widespread survey to determine whether *Tenkile* existed elsewhere in the ranges. I began by questioning hunters about tree-kangaroos and collecting whatever pieces of jaw, skull and fur they had kept as trophies of the hunt. Through this I hoped to learn about its distribution and abundance, as well as a little of its biology.

My stays at Wilbeitei and other villages were often enlivened by stories of past hunts and of the excitement of tracking and killing *Tenkile*. The males, I was told, were far larger than the females and were very powerful adversaries. They also possess a pungent odour. Hunters said that it is impossible to keep a successful kill secret, for people can smell *Tenkile* on your hands for a week afterwards.

It became clear that *Tenkile* was a very distinctive animal. Measurement of the jaw and skull fragments established that it was indeed a large tree-kangaroo. They also showed that it was related to Doria's Tree-kangaroo (*Dendrolagus dorianus*), the species distributed along the central mountain range of New Guinea. *Tenkile* differed from Doria's Tree-kangaroo in being black rather than brown, in aspects of its skull and dentition, and in possessing a more powerful, although not entirely unpleasant odour.

Following this initial investigation, I began to search for a living animal. I only ever saw one adult *Tenkile*, a male captured by a hunter in 1990. This was a precious moment.

Examining the rare creature, I discovered that what hunters had told me of its odour was no exaggeration. And even a week later, in Sydney, the smell was still clinging to me—a mixture of pine needles, musk and something I can only describe as 'tree-kangaroo'.

It was disheartening to learn that this beautiful and distinctive tree-kangaroo was fast becoming endangered in the Torricellis. I questioned older hunters, and sometimes accompanied them to places where they had captured *Tenkile* in their youth. Many of these sites were now adjacent to gardens and quite close to villages. In some instances, *Tenkile* had not been seen in these places for fifty years. Its modern distribution was centred solely upon the sacred site at Sweipini and a remote ridge called Mungople, which was the most distant country from the settlements in the Fatima area.

Discussions about *Tenkile* drew talk of other creatures inhabiting the forests of Olo country. From Kaspar Seiko and some of the older hunters of Wilbeitei I heard stories concerning a creature they knew as *Weimanke*. *Weimanke*, they said, was somewhat like *Tenkile*, but its face was pale, like a white man's. Kaspar said that although he himself had never captured *Weimanke*, his father had once brought one to the village from Sweipini while Kaspar was still a child. I was confused as to what kind of creature *Weimanke* might be—if it was indeed anything more than mythical. In any case, I needed to concentrate my efforts on tracking down the more tangible *Tenkile*. I dismissed *Weimanke* from my mind.

Yet it was during our extended survey of the North Coast Ranges that the mystery of the mythic creature with the white man's face was solved.

We divided the survey work up between the team of researchers employed on the project. Lester Seri and Pavel German (of the Australian Museum) were to cover the far eastern and western portions of the ranges, while I was to cover the high, central blocks of Menawa and Somoro.

Lester and Pavel began in the east. They arrived at the airstrip at Sibilanga with the objective of surveying Mt Sapau, an isolated peak which defines the eastern end of the high Torricellis. As they were preparing for the climb, Lester fell sick with malaria. Unable to walk, he instructed Pavel to carry on without him and to accompany some hunters to the peak.

A week later Pavel returned with a very strange tree-kangaroo. The hunters who captured it called it *Weiman*. It was reddish, with a whitish-pink face. Immediately I knew that all I had been told of *Weimanke* was true. Amazingly, here was yet another kind of tree-kangaroo living in the Torricelli Mountains which was unknown to science!

At Wilbeitei I opened the drum in which Pavel had preserved this animal's skin. Kaspar saw *Weimanke* for the first time in at least sixty years. His eyes filled with tears. How good it would be to see *Weimanke* back at Sweipini again, he said. Yet the chances of this ever happening seem slim, for *Weimanke* is nearly extinct even on Mt Sapau, its last stronghold.

In assigning myself the Menawa block to survey, I had selected an area of singularly difficult access. There are few villages and no airstrips near the highest peak, Mt Menawa, and the community I suspected to be the traditional owners of the mountain seemed to be concentrated near a small village marked on my map as Fas. The distance between human settlement and peak was heartening in one sense: tree-kangaroos tend to live where people do not. The nearest airstrip appeared to be at a place called Utai. I would need to charter a small plane. Accordingly, I explained to the pilot that my destination was Fas village, and that Utai appeared to be the closest airstrip.

To my delight, he said that a new airstrip had just been opened at Fas itself. We could fly directly there, saving me a walk.

A mere fifty minutes later I stepped from the aircraft into the middle of Fas village. As the Twin Otter taxied back up the airstrip in preparation for take-off, I was greeted by the village head-man.

He strode forward and we shook hands. I introduced myself and explained that I wished to climb Mt Menawa. How long did it take to walk there? The head-man smiled and shook his head sadly. Mt Menawa, he said in perfect Pidgin, was about five days' walk away. With a sinking feeling I got out the map and pointed to Fas's position, within, I thought, about half a day's walk of the mountain. 'Ah,' he said, 'that is 3Fas. This is 2Fas.'

We looked up as the Twin Otter soared overhead, on its way to Vanimo.

Our situation was made all but irreversible by the state of the new Fas airstrip. It acted like an ant-lion trap: very easy to slide into with a load of cargo, but extraordinarily difficult to get out of. The trouble was that the strip was boggy and short. Any aircraft could land a large volume of cargo into the place, but only a Twin Otter was powerful enough to lift it out. I knew that the Twin Otter now flying away was the only one working in Sandaun Province—and that it was booked for weeks in advance.

To make matters worse, the local two-way radio used to arrange aircraft landings was broken. To get a message out, someone had to walk across the range to the next village, or else use the school radio and hope that whoever they made contact with would pass on our request to the airline.

This situation was particularly galling to the crew (employed by Gary Steer, an Australian documentary film-maker) who were travelling with me. For them time was money, yet they were well and truly stuck. There were simply not enough porters in 2Fas to lug their 200 kilograms of film equipment anywhere.

We were destined to spend two weeks in 2Fas, awaiting an aircraft to take us on the twenty-minute journey to Utai.

Our misery at being detained there was increased by the plague of cockroaches which infested our hut. These were thick even by day. If a notebook was left open on the table for any time at all, you returned to find it covered in small black blobs. These were cockroach droppings, which rained incessantly from the thatched roof. My breakfast of sweet potato suffered the same fate.

By night the minor inconvenience caused by the roaches developed into a major problem. We relied on a decrepit hurricane lantern for light, and every now and again it would splutter and go out. One evening this happened just as we commenced dinner. I put down my plate to attend to it. The lamp, however, had other ideas and despite my best efforts it failed to spark into life. Disgruntled, I reached glumly for a dinner to be eaten by torchlight. I was saved the trouble, however, for when I swung the beam onto the table I found not a meal, but a plate piled high and spilling over with cockroaches. They scrambled wildly away from the light, taking my appetite with them. There were at least four species in the feeding frenzy.

Our time was not completely wasted, though. I engaged in numerous dart tournaments with the villagers and spent several delightful evenings with Tom, the local schoolteacher, whom I had met previously at Yapsiei. I am more than impressed with the job teachers like Tom do. Their life, if posted to such remote villages, is largely one of deprivation, yet the service they do their country and community is invaluable. I left almost all my pencils, biros and paper with Tom when I departed—although the school year was well advanced he was yet to receive his supplies from head office.

The stay was not wasted scientifically either, for by questioning villagers I learned a little about the rare Black-spotted Cuscus. I also discovered an undescribed subspecies of horseshoe-bat roosting under a landslip near the village.

The Twin Otter arrived just as I was about to set out across the mountains on foot to Sissano Lagoon to arrange for its return. I left 2Fas with a small but interesting mammal collection from this hitherto unknown region.

We arrived at Utai airfield at about midday. As it would only be a four-hour walk from there to 3Fas (and an additional half day to the base of the moutain itself), I decided to go on to the village that day, leaving most of my cargo and the film crew to catch up later.

Some men from 3Fas were visiting Utai at the time and I asked them for help in reaching their village. I was amazed to find them reluctant to assist me; one even went so far as to suggest that, for my own safety, I should not go to 3Fas at all.

This entirely unexpected situation threw my plans into chaos. I had come all the way from Sydney to Utai, with an unwanted detour via 2Fas, in order to reach Mt Menawa. The two lost weeks had put me in no frame of mind to abort the project. Moreover, Mt Menawa is the tallest mountain in the entire North Coast Ranges. To return without surveying it would throw the validity of the entire project into doubt.

It was late in the afternoon by the time I decided to make the walk unaccompanied to 3Fas, despite the ominous reception at Utai. I found it difficult to believe that the disaffection with my proposed visit was shared by more than one or two individuals.

It was a long, wet walk up a river bed before I reached the village some time after the last rays of sun had left the sky. From what I could see, it looked to be a very traditional place, for there was no evidence of basic amenities such as a school or first aid post. A few men came into the village square to meet me. They seemed genuinely surprised and disturbed to find me standing there. I explained who I was and what I had come for, and was then led to a hut on the edge of the village.

I remained there, alone in the torchlight, sorting the equipment in my pack. No-one brought food or water, or even offered to light a fire. This extreme break with basic Melanesian etiquette set me on my guard. Never before had I been treated so badly in New Guinea.

That night a large bonfire was lit in the village square. Men began to gather around it and debate vigorously. I strained to hear what they were saying, but mostly they spoke in their own language. As the debate heated, however, a few Pidgin phrases were interspersed with the *tok ples*.

'If we kill him, the Government will be on our side…He is a "wildlife", we should kill him.'

Then another voice: 'The Bible says it is wrong to kill. We will get plenty of trouble if we kill him.'

The debate went on long into the night. Shocked at the nature of the discussion, I got no sleep until the small hours of the morning, when, during a lull in the proceedings, I dozed briefly.

Before first light I slipped out of the hut and began to walk downriver. No-one was stirring in the village.

On my way upstream I had passed a village about two hours' walk from 3Fas. By the time I reached it again that morning, people were already going about their early tasks. In the village square there was a fine, half-grown pig. I inquired after its owner and asked if he would sell it to me. We settled on a price of 40 kina and I asked the owner for his assistance in carrying it back to 3Fas.

We arrived mid-morning to a village which still seemed

strangely quiet. I ushered the piglet into the village square and there commenced a speech in Pidgin.

I began by saying that I felt that the people of 3Fas were *bel i hat* (angry) and had a grievance with me. I had no idea what the basis of the grievance was, but I had brought this pig as a 'talking pig', so that we could sit down and eat it, then discuss the nature of their problem.

After a few minutes an elderly man approached me, telling me that my gift had been accepted by the village. Slowly a group of men gathered around and sat down to talk as the women and youths prepared a *mumu* to cook the pig in, along with some sago and greens.

One of the younger men was more eloquent than the others. His name was Simon and as we talked the story of the villagers' anger began to emerge. It had, at its base, the poor treatment they felt they had received at the hands of previous wildlife researchers.

Simon related that the first 'wildlife' to visit their village was an American ornithologist who arrived about 1974. At that time, the villagers had had very little contact with the outside world. The researcher explained that he wished to climb Mt Menawa. The locals were worried by this as Mt Menawa is their sacred place, inhabited by *masalai*. They agreed to carry his cargo as far as a spur just below the summit, but refused to go any further. The ornithologist went on alone, and when he reached the summit he discharged his shotgun. At this, a couple of the bolder village men followed his track to the top.

The *ples masalai* had been conquered, but many villagers still felt equivocal about this intrusion into the realm of the spirits.

When the ornithologist left the village, he paid everyone with what they described as 'sixpences'. The villagers were elated, believing that each had received a veritable fortune because of the large number of small coins they were given. Imagining themselves to be wealthy, they went to the trade store at Utai—only to find that their coins were barely sufficient to purchase a bag of rice or a tin of fish.

A second 'wildlife' visited Utai in the 1980s. This one (who was also an American) wanted to carry out a full wildlife survey on the mountain. According to the villagers, he collected literally thousands of birds, mammals, reptiles and insects—enough, they said, to affect their food supply. And, according to those who worked with him, he bullied his employees and paid the people very little for the vast number of animals he took from their land. His attitude was one of arrogance and suspicion. He told the locals that they were lazy and had not collected enough.

This infuriated them.

Finally, the people of 3Fas had had enough. They hatched a plan to murder the visiting American. On his last morning on the mountain, Simon planned to follow him as he moved along his trapline, slowly picking up and storing his traps. When he was deep in the forest, Simon would drive a machete through his skull as he bent, vulnerable, over a trap.

The plan, however, was foiled when the researcher sent someone else out to retrieve his traps, explaining that he was too busy packing to attend to them himself.

After these dismal encounters with those they knew as the 'wildlife clan', the people of 3Fas decided to take revenge. They were determined to kill the very next member of the clan to visit them. That person was me.

Although this idea that justice can be served by killing an innocent party might seem foreign to Europeans, it made enormous sense to the people of 3Fas. In Melanesia, the clan is the all-important entity. Retribution for an offence can be ventured upon any member of the offender's clan.

This system, known widely as 'payback', works because it keeps equivalence in numbers between competing groups. In this system, if a man dies suddenly of natural causes, a ceremony is held to determine who enacted the sorcery responsible for his death. The offenders are invariably found to be a competing, usually adjacent group. The revenge killing must restore the balance between the groups. What is important in this system is not the doing of justice to the individual, but achieving a balance between competing clans.

Hearing myself classified as a member of the 'wildlife clan' on that first night should have alerted me to the fact that I was carrying a communal responsibility. Unfortunately it had not, and it was only after Simon's lengthy explanation that I understood the nature of the problem. I have little doubt that justice would have been visited upon me had I not settled the matter in a more or less Melanesian manner.

Our pig feast ended in a formal, written agreement. I explained precisely what I wanted from my work (basically, knowledge about tree-kangaroos and a sample of each species found in the region) and in turn I wrote down a rate of pay for services, food and specimens which was acceptable to the villagers. This would be used by them in future if members of my clan ever visited again.

Soon afterwards the rest of the crew arrived, and were incredulous when I told them of the events of the past twenty-four hours.

So I spent a couple of weeks at 3Fas. I learned there that a population of tree-kangaroos somewhat similar to, although distinct from *Tenkile*, existed atop Mt Menawa. Yet that knowledge was among the most hard-earned that I have gleaned in Melanesia. Not only had it almost cost me my life, but I have never eaten so poorly while in the field.

The people of 3Fas are sago-eaters. They plant no gardens, and so even a banana was an unheard-of luxury. Like them, I had to subsist on sago processed into a grey jelly that resembled snot in colour, texture and (I assume) taste. I revolted at it and could barely get a mouthful down. As a result, by the end of my time at 3Fas, I was greatly reduced in bulk and began to worry for my health. The only variety I had after my meagre supplies ran out was the occasional, near-rancid piece of pork. On one occasion, I ate a piece of bright orange cassowary fat which was brought to me as a gift. The fact that it was fly-blown did not add to its charms, yet did not deter me from consuming it.

When I left 3Fas, Simon was among the people who offered to help carry my cargo to Utai. Just before we reached the settlement we stopped to rest in a hut. There were several women in occupation, including a young mother with her beautiful, newborn child. I asked who the baby's father was, and to my enormous surprise learned that it was Simon. Remarkably, Simon studiously avoided the woman and child during the entire time we were there. I asked one of his friends whether Simon had seen his child before. Apparently he had not.

I never got to the bottom of this matter. Perhaps Simon was following a cultural practice which I have not met elsewhere, or perhaps he was displeased with his wife. Whatever the case, it served to reinforce my feeling that the culture of the Utai people is very different from that of other groups I have encountered during my fieldwork.

Descent from the Neon Basin. Ken Aplin and Goilala youths from Kosipe ferry some of our equipment, including the all-important liquid nitrogen cylinder, down a steep slope.

Kebuge (above) kills a pig for a feast at Yapsiei. Despite being afflicted with elephantiasis, Kebuge walked from Yapsiei to Yominbip in order to construct a helipad for us there.

This makeshift shelter (left) was erected near Kosipe in 1981 to house myself and a few local men who accompanied me as I laid traps. It was roofed with strips of bark from a *Papuacedrus* tree which was at least half a millennium old. After it was felled, the tree was left to rot. All day the forest rang with the sound of the axe, as the Goilala cleared land for a new garden.

Opposite: Anaru on Mt Boobiari, returning from the hunt with two *Kuyam* (Ground Cuscus).

Opposite: The Hindenburg Wall, Ok Tedi area, western Papua New Guinea. The wall, as it is known locally, is one of the natural wonders of the world.

Crossing the Yapsiei River by canoe in 1984, I imagine my liquid nitrogen cylinder, my notebooks and myself are about to be dumped into the crocodile-infested waters. Miyanmin canoes lack outriggers and are thus highly unstable. If you are not to overbalance, you must pretend to be a sack of potatoes, which I'm trying hard to do. Photograph by Robert Attenborough.

Syme, a tree-kangaroo hunter of reknown, wearing a wreath of victory at the close of our 1992 field season. Syme was old, his canines worn to stumps, but his presence seemed to be essential to find *Tenkile*.

These large objects (right), being worn by Olo tribesmen, are *tumbuans* (spirit masks). The black and red one in front represents the *Tenkile* ancestor spirit. They were brought out of the *haus tambaran* to participate in a festival upon completion of our 1992 field season.

The young men (below) from Bultem village, near Tabubil, are going through male initiation rites. Telefomin, a few days' walk away, was once the centre for such rituals, but since the arrival of the Baptist mission they have largely ceased there, and now more often take place in Catholic areas such as Bultem.

Tenkile (Dendrolagus scottae). For three years, the only evidence I had for the existence of this new species of tree-kangaroo was a single claw. In 1988, after scraping together funding to revisit the Torricelli Mountains, I found that the claw was indeed from a rare and previously unknown species, and that a conservation program was necessary to ensure its survival.

The rhythm of life at Yapsiei seems to have remained unaltered for millennia. Each evening the women return to the village, loaded down with children, pigs, firewood and food.

OPPOSITE PAGE

A. D. Hope and Goilala friends outside a Swiss-style chalet at Kosipe.

This group of Western Dani men walked from Ilaga to Wamena to trade salt.

Amunsep in his prime, with one of his hunting dogs. In his left hand he holds some hunting charms.

With Femsep, a year or two before his death. Photograph by a local man.

During our weeks trapped at 2Fas we played numerous darts tournaments with the locals. Despite their proficiency with bow and arrow, we usually won at darts.

Willok's habit of eating tapeworms disgusted the Telefol. He took this one from the gut of a ringtail possum. I was eventually to bear the dubious distinction of having the worm named after me.

Peter (above) was chief assistant to Anton, our cook, while we worked on the *Tenkile* radiotracking program in the Torricelli Mountains. Peter never lacked a smile, even after spending weeks in our sodden jungle camp.

Did this pig (above) save my life? I bought it as a peace-offering to the people of 3Fas, so that an explosive social situation could be defused. Photograph by a local man.

Opposite: This tiny boy, sitting below Anaru's drum, had been recently orphaned. His distended belly indicates malnutrition, malaria, or both. His skin is covered in *grile*. Both Don Gardner and I worried over his poor physical condition. I do not know whether he survived.

Kwiyawagi dandies. These young Lani men beautified themselves with leaves and flowers from the forest during our walk to Kelangurr Cave.

Opposite: This Lani man is setting a deadfall trap in forest near Kwiyawagi. Traps such as these catch giant rats, quolls, possums and even wallabies. The *noken* on his back holds sweet potatoes.

Our camp in the Meren Valley was dwarfed by the vast limestone cliff carved by a glacier 15,000 years ago. Arianus Murip was assaulted by security guards a few hundred metres from here, and left to die in the desolate valley.

The *rumah tuan tannah* (house of the earth spirit) discovered by Yonas on the Meren Glacier. I am crouching by the entrance of the ice cave. Photograph by Yonas Tinal.

The last reminder of an ice age. The Meren Glacier, sitting atop the Carstensz Mountains in central Irian Jaya, is one of a handful of equatorial glaciers remaining on the planet. Global warming is causing it to melt so quickly that it may die before I do.

A vast area of lowland forest will eventually be smothered by tailings from the Freeport mine. Here, dying forest along the tailings levee, near Timika, has been clear-felled.

This transmigrant settlement, bulldozed into the jungles of southern Irian Jaya is, like countless others, laid out with military precision. It is difficult to grow rice here, so the camp inhabitants survive as best they can. Some find work with logging companies, while others trap wildlife for sale. Many make a few rupiah selling fruit and vegetables in town.

The central square of Kuala Kencana, southern Irian Jaya, in February 1996. The city was newly constructed but not yet inhabited. It has been built where lowland jungle existed only a year or two before. It is expected that a quarter of a million people, mostly non-Irianese, will live here.

Dingiso (*Dendrolagus mbaiso*). The discovery of this black-and-white ground-living tree-kangaroo in 1994 was the high point of my career as a biologist. The animal is found on the mountain summits of Irian Jaya. The Moni people revere it as an ancestor.

TWENTY-TWO

Trail of the *Tenkile*

So—*Tenkile* were indeed to be found only in the Torricelli Mountains near Wilbeitei, even though a related tree-kangaroo lived atop Mt Menawa.

I therefore had no choice but to concentrate my research and conservation program in the Wilbeitei area. We were to make many visits over the next few years.

As we began, disaster struck. The sacred *ples masalai* at Sweipini was one of the last strongholds of *Tenkile*. But in 1990 some villagers asked Father Pat to exorcise the spirit eels which are believed to guard the sacred site. This he did, in a ceremony at Sweipini attended by hundreds. And then, with the powerful spirits effectively banished, hunters were free to enter the place—and they killed many *Tenkile* in just a few months.

When I visited Sweipini with Kaspar in 1991 we were dismayed to find all almost traces of *Tenkile*—such as fresh

claw marks on trees, scats, tracks and chewed vegetation—
gone. *Tenkile* had lost its last safe haven.

I still struggle to understand what prompted the people of
Wilbeitei to request the exorcism from Father Pat. Was it, perhaps, a result of the new and exhilarating Catholicism which
had swept through the area? Or were they, in some way, trying
to help me by opening access to an area where *Tenkile* was still
abundant? If this was the case, then I had made a truly disas-
trous blunder in expressing interest in studying *Tenkile* at all.

The development of conservation programs in countries
such as Papua New Guinea is fraught with difficulty. Western
notions of conservation often appear to be completely non-
sensical to the local people. Many villagers believe that the
animals of the forest have always been there and that they will
always remain. When faced with clear evidence of a decline in
abundance, or even extinction, they will point to a place over
the mountains, saying, 'There's still plenty there.' Little do
they realise there is always a village 'over there', inhabited by
people who, when asked the same question, point back in
their own direction.

The problem goes much deeper than that, for the Melanesian
world-view incorporates humans and animals, the seen and
unseen, the living and the dead, in a way that is vastly different
from the European outlook. What Europeans call 'supernatural'
factors are for New Guineans simply the non-visible parts of a
single continuum of life. Indeed they are eminently 'natural'.
Such considerations often determine the fate of species, a point
brought home to me during my time at 2Fas.

The men of 2Fas wear head-ornaments made from the fur
of the Black-spotted Cuscus (*Spilocuscus rufoniger*), the species
I had first encountered on that trip to Mt Boobiari many years
before. It is an extremely rare cuscus which quickly vanishes
under anything but the slightest hunting pressure. By the
1980s it was already extinct throughout most of its distribution
in Papua New Guinea, with all recent records coming from
extremely remote places such as Mt Boobiari.

When I asked the people of 2Fas about the Black-spotted Cuscus, the answer was invariably, '*Planti i stap*' (There are lots of them here). I began to doubt this statement, however, upon inquiring into the history of individual ornaments made from its fur. Many were very old. Some had been inherited from a grand-parent. If the species was so common, I wondered, why were the ornaments virtual heirlooms?

The answer was finally revealed when I spent an afternoon yarning with a group of older men. In response to my many questions, one of them said: We have told you this cuscus is very common, but it is also very difficult to catch. If a man wants to catch one, he must possess very strong magic. To make this magic, he must spend six months in the men's cult house. He must eat only certain foods, and all the time he must abstain from sexual intercourse. Then he must travel to the big bush, two day's walk from here. If he is lucky, he will find a cuscus there.'

When I asked how long it had been since someone had suc-ceeded in the hunt, I was told that no-one had caught one for many years. In the eyes of the elders, the village youth were a degenerate lot who lacked the moral fibre to endure the arduous preparation necessary for a successful hunt.

But this is not the whole story either. In 1987 I visited Woodlark Island off the coast of eastern New Guinea to study the unique spotted Woodlark Cuscus (*Phalanger lullulae*) which is found only there. This visit coincided with a similar visit by a team of students from Oxford University. Woodlark is a remote island with no regular air service. It gets few European visitors, so the arrival of two large groups, both bent on a study of the same cuscus species, caused quite a stir. We all worked hard during the two or three weeks of our visit. At the end we had collected a few specimens of the cuscus for the museum to confirm our identification and thought no more of it.

Just recently, though, I received a letter from the person who had led the Oxford University expedition. He had heard from a visitor to the island that the cuscus was now much rarer than before and that the local people firmly believed that this was due to the terrible ravages our expeditions had committed upon the population. Woodlark is an enormous island (some 800 square kilometres in extent) and it is inconceivable that our small collection could have had any impact on the cuscus population, for it was an extremely common animal. Yet the arrival of our expeditions clearly had an enormous social impact, which has perhaps coloured people's perceptions of the animal's abundance.

After experiences such as these, as well as watching the attempts of other well-meaning researchers to develop conservation programs in Melanesia, I believe that it is a rare bird indeed who can devise a successful program. This is because, in order to do so, one must have the trust of the local people as well as a genuine depth of understanding about how they view the world. It is my hope that the Papua New Guinea Department of Environment and Conservation will be able to develop local, innovative solutions to this problem, for they have an intimate understanding of Melanesian ways of life and thought, as well as the necessary scientific framework to know where the conservation problems lie.

Our problems in the Torricellis were complicated at times by the presence of the film crew. Gary Steer was interested in making a film of our search for *Tenkile*. Gary is a wonderful companion in the field, but the vast amount of equipment he needed sometimes transformed our small camp into a bursting metropolis.

And Gary's needs were quite different from our own. We were happy to track our animals from a distance, for it was far worse to be continually disturbing them than never to see them but to know approximately where they were. The film crew, in contrast, needed footage of tree-kangaroos.

We also found that the issue of film-making introduced a new financial concern among the local people. They had been happy to help me learn about *Tenkile* and to be paid average rates for their work. They perceived the film-making venture differently, for they felt that it would result in a financial windfall to Gary. If that were to happen, then they, as landowners, wanted their fair share. Although I was not directly involved with this issue, the problems it raised (such as distrust of Gary's and at times even my motives, along with ever escalating demands for money) brought about social strains which we would have been much better without.

But relations were good in other ways. From the very first we had been slotted into a series of relationships in the village. Kaspar Seiko and the two best local hunters were our main helpers. It was they, with their dogs, who worked intimately with us locating *Tenkile*. They also became our closest friends. Each time we set off into the bush with them, our line of carriers erupted into a glorious chorus of whooping cries, 'Yi, yi, yi'. It went on and on, only the fatigue of carrying the heavy loads finally bringing silence. The sound reminded me of the melodious call of the New Guinea singing dog.

Relationships with other villagers took root and flourished. Anton, a man in his early sixties, became our cook. From the moment of our arrival for each expedition, to the last farewell, Anton was there. His qualification for the position was that he had once cooked for the priests in Aitape. On tasting his first meal I was suitably impressed, for the mixture of tinned fish, fresh greens and rice was at least palatable. Qualms arose when the same dish was served again at breakfast, and these qualms turned into a terrible sense of foreboding at lunch that day when it became apparent that Anton could cook but one meal.

Despite enormous encouragement, including sundry gifts of herbs, spices and other ingredients, Anton never swerved from his speciality. Perhaps the priests had devised culinary monotony into a sort of penance, and Anton had assumed it was a European tradition.

In a desperate attempt to overcome his culinary limitations, I even hired a cheerful assistant for him named Peter, who seemed, alas, to have studied at the same school of cookery. And yet there was no way that I could fire Anton. To the villagers, he was a cook by profession. To fire him and hire someone else would have led to a terrible loss of self-esteem. It was something one just could not do to him, for Anton was a lovely person. I held out in this resolution even when a member of the film crew came to me in horror one day, saying that she had just seen Anton in the cook house, attempting to burst a large and very angry looking boil in his groin, with *her* fork. My feeble response—that she could wash the implement in some Dettol I had secreted away (the public stocks tend to evaporate quickly treating a village-full of cuts and scratches)—seemed only to add to her outrage.

I engaged Viare Kula, a Papua New Guinean with a degree from the University of Papua New Guinea, to undertake most of the radiotracking. In preparation for this he spent the previous eight months in Australia working with Roger Martin radiotracking Bennett's Tree-kangaroos (*Dendrolagus bennettianus*). Viare was a competent and hard-working researcher. What success we had with the project was largely due to him.

Our radiotracking program began with Viare, Kaspar and the hunters working to capture some *Tenkile* in order to place radio collars on them. I was busy in Australia at this time and could not be with them. To my surprise and relief, Viare achieved this goal successfully within a few weeks. Given the rarity of the species, it had seemed certain that this would take far longer. A spell of good weather (unique during the time of our study) allowed the dogs to work efficiently and Viare placed collars on three individuals. There seemed high hopes of success when we contemplated our three wired *Tenkile* roaming the forest around Sweipini.

By now I was back in the Torricellis. Our base camp was situated on the only relatively level piece of ground on the Sweipini track. It was also the last point at which water could be obtained, although this necessitated climbing down a 150-metre near-vertical drop, then lugging the bucket up to the camp. The camp was located at about 1,200 metres elevation, and beyond it the track rose abruptly for 350 metres.

Our day often began with a descent to the water to wash and brush our teeth, then a climb back up to the camp. Since we were tracking animals that lived beyond the ridge crest, we had to make the ascent to the summit each morning, then climb and drop several hundred metres further before we began our work. We would spend the rest of the day traversing the steep ridges of the range in our attempts to pick up signals. Carrying our receiver and aerial, as well as some supplies, this soon became an arduous routine, as we ascended, on average, approximately 1,000 to 1,500 vertical metres each day.

It rains or is misty virtually every day at Sweipini. This keeps the vegetation damp, which, combined with the extremely rugged topography, tended to deflect and break up our radio signals. When we tried to approach an animal to get a better fix, we found that it usually fled headlong downslope long before we saw it. This flightiness had doubtless developed because we were dealing with a population of animals which had been heavily hunted. Only the most skittish had survived, for those which stayed where they were when they heard a human approaching—either through curiosity or laziness—ended their days in the stew-pot.

These problems led to an unacceptable level of disturbance to the animals we were tracking. They appeared to be travelling up to two kilometres in a day. This is highly atypical of tree-kangaroos. We felt that it was simply not ethical to stress the animals to this extent. Furthermore, any data we would collect on home ranges would be meaningless in these circumstances.

For a while we tried to circumvent these problems by using a technique known as triangulation. Two receivers are used (or two fixes taken) at a distance. This system has the advantage of being able to fix the position of an animal from a distance, thus minimising disturbance. We found this approach unworkable in the Torricelli Mountains, because the jagged topography and wet vegetation broke up and bounced the radio signals to such an extent that we could rarely obtain a reliable reading.

Throughout the entire time we radiotracked the three *Tenkile*, we saw a collared animal only once. Over the hour I observed it, the animal sat impassively, occasionally twitching an ear.

Added to these technical problems were the logistical difficulties of life at the camp. It was almost impossible, for example, to dry anything. For weeks Viare and I went to bed wet and woke up wet. After a month or more, the strenuous activity and poor diet began to affect our immune systems. I became troubled with an ear-infection which made it difficult to hear and sleep.

Worse, we became prey to tropical ulcers and deep, incredibly painful boils which added further to our misery. The boils are caused by a bacterium which normally inhabits the nasal cavity. You are commonly infected by scratching yourself after shaking hands with someone who has just picked his nose. I began to dread the necessary ritual of shaking hands with everyone upon entering a village.

These boils tend to creep upwards on the body. One might form near the knee and when it is healed another will appear on the thigh. After that, a boil will develop in the groin—and in this position, these egg-sized, pus-filled buboes can produce immobility and the most dreadful pain. When they have burst they leave a gaping cavity. It is rather unnerving to see metres and metres of disinfectant-soaked bandage disappear into a gaping hole in your body.

There were, however, compensations to it all. I remember climbing to the ridge crest one morning when a light mist hung in the low forest canopy. The trees were covered with moss—great wisps of it—their gnarled trunks reaching barely seven metres above the ground. One of the tallest plants was a palm which grew only on the ridge tops, its graceful, feathery fronds rising free of the dense, small-leaved canopy. At this season it was heavy with fruit, the great bunches of bright red berries hanging in clusters which seemed to glow in the diffuse light.

Suddenly I saw a movement. A large black bird with a long tail and beak dashed round the trunk of a palm. A second later I heard its call—a loud *blak, blak*—and it emerged again into view. It carefully chose one of the ripe red fruit and, breaking it off with its long, curved bill, swallowed it whole. This was the near-mythical (at least to me) male Black Sicklebill Bird of Paradise (*Epimachus fastuosus*). Flashes of deep blues and reds burst from the iridescence on its feathers. Enchanted, I watched it for long minutes before it flew out over the valley. Its calls could often be heard, coming from near and far, during that palm-fruiting season.

Events nearer camp also brought variety to our often miserable days. Occasionally a great, metallic blue butterfly would land on my skin, seeking sweat to drink. Or, when I laid my socks out to dry, they would sometimes be surrounded by clouds of smaller yellow butterflies, seeking I know not what. And, following evening rain, a profusion of frogs would appear. Some were tiny, with bright red or yellow thighs. They would climb on the netting of the tent at night, catching insects attracted to the light, and I would watch their silhouettes from my damp sleeping bag before dozing off.

One night, while spotlighting near the tents, I heard a loud scream. As I lifted my foot, I found a puffed up and very angry ball of a frog which I had inadvertently punched into the mud. It was black and covered in long, fingery papillae. It looked like nothing more than a black, prickly golf ball. I subsequently found another of these bizarre creatures in exactly the same way. They still remain unidentified.

One evening, while at the very summit of Mt Somoro, I found yet another strange frog. It seemed to be all head with spindly, barred legs. This was a species of *Lechriodus* or barred frog. It looked as if it could swallow a creature as large as itself.

Frogs and birds were not our only visitors. One morning Lester Seri (who worked with us on the early expeditions) awoke to find an enormous black, phallic-looking worm in his sleeping bag. Ribald jokes rocked the camp for weeks. Someone ventured that it had probably been attracted there in search of a mate! The worm experts at the Australian Museum, though, were grateful to receive this specimen, and I requested that, if it turned out to be an undescribed species, then it should be named for part of Lester's anatomy. I am yet to hear the result of their researches.

By night we were frequently visited by Painted and D'Albertis Ringtail Possums (*Pseudochirulus forbesi* and *Pseudochirops albertisii*). Kaspar said that our camp was on a '*rot bilong kapul*' (possum road), and that the animals crossed from one valley to another at this point. One morning a Three-striped Dasyure (*Myoictis melas*) wandered into camp, giving Viare his first glimpse of the species. This rat-sized marsupial predator is marked with three black stripes which run along the back, but its most conspicuous features are its fiery red rump and head. It is one of the few New Guinea mammals which is active by day.

And then there was the view.

On a clear morning, from the crest of the Sweipini ridge, we could see all the way to Sissano Lagoon on the north coast of New Guinea. This view alone provided incentive to remain on the mountain, even though the tree-kangaroo radiotracking was not progressing as it should. Indeed, the difficulties with detecting signals, along with the flightiness of the collared animals, were appearing more and more insurmountable.

We finally agreed to take a break for a couple of months to rethink our strategy. I returned to Australia and Viare to Port

Moresby, where we each talked with experienced radio-trackers who had faced similar problems. Unfortunately our consultations provided no new ideas which might offer success. Nonetheless, we decided to return to the mountains for one last attempt. Our hope was that the animals might have calmed sufficiently in the interim to allow the tracking to proceed without unduly disturbing them. If this failed, we would terminate the program.

Within a couple of days of arriving at our old camp we once again located the signals from two of our animals. By not approaching too closely, we hoped they would remain settled. So we were delighted when the source of the signals continued to come from one area, even as we drew, cautiously, ever nearer. After a week or so, when the signals were still coming from the same place, we felt we could close in for a look.

Imagine our dismay when, that morning, Viare found the remains of one of our radiocollared animals. A day or two later we found the bones of a second. The last animal, judging from movement in its transmitting position, appeared to be alive—but was reacting to our presence as badly as before.

What, we wondered, could have killed our precious *Tenkile?* After considering all the possibilities, we concluded that the two animals which died had probably been bitten by dogs when they were originally captured for collaring. Viare had seen no bite marks on them and had even given them antibiotics as a precautionary measure on their release. Still, it is possible that their long, dense fur had obscured a bite and that the antibiotics were insufficient to fight off the deep muscle infection which a laceration might introduce.

I was doubly upset at this catastrophe, for we had posted muzzles to Wilbeitei some months before Viare's first visit, in order to get the dogs used to wearing them while hunting. The muzzles had never arrived, but Viare did not realise this until he reached Lumi to begin searching for animals. Some corrupt postal clerk may well have sealed the fate of our conservation program, if not an entire species.

Dogs are essential to locate *Tenkile*. We did not consider the danger of using them great, despite the lack of muzzles, for we had assumed that *Tenkile* would stay in the tree-tops when they saw a dog, just as other tree-kangaroos do. But now we began to suspect that the dogs often encountered individuals on the ground. These might then be bitten before they could regain the safety of the tree-tops. So, one thing we learned was that *Tenkile* was more terrestrial than other tree-kangaroos.

The despair that comes with killing rare animals defies adequate description. It was as if the continuous chill drizzle of *Tenkile*'s habitat stayed with me, deep in my bones, for months after I returned to Australia.

At the termination of the *Tenkile* project, Gary and I arranged for Kaspar to visit Sydney. I was recovering from cerebral malaria at this time, so unfortunately could not show him around as much as I would have liked. We had arranged the visit as a token of our appreciation for the enormous assistance he had extended to us. For a man who had never travelled further afield than Wewak, it was an extraordinary experience, though he accepted with great equanimity much of what I thought might astound him.

On his return Kaspar was given a hero's welcome. The village truck, complete with a *Tenkile* painted on its door and wreathed in bush leaves, was dispatched to Lumi airport to pick him up. It was particularly pleasing to see him so honoured by his community, for he is a man with great traditional knowledge. Despite their wisdom, such people are sometimes thought of as 'bush kanakas' by other

Melanesians with greater contact with the outside world.

Kaspar's joy was short-lived, however, for a few weeks after he returned his wife died. It was clear to everyone in Wilbeitei that some jealous, malicious sorcerer had been at work.

PART VI

JAYAPURA AND BEYOND

TWENTY-THREE

Peace and prisons

The island of New Guinea is divided into two nearly equal parts. The eastern section consists of the mainland of Papua New Guinea, while the west comprises Irian Jaya, the former Dutch colony that is now a province of the Republic of Indonesia.

Since 1969, when Irian Jaya was incorporated into Indonesia, it had been difficult and at times impossible for researchers to work there. I made my first attempts to go to Irian Jaya in 1984, writing to LIPI (the Indonesian Government science organisation) requesting permission to undertake a program of wildlife research there. But no reply ever came to my letters. I now know that at that time obtaining permission for such work was, to all intents and purposes, impossible. And without a formal permit to undertake research, one cannot obtain funding—so I was unable to proceed with my plans.

By the late 1980s, however, the political situation had relaxed to the point where it was possible to consider carrying out faunal survey work in the province. This was a most exciting prospect, for Irian Jaya was (and indeed remains today) a great blank spot on the map of zoological exploration.

Even today, Irian is not the kind of place where one can wander at leisure. All visitors (be they researchers, tourists or Indonesians from outside the province) need a police travel document to enter. The document (called a *surat jalan*) lists the localities which may be visited by the letter-holder and is checked and validated at every town or community through which one passes or visits.

Geoff Hope once again played an important role in my life in providing yet another research opportunity. He had opened the door to Papua New Guinea for me—and now, in 1990, he also handed me the keys to Irian Jaya.

Geoff had been invited to Irian Jaya by the University of Cenderawasih (remarkably, the province, which has just over a million inhabitants, boasts two university campuses). He was intending to set up a unit to study alpine ecology. This invitation was extremely useful, as it allowed him to travel to many areas he could otherwise not reach.

Both of us had long been aware of some fossils discovered by a missionary high in the mountains of the central range. The fossils were reportedly found in a cave, which was rumoured to be full of the bones of large extinct marsupials.

In 1989 Geoff and his partner Bren Wetherstone had visited the site, and thought it might be a significant fossil locality. To reach it they had undertaken an exhausting round trip, on foot, of over 250 kilometres through the rugged mountains of central Irian Jaya. The first-hand knowledge they thus gained of the site was to provide the opportunity I then needed to make contacts both within LIPI and Irian Jaya which would allow me to undertake fieldwork there.

Investigating a fossil site is quite a different prospect from undertaking wildlife research. Wildlife is protected in Indonesia and one needs a number of permits from various agencies in order to undertake such work. Fossils are not covered by this legislation. So I could quite justifiably ask for funds to visit Irian to look at fossils and not be hampered by the need to obtain a visa to research wildlife.

In early 1990 I received the funding necessary to mount an expedition to examine the cave and Geoff, Bren and I were ready to set off. This was the beginning of the greatest adventure of my life. Indonesia seemed incredibly exotic, and once again I experienced the thrill and frustration of entering a culture whose customs and language were entirely new. Not since my first visit to Papua New Guinea had I felt such a rush of anticipation and high adventure.

As I flew into Jayapura, the provincial capital, I was struck by just how similar it is in its setting to Port Moresby. Both were established in rain shadow areas where grassland predominates. Around Jayapura, very poor soils derived from oceanic crust rocks help exclude forest and promote grassland. Also, both Port Moresby and Jayapura are set on the edge of beautiful harbours and framed by a backdrop of mountains.

Despite these similarities in natural setting, I find Jayapura incomparably more beautiful. As one lands at the great, American-built airstrip of Sentani, the green Cyclops Mountains seem to rise impossibly abruptly from the coastal plain. They reach a height of 2,000 metres before plunging dramatically into the sea a few kilometres to the north. Between mountains and town lies Lake Sentani, a complex freshwater lake which resembles Sydney Harbour in its profusion of bays, beaches and inlets. It is surrounded by a low, undulating plain, which can become unbearably hot during the middle of the day. Near the lake or sea, however, one is often cooled by delicious evening breezes.

Nestled into Lake Sentani's bays and perched upon her islands are myriad little settlements composed of traditionally thatched houses. These are often all but obscured by the coconut palms, hibiscus, breadfruit trees and sundry other plants that surround each cluster of huts. The steep, grassy slopes leading to the water are everywhere punctuated by neat gardens. The waters of the lake are still relatively clean (although they are increasingly threatened by pollution), and are home to such exotic creatures as the gigantic freshwater Sentani sawfish (which reaches several metres in length) and tiny, jewel-like Sentani rainbow fish, both of which are unique to this body of water.

Jayapura is perched near where the lake approaches the sea. There, a series of pretty white-sand beaches, hills and islands stretch into the distance. The town itself is unfortunately built around a creek which is now horribly polluted, resembling in sight and smell the filthiest open drain in Jakarta. A ramshackle collection of tin-roofed huts on stilts cluster around this drain, while more modern buildings (including a comfortable large hotel) line the main streets.

We found simple, clean accommodation in an old Dutch colonial house in a suburb called Dok Lima ('Five Dock' in English), which received its name during MacArthur's occupation in 1944. The house, which overlooked the bluest of seas, was shaded by great, orchid-filled banyans. Its verandah received a cool evening breeze.

Buying spicy, freshly cooked satays from a passing street vendor and enjoying them while taking in the view, I felt I was in paradise. Later I learned that the satay seller was rumoured to be in the employ of the Indonesian military, and was paid to keep a watch on foreigners. Ah, the bittersweet nature of Irian.

As I began to explore Jayapura on that first trip, my sense that I had been transported into some kind of nirvana was only strengthened. Throughout the week we spent there, the weather was balmy. Transport and accommodation, although basic, were inexpensive and clean, and fragrant Asian food was available almost everywhere at ridiculously low prices.

One of the best fish restaurants I have ever eaten at is perched over the waters of the bay, right in the centre of the town. The attentive owner, a man from Flores, insists that his customers choose their fish fresh from an ice-filled barrow kept at the restaurant entrance. Coral trout, potato cod and a dozen kinds of brilliantly coloured reef fish lie beside trevally, mackerel and flounder. Your selection is barbecued instantly over hot coals, and served with a delicious sweet black sauce. Washed down with icy beer (which even today is brewed according to Dutch tradition), the repast is worthy of the best restaurant of any great city. But no great city could ever provide the brilliant phosphorescence of Humboldt Bay, or the mild breezes and myriad stars of a clear tropical sky.

Having spent a great deal of time in Port Moresby, I was struck most forcibly by the fact that Jayapura was a *safe* town. I did not see high fences topped with razor wire, or hear vicious dogs barking behind them. There were no armed guards in front of shops, and no heavily fortified compounds protecting a besieged elite. On several occasions we found ourselves walking the streets at 3 a.m. in perfect safety. For anyone used to life in Port Moresby, this was an impossible luxury.

But even during this first visit, when language was such a barrier, and I was viewing this new world through rose-coloured glasses, the cost at which this security was purchased did not entirely elude me. As we drove from the airport to town we saw an imposing prison beside the road. A few freshly dug graves were prominent at the end of a row of older mounds. They were undoubtedly meant to be a warning. The police and military were evident in every street (although in this respect Jayapura is not so different from the rest of Indonesia), and armed military posts were located on all of the major roads leading to and from the town. The arrogant young soldiers who manned them could be incredibly rude to approaching Melanesians.

The other striking thing was that, after a mere twenty years of rule from Jakarta, Jayapura had become a truly Asian city.

Just as the food was delightfully Indonesian, the shops had a distinctly Asian appearance. The *pasar* in the middle of town is as labyrinthine and crowded as any in Java, while the stream outside it is as polluted as Jakarta's Ciliwang River. Melanesians are loath to foul their waterways, and one rarely sees such a disgusting sight elsewhere in New Guinea.

In typical Indonesian manner, concrete policemen stood at busy intersections, their stern, unblinking eyes staring out of their pink faces, while black-painted guns bulged at their hips. Street vendors with their *warung*s (Indonesian versions of Harry's Cafe de Wheels) dotted the street, while *becak*s (trishaws) and minibuses crowded the pot-holed roadsides.

Melanesians were still in evidence, but it appeared that over half the population of the town already consisted of trans-migrants from elsewhere in Indonesia. I saw no signs of hostility between the two groups. Indeed there appeared to be some remarkable signs of racial harmony, such as pairs of Melanesian and Asiatic men walking down the street together, engaged in friendly conversation.

Another striking thing about Jayapura was the number of illegal immigrants from Papua New Guinea I met there. At first I could not understand why they had left their own free country to live in a nation where Melanesians did not rule, and where their lives, if they were discovered, might be endangered.

Gaining entry to Irian was certainly no problem for them. Jayapura is located only a few kilometres west of the border. The opportunities for crossing are many, for the border is poorly marked and runs through jungle for much of its length. Once in town, the immigrants readily blended in with the population, since many already spoke a smattering of Bahasa Indonesia.

The Papua New Guinea border crossers seemed eager to meet Europeans. Those I encountered in Jayapura usually approached me secretively on a bus or in a market, whispering a few words of Pidgin to test how I might receive them. Most were from the border areas, such as Vanimo or Yapsiei, where I had worked extensively, and we often had a few acquaintances in common. They had been drawn to Jayapura by cheap food, clothing and other goods. These were to be had for a fraction of the price paid in Papua New Guinea, and doubtless a thriving illegal trade is plied across the border.

Some of these people were in Jayapura for a brief visit, but others had already stayed for many months. All lived in great fear of detection, and more than one expected death if discovered.

The few days we spent exploring the environs of Jayapura were full of excitement. One day we hired a minibus and drove to the site of General MacArthur's headquarters in the foothills of the Cyclops Mountains. MacArthur had a mansion built on the spot, and based himself there for many months during the Second World War. Although there is nothing left of his house today, the visit made a deep impression on me, for the commanding view from the place explained something essential about this extraordinary man.

The site permits a sweeping panorama of the Sentani plain. There, way below, stretches the airstrip. When seen from this point, it is clear that the single runway still in use at the modern airport of Sentani is just one tiny portion of a vast, now largely abandoned airfield complex which was built during the war. About five enormously long landing strips appear to have been constructed for the Americans' use. The present runway, long as it is, takes up less than half the length of just one of these strips.

Standing there, I imagined the scene as it must have appeared fifty years ago. Hundreds of great silver bombers, filled with thousands of tonnes of lethal cargo, would have lined up on the tarmac. I imagined MacArthur standing on his balcony, radio in one hand, the other raised ready to give the command for take-off. With a gesture he sent the huge bombers on their mission to wreak vengeance upon those who had shamed him so vilely at Corregidor. Musing on the imagined scene, I began to feel in my bones the megalomania which must have driven the general.

We drove back along the shore of Lake Sentani, passing a number of well-constructed, colonial-style houses perched by the water. Each was surrounded by gardens of croton, frangipani and hibiscus. They were, I was informed, one beautiful brothel after another. Another army is now occupying the Sentani plain, and apparently several of these establishments are reserved for its exclusive use.

Years later I was to learn from a medical orderly that the crew of a Thai fishing vessel caught illegally in Indonesian waters was held in Jayapura for almost a year. During that time its members roamed freely through the town. Prior to being released, they were all given a medical check. Twelve of the fifteen crew tested positive for HIV.

As we drove along I wondered how rapidly change would come to Jayapura. I thought of the great Sentani sawfish, which is already threatened by pollution and overfishing, and of the picturesque, sleepy Melanesian villages which were all that existed here just half a century before.

TWENTY-FOUR

Traces of tundra

After waiting for several days, we were informed that our *surat jalan*s were ready to be picked up at the police headquarters in Jayapura. We were permitted to proceed to the mountains!

But we had still not jumped through all the official hoops set for us. At Wamena, we would need to secure yet another travel pass to continue on to the tiny settlement of Kwiyawagi. From there, the fossil cave which was our objective was only half a day's walk away.

Sentani airport is a chaotic place. There are no queues and few clues at the counters as to which flights are going where, or when they depart. On some secret signal, which we apparently failed to perceive, crowds of people rushed the counters—only to be ignored by staff.

Finally, our height (and probably our colour and helplessness) brought rescue in the form of a courteous official, who took our tickets and luggage and handed us our boarding passes. Our *surat jalan*s were stamped, and hand luggage checked to ensure that we were not carrying alcohol into the highlands. Concern that the Irianese may obtain alcohol prompts such measures, which even extend to the numbering of beer bottles in Jayapura. Only a bureaucracy as byzantine as Indonesia's, surely, could try to keep track of the fate of individual bottles of beer!

In terms of its location and infrastructure, Wamena is Irian Jaya's equivalent to Mount Hagen. With the exception of the mining town of Tembagapura, it is the only substantial settlement in the Irian highlands. It is still entirely reliant on aircraft to maintain contact with the outside world, and this relative isolation means that it retains a more Melanesian character than Jayapura.

This will soon change, though, for the Indonesian Government is rapidly constructing a road from Jayapura to Wamena. From there it will turn west, running the entire length of the central highlands, and terminate at the town of Nabire on Geelvinck Bay. The very heart of Irian will be exposed to the outside world by this highway. The task of construction in the vast expanse of forest, floodplain and abrupt foothills which lie between Jayapura and Wamena is enormous. And, while building the road might be technically feasible, one wonders at the cost of keeping it open in tectonically unstable Irian Jaya.

From the air, my first view of Wamena was a broad, grassy valley dotted with traditional Dani hamlets surrounded by incredibly neat and extensive sweet potato and vegetable gardens. Then came the town itself: an untidy, rusting conglomeration of tin-roofed buildings whose streets were laid out in a grid pattern. The silver minaret on the mosque gave it a distinctively Javanese appearance, even from above.

In the streets of Wamena, you see an extraordinary mixture of humanity. Proud Dani men, still holding fiercely to their traditional dress of *koteka* (penis gourd) tied at its base to a

protruding testicle, stalk down the street, beards thrust forward and hands clasped behind their backs. Nervous-looking
Muslim women, the oval of their face the only flesh visible in a
sea of cotton, whisk gracefully by, while military men in
immaculate and tight-fitting uniforms swagger confidently
down the middle of the road.

Surely it is a perverse twist of fate that has put a nation of
mostly Muslim, mostly Javanese, people in control of a place
like Irian Jaya. You could not imagine, even if you tried, two
more antipathetic cultures. Muslims abhor pigs, while to highland Irianese they are the most highly esteemed of
possessions. Javanese have a highly developed sense of mod-
esty. They dress to cover most of their body and are affronted
by overt sexuality. For most Irianese, near-nudity is the univer-
sally respectable state. Moreover, men from the mountain
cultures of western New Guinea wear their sexuality proudly.
The long penis gourd often has the erectile crest of the cocka-
too attached to its tip, just in case the significance of the
upright orange sheath is missed.

Javanese fear the forest and are happiest in towns. They
attach much importance to bodily cleanliness, yet pollute
their waterways horribly. Irianese treat the forest as their
home. Many are indifferent to dirt on the skin, yet, through
custom, protect the ecological health of their forests and
rivers. Javanese respect of authority is typically Asian in its
obsequiousness. Irianese are fiercely intolerant of attempts at
domination. No Dani man would ever let another lord
it over him as a *tuan* (prince) does a Javanese *petani* (peasant).

It is hardly surprising that these differences have led to an
explosive social situation. Unless these two very different cultures can come to respect each other and find some common
ground, the situation can only lead to an escalating conflict.
Indonesia will then face a protracted civil war which will make
East Timor look insignificant by comparison.

At present things are not entirely hopeless. I have met a few
Javanese (usually the better educated) who understand and

truly like the Dani, and who do not wish to change them. Likewise, I have met some Irianese (particularly coastal people) who feel some allegiance to Indonesia. These rare exceptions, however, are frail beginnings upon which to build a nation.

For many years the Indonesian military has been trying to get the Dani to replace their traditional dress with western-style clothes. During the 1970s this 'persuasion' took the form of an official policy called 'Operation Koteka'. The coercion used was often brutal, and many Dani who came under its influence still complain of their ill-treatment. It is, I suspect, no coincidence that many of the Dani living at Wamena, which is the centre of Javanese influence in the mountains, have most strongly resisted the pressure to don trousers. It was they who suffered most intensely in the past and, in a typically Melanesian way, they have refused resolutely to be bowed.

Everything is cheap in Wamena. The military flies food into the isolated town gratis, so that rice can be purchased there for little more than one pays for it in the streets of Jakarta. Clothing is ridiculously cheap by Papua New Guinea standards, as are all of the other little luxuries of life. This, I suppose, is some small recompense for the outsiders (many from Java) who are sent to work in this remote and sometimes hostile outpost of empire. The Melanesians, however, who have no experience of any other economy (and whose cash reserves are minuscule), complain of the prices and strongly suspect that they are being exploited by the shopkeepers and the Government.

Despite my interest in the dynamic social mix at Wamena, I was anxious to leave the town and visit a truly Melanesian part of Irian Jaya. So it was a relief when, after a day-long wait at the police station to obtain permission to travel to Kwiyawagi, we finally held in our hands the last, necessary, profusely stamped piece of paper. Our flight (which we had to arrange months in advance) would be waiting for us in just a day or two's time.

The flight from Wamena to Kwiyawagi is unforgettable. As the aircraft climbs slowly to the west, mountains rise sharply from the valleys, their upper slopes clothed in beech forest of the darkest green, while their summits stand out above the vegetation as pointy limestone peaks and spires. Below, the Baliem River rushes through yellow grassland, past hundreds of settlements and gardens. There is something very 'Irian' about the view with its round houses and limestone topography. I could never mistake it for somewhere in Papua New Guinea.

Soon the aircraft enters a narrow valley where the river becomes a foaming torrent. At the head of the valley stands an abrupt limestone wall. It was astonishing to see that the huge river we had been following was issuing from a fissure at the base of this cliff.

Our aircraft struggled to gain elevation to clear the 3,000 metre-high limestone crest above the fissure. It did so with the barest of margins, and we swooped over tree-tops and spires of jagged, grey limestone karst which seemed to be just a few metres below us.

The conical limestone towers and dark trees soon dropped away abruptly at yet another steep cliff-face. Beyond it lay a glorious, undulating valley, stretching away to the east and west. This great, isolated valley is a gentle and fertile land dotted with hamlets. Two vast rivers cut their way through it. Even though the rivers are at nearly 3,000 metres elevation, they are lazy, meandering and muddy, resembling the type more often seen at sea-level than at such altitudes.

These are the East and West Baliem rivers. They converge just a few kilometres from the base of the cliff we had just passed. Looking back, I saw one of the most extraordinary natural features ever encountered in a lifetime of travel—the Baliem swallet—a vast hole in the earth which lies at the cliff's base. Into it disappears the entire combined flow of the East and West Baliem rivers. To see such an enormous volume of water disappear from the face of the earth, as if it was entering some great plug-hole, is awesome. The water swirls furiously, sending up great spurts of spray as the river and all it carries enter an underground cavern. It exits on the other side of the range, at the great spring we had flown over.

The swallet is made all the more striking by evidence that this sink-hole occasionally clogs up. Around it, in ever wider concentric rings, are ridges which mark the shorelines of old lakes. These form whenever debris, such as trees, boulders and mud, temporarily clogs the entrance. The water forms ponds until the blockage is breached. Then the lake is emptied by a vast, sucking whirlpool in what must surely be one of nature's great spectacles.

The limestone range at the swallet cuts the valley off entirely from the outside world. The basin is completely enclosed, and the only access into it by foot is by scaling one of the rugged ranges which surround it. I was to discover that this topography had protected the region, almost miraculously, from major incursions by the outside world. In a sense it is a little Melanesian Switzerland, peopled by patriots as fiercely jealous of their independence and security as any Swiss, and equally well fortified by nature.

This world enclosed by the limestone ranges is remarkable for its gentleness and beauty. Warm air rising from the valley prevents the formation of cloud, so there is often a clear blue sky overhead. The temperature is pleasantly warm by day, reaching the low 20s, but the nights are cool, and in May to July frosts are not uncommon.

The East and West Baliem rivers meander through this valley in great, easy loops. They flow through a rustic landscape of gardens and grasslands studded with tall, palm-like mountain pandanus. These striking trees, with their heads of radiating, strap-shaped leaves towering up to thirty metres above the valley floor, are supported on stilt roots, giving them a rather bizarre appearance. They are remnants left when the forest was cleared, and many are clearly ancient. The football-sized clusters of nuts they produce are by far the most highly esteemed plant crop the mountain people know. Smoked, they can keep for weeks or months. When the pandanus season comes, the Dani develop a single-minded obsession to gorge on the oily nuts. This has been referred to as 'pandanus madness' by some visitors.

The backdrop to this scene is one of forested hills, behind which, to the south, rises the awesome barrier of the Prinz Willem V Range. This is the highest point on this part of the range, and the grey-white limestone summit gives an illusion of snow-capped mountains, although snow is usually absent.

The Cessna began to descend into this dream-like valley, towards an airstrip perched on a rise beside the West Baliem River. Between it and the river, a small collection of tin-roofed shacks, interspersed with huts roofed with original thatch, marked the settlement of Kwiyawagi.

This settlement, and indeed the entire valley, is inhabited by the Lani, a large tribal group who are closely related to the Dani of the Baliem Valley.

On landing we were immediately surrounded by a small crowd of Lani youths, which quickly swelled as we unloaded our cargo. Almost all of them were dressed traditionally, wearing short, very broad penis gourds, and hair-nets.

By this time I was intrigued by the variety in shape and size of penis gourds in New Guinea. Many older Lani men wear extraordinarily long ones, which are in some cases so extreme that they threaten to poke the wearer in the eye. Youths, on the other hand, prefer the short, broad gourd I came to think of as the 'sporting model'.

There is a functional reason for these preferences. The gourd worn by the young men serves as a pouch. They remove the plug of fur or cloth at its end, and retrieve from it tobacco, matches or other small knick-knacks. Being broad, it has considerable capacity. Being short, it does not get entangled during a dash through the forest in pursuit of a possum. Such an accident, by the way, could be rather painful, considering the string that ties the gourd at its base to one testicle.

Older men, of course, have different needs. Their hunting

days are over, and politics and diplomacy are their business.
Here, the truly long gourd comes into its own. Few manner-
isms command as much attention as majestically waving an
elongated codpiece away from the face as one prepares to
speak.

Later I showed some Lani men and women photographs of
Miyanmin dressed in their tiny, pendulous gourds. The
women were immediately thrown into gales of hysterics, which
erupted over and over each time my photographs were borrowed and handed around the room. The men, on the whole,
looked a little embarrassed, but nonetheless often joined in
the laughter.

Standing among the youth in their 'sporty' gourds who met
us on that first day was one older Lani man dressed in shorts
and a shirt. His European clothes set him apart, and he introduced himself as Manas, pastor to the community.

Manas led us to a surprisingly western-style house, complete with guttering, water-tank and chimney, which lay a few
hundred metres from the strip. It contained, amazingly, a fine
cast-iron stove, a shower and even a flush toilet! These unexpected luxuries had been imported, and the house itself built,
by Pastor Doug Hayward of the Unevangelized Fields Mission
(UFM).

The UFM is an American organisation which specialises in
bringing the word of God, as it is understood in North
America, to the few remaining 'unevangelised' tribal groups
still inhabiting the planet. The organisation is clearly not short
of cash, and does not believe that its missionaries need to
suffer as they bring light to the heathens. Despite its luxurious
accoutrements, the house was not Hayward's main base, but
was used only occasionally during his brief visits to the area.
Hayward had left Irian Jaya some years before, and now the
community at Kwiyawagi made a little cash by renting his
abode out to visitors.

It was soon clear that in travelling from Wamena to
Kwiyawagi we had crossed some sort of invisible frontier.

Wamena is an Indonesian town, complete with its mosque, army and police. Kwiyawagi, however, is completely Melanesian in character. In 1990 there was almost no sign of government control or influence. There were no outsiders at all living in the valley, and there was no government hospital, police post, or even school. All of these services were instead provided by the Lani people for themselves. It was as if Kwiyawagi was a small, independent nation-community, which somehow survived despite being surrounded by a vast, powerful and potentially hostile state.

These impressions were reinforced by seeing more of how the people of Kwiyawagi organised their lives. Although their needs were few, they still had to find the cash to purchase basic medical supplies, materials for the school, and to pay a few wages. In addition, the licence fee for their radio, an essential piece of equipment, cost the community an incredible three-quarters of a million rupiah (five hundred Australian dollars) per year. Unless this inordinate sum could be met, there would be no radio schedule, and therefore no aircraft landings, no access to emergency medical care, no export of produce, and no news of the outside world through the mission network. The mission radio network, incidentally, is carefully monitored by ABRI, the Indonesian armed forces, so news is hardly uncensored.

The necessity of raising cash for these purposes has engendered innovation and a strong sense of cohesion among the Kwiyawagi Lani. Manas seemed to be a responsible man who handled the community finances capably and fairly. One of his innovations was a project to grow garlic, a light, relatively high-priced product, for export. The community finds it economic to charter an aircraft and fly the garlic to Jayapura. There, a villager sells it head by head on the street. This project, plus rent from the Hayward house, were the principal sources of community income at the time of my visits.

It was soon made clear why the Kwiyawagi Lani guarded their independence so jealously. They remembered the last time 'Indonesians', as they referred to the army, had come to their land. That was in 1978, when, they said, troops made an incursion as far as the headwaters of the West Baliem River. The Lani told me that 'hundreds' of people had been slaughtered, many houses burned and pigs shot. Casualties on the other side were limited to two Indonesian soldiers who drowned while crossing the West Baliem River. The young men of Kwiyawagi assured me that, were the army ever to return, they would not escape so lightly again.

Our stay at the mission house was among the most pleasant I have ever spent in Melanesia. While there, we were cared for by a delightful, impish man named Jot Murip. He lit our fires and maintained a semblance of order in the kitchen. Each afternoon Lani women, dressed in their traditional grass skirts, would arrive carrying *noken*s (string bags) full of European potatoes, carrots, cabbages, beans, garlic and onions to sell to us. Each morning they would return with baskets filled to the brim with live yabbies, individually wrapped in grass, which had just been fished from the West Baliem River. Fresh yabbies in garlic, accompanied by potatoes and carrots, soon became an absolute culinary favourite.

By day, a sprinkling of Lani would remain in the house, but each evening it overflowed with visitors. At times it became so crowded that we could hardly move. Noses and eyes crowded at every window and door, while even cracks in the walls were not despised as vantage points by latecomers.

In these conditions I would often trip over children who were crouched under my chair munching on yabbie heads, or spill coffee over a dark arm that I had failed to perceive beside me in the dim light of our kerosene lamp. Occasionally, I would even accidentally sit on someone who had taken occupation of my chair. Still, my bedroom was a sacrosanct refuge, and because of it I rarely felt driven to desperation by the crowds as I had in Betavip.

After spending a few days getting to know the people and exploring the layout of the valley, Geoff, Bren and I explained to Manas that we wished to visit the cave where Pastor Hayward had found the fossils. Manas promised to organise some guides for us, and we prepared to set out the next morning.

The cave, known locally as Kelangurr, lies about half a day's walk north-west of Kwiyawagi. The track is initially good, but soon degenerates. We started by crossing a sturdy wood and steel cable bridge spanning the lazy, brown West Baliem River. Beyond that, a well-formed path led through an expanse of sweet potato gardens.

Lani gardens are quite the largest agricultural enterprises that I have ever encountered in Melanesia. At Kwiyawagi, entire hillsides were occupied by one vast garden. Their roughly rectangular area was bordered by fences and subdivided by shallow drains into smaller rectangles. Each of these smaller patches was the property of one woman. As we trudged the paths which bisected these great gardens, the women appeared as ant-sized figures in the distance. Each was bent over, digging stick in hand and *noken* slung from her forehead, intent on weeding, planting or harvesting.

Every few kilometres we came across a small Lani hamlet. The huts are of the round 'bee-hive' type, and are exceptionally well constructed and warm. The floor is sunk below ground level and there is a fireplace in the middle. This space is shared by the women, children and pigs. An internal platform provides an upper level on which the men sleep (now that men's houses have been abandoned through Christian missionary influence).

As we passed by, people would come out to greet us. On one occasion, a veritable Methuselah, dressed in dirty jumper and long penis gourd, was led to us with a request that we photograph him. By the time I returned to Kwiyawagi in 1994 the old man had passed away. I gave the photographs to his family, who were delighted to have them to remember him by.

Although Lani huts appear basic from the outside, they are built of a double-wall of split palings, with an insulating layer of dry moss packed between. The roofs are thickly thatched, and as there is no chimney the smoke can escape only by seeping through the thatch. I often woke to look across a misty valley in the early morning and watch the plumes of blue smoke as they trickled from the hut roofs on a hillside.

The arrangement, however, is not entirely safe. We were provided with spectacular proof of this as we passed through the last of the gardens on our walk and approached a small hamlet nestled against a hill which carried remnants of forest. The thatch of one of the houses was smoking rather more than usual. Within seconds, billows of smoke were rising above it, followed shortly by licking flames. People seemed to rush from everywhere, and soon several men were atop the hut, grabbing desperately at the flaming thatch and throwing it to the ground. Minutes later the fire had been extinguished. By evening, a new roof would doubtless be assembled and the occupants would once again be snug inside their renovated home.

After leaving the gardens, the track took us through swampy forest, where we struggled knee-deep in mud for several hours. The *Podocarpus* (Plum Pine) trees were fruiting, and under each lay masses of purple-black, plum-like fruit. The fruit of these curious pine trees comes in two parts. The seed is ovoid and about the size of a marble. Above it is a fleshy drupe the size and colour of a large muscatel grape. This is formed from the much-inflated stalk of the fruit itself. Birds had been busy eating the drupes, and many either had the seed detached, or had been damaged, spreading a purplish stain everywhere.

We finally emerged in a clearing in the forest. A boggy creek meandered through it and a hut, which acted as a kind of halfway house on the track, stood in the middle. It was of typical construction except that it lacked the internal 'mezzanine' level. From here it was only a twenty-minute walk to the cave.

Kelangurr Cave is not easy of access. The entrance through a tall, narrow fissure is about seven metres up a sheer limestone rock-face. At first I thought this would thwart us at the very last in our attempt to visit the cave, but a Lani youth felled a sapling against the rocks. By climbing it we were soon at the entrance.

The mouth of the cave forms a small antechamber, where we rested in the twilight before venturing further. Beyond it, the cave narrows to a crooked slit, wide enough to admit a Lani boy, perhaps—but far too thin, I feared, for me. As I sat in the antechamber pondering my next move, I noticed thousands of tiny bones scattered about on the cave walls and floor. They seemed to be weathering out of the limestone rock-face. Among them were the remains of rats, bandicoots and a pygmy species of ringtail possum. Many were black and heavily mineralised, and were clearly very old.

I was pondering on how these remains could have accumulated and become fossilised in this part of the cave when I saw a much larger bone lying in a fissure near the inner entrance. It looked like a human shoulder blade, and it was with very little enthusiasm that I reached down for it, dreading to find evidence that the cave had once been used as an ossuary. Apart from my personal aversion to working in such places, any investigation of a cave used for these purposes could lead to misunderstandings with the local people. After all, almost anyone would be sensitive about strangers poking around and taking bones from their ancestral cemetery.

But, as I picked up the bone, these dismal thoughts flew instantly from my mind. It was heavy and mineralised, different in shape from a human shoulder blade. It was, I realised, an ancient fossil which bore unmistakable signs that it had once belonged to a marsupial. My skin tingled with excitement.

In my hand lay the bone of a long-extinct, gigantic marsupial! Here was my ticket to New Guinea's ice age.

My elation was tempered by thoughts of negotiating the squeeze to enter the cave proper. Still, I seized the moment and started to force myself into the claustrophobic cleft. The squeeze was roughly Z-shaped in plan section; broadest on top, but narrowing alarmingly at the bottom. I went in head

first, and had managed to contort my body into the obligatory
Z-shape when I felt myself losing my grip on the walls and
sliding down into the narrower part of the opening.

Suddenly, I was entirely trapped.

Gravity had wedged me into the crevasse—and my strug-
gles were fixing me ever more tightly into it. My face was hard
against a cold, wet, slimy rock-face, my head twisted at an awkward angle. Irregularities on the rock-face seemed to catch at
my knees, ankles and back, while my left arm dangled helplessly free in the lowest part of the crack, which widened
perversely to deny me a grip.

I was pinned halfway into a cave at 3,000 metres elevation
in the mountains of Irian Jaya, half a day's walk from the
nearest airstrip. Help, if it ever arrived, would be slow in
coming. There would be little Geoff and Bren could do in this
situation.

I fought off rising panic.

After several minutes I decided to try an experiment. I
emptied my lungs as thoroughly as I could and, holding myself
in place with my head and knees, tried to shift my body
upward. I then expanded my lungs as far as possible, hoping
to wedge myself in the higher position. After a few such efforts
I had risen a few centimetres and freed my knees. Now I had
some room to manoeuvre and continued to push upward and
forward. Soon, my head emerged into a large chamber.

Into this I clambered with relief and wonderment.

The inner chamber of Kelangurr Cave is a beautiful place.
Stalactites hang from the ceiling, while stalagmites, great frac-
tured lumps of fallen stalactites and small rills of limestone cover
the floor. Like a palaeontological Aladdin's cave, large bones lay
everywhere between the glinting calcium. At my feet was a jaw,
beyond that a skull, and over there, leg bones and ribs.

Elated again now, I realised that we had stumbled across a
treasure trove of ancient remains.

As we went further into the cave, I was disappointed to
discover that there were fewer bones. The main deposit, we

surmised, must have lain outside the existing cave. A vast landslide would have carried away the main chamber in prehistoric times, leaving Kelangurr Cave behind as a mere remnant. This would explain its entrance being high in the cliff-face, as well as the predominance of bones near the mouth. The fallen and broken stalactites told another tale. Earthquakes had rocked through the chamber at least three times, sending spears of calcium raining towards the floor. Perhaps one of the quakes had been powerful enough to have carried away the main chamber.

Studying the bones some time later in the museum, I would discover that the larger ones belonged to two kinds of marsupials. The majority were from the creature whose shoulder bone I had first found. A distant relative of wombats and koalas, the extinct marsupial was about the size of a panda. It may also have looked rather similar to a panda, for it had a small pushed-in muzzle, forward-pointing eyes, a very short tail, and it inhabited high mountain forests, as do pandas today.

From its teeth it was plain that it was a plant-eater, and of a genus and species completely unknown to science. Here was an extraordinary discovery indeed. Perhaps the largest creature ever to have trudged the high mountain forests of New Guinea, its remains had, until that day, lain undisturbed and undiscovered in the cave for millennia. Several years later I had the pleasure of naming the new genus and species *Maokopia ronaldi*. The first part of the name recalls its habitat, the Maokop Range, as the Dani know Irian's mountains. The second part honours a friend and fellow scientist, Ronald Strahan.

The second large creature to leave its remains in the cave was an extinct kind of wallaby about the size of a grey kangaroo. It, too, belonged to an undescribed species, although its genus, *Protemnodon*, had been described more than 150 years earlier from remains found in Australia. I named the species *Protemnodon hopei*, after Geoff Hope, to whom I owe so much. Although its remains were less common than those of *Maokopia*, there were sufficient to determine that it too was a plant-eater, and that, unlike the living large Australian kangaroos, it could hop only slowly.

So occupied was I with these fossils that I almost failed to notice a neat nest made of freshly picked leaves pressed into the clay floor of the cave, just inside the entrance. From the warmth remaining in it, I concluded that whatever was using the nest must have only just vacated it. Searching the cracks and crevices for evidence of the occupant, I saw a large black blob perched on a distant ledge. From the tip of its nose to the end of its tail, the creature was the best part of a metre long. As the beam of the torch caught it, it let out a loud, dog-like snarl which reverberated round the cavern.

'*Keneta*,' one of our Lani companions whispered in my ear.

The English name of the animal the Lani know as *Keneta* is the Black-tailed Giant-rat (*Uromys anak*). I had seen the species just once before. One day on the Sol River a Telefol hunter had come into camp, his hand tightly bandaged. He opened his *bilum*, and angrily threw down the body of an enormous black rat. Clearly, before examining the catch, I had to treat his wound. As I began to unwind the bandage, I realised that the inner layers were dripping with blood. Its source was a horrific injury to his right thumb. The last joint had been bitten right through, and the nail was shattered with punctures. So severe were these that the end of the thumb appeared to be pulp, which wobbled as I dropped antiseptic onto it.

'*Quotal*,' he said, as he explained how he had been feeling in a tree-hollow for a possum. Instead he had come across *Quotal*, as Telefol know the species. The bite of no other animal is feared as much by them. Its incisors are razor sharp and up to two centimetres long. The terrible damage done by repeated bites to this hunter had been inflicted by an immature rat.

Now, despite its fearsome reputation, I wished to get a closer look at this remarkable animal in the cave. I asked my Lani companions to help me by blocking a possible escape route while I approached the beast to take some photographs. The Lani youths were, however, wavering in their resolve, and scampered quickly away when the rat moved leisurely towards them. They were nervous about being in the cave in any case, and seemed to be reluctant to tackle the rat. I tracked it to a new position, from where I could tell that it was an adult male. After taking my photos, I left the lads, whose resolve had stiffened, and went to explore the deeper recesses of the cave. I could see one Lani youth outlined in the spotlight of Bren's torch, wielding a detached stalactite at a dark object whose snarls shattered the quiet of the cave. It looked for all the world like a scene from the Stone Age as pictured in one of the *How and Why* books of my childhood.

The cave ended in a large chamber which, although impressively hung with stalactites, contained neither fossils nor fauna. Enchanted with its beauty, but disappointed with the results, I realised that the time had come to negotiate the squeeze yet again and return to our camp. This time things went more smoothly, and I was soon in the outer air. A shaft of sunlight illuminated the bones in my hand, which had known nothing but darkness for at least 40,000 years.

Geoff, Bren and I spent a few more days in the area examining fossil-bearing deposits exposed in the banks of the West Baliem River. Unfortunately the river was high during our visit, and most of the deposits were under water. We did manage to retrieve a few bones, however, largely from pebble banks near the bridge.

I obtained bones *in situ* on only one occasion. A couple of youths showed me the place where they had found bones when the river was low. It was on a bend below a high, abrupt bank. I waded out into the river, which was murky, thigh-deep and freezing. I began to grope in the mud with my toes for anything which felt like a bone. If I encountered a shape which felt interesting, I would try to reach it with my hands. After about fifteen minutes, getting close to my limit for exposure to near-freezing water, I felt a long, thin object between my toes. I reached for it, and came up with the lower leg bone of an extinct wallaby. So fragile was it that it broke in half as it came to the surface. After a few seconds I located a second bone, which proved to be the upper leg bone of the same animal. The site was clearly a promising one and I intended to return to it the next day with Geoff. The river rose overnight, however, making this impossible.

The river sites were interesting, for their sediments provided evidence that they had formed more than 40,000 years ago when glaciers reached near to the valley, which was then probably covered in periglacial tundra. Interestingly, the same two marsupial species (*Maokopia* and *Protemnodon*) present in the cave were also the only ones which we found in the river deposits.

By now, our rather extensive trekking in the valley, the base of which lay at 2,900 metres elevation, had prepared us for the thin air of the mountains.

The Prinz Willem V Range beckoned.

Our objective in climbing the range was to examine a rock-shelter known as Billingeek. The people of Kwiyawagi have used Billingeek as a hunting lodge for countless generations, and we hoped that we might learn something of the high-elevation fauna by visiting it.

The walk began spectacularly. We followed the *Jalan Raya* ('great road', which was in fact a foot track) westward for several hours. This magnificent pathway, which traverses east–west along Irian Jaya's mountain spine, is an ancient trade route. In parts it is so well constructed that it resembles an Inca road, and would certainly be capable of admitting a small vehicle. In others, however, it dwindles to a muddy track which descends steep declivities, or else a line of slippery logs leading through a morass.

As we strode along a fine section of the track, I pondered the role it has played in the lives of the Kwiyawagi people. The *Jalan Raya* is one of the world's great foot-only trade routes. Produce, such as the plumes of birds of paradise, has probably travelled along it for millennia on its journey to places as far afield as Sri Lanka and China.

Kwiyawagi lies smack in the centre of the most deserted part of this route—about halfway between the major population centres of Ilaga and Wamena. Perhaps the people of Kwiyawagi have always opened their doors to weary travellers, operating a kind of mediaeval hostelry business. If so, then the idea of renting Pastor Hayward's house to visitors would be nothing new to them.

At mid-morning, we ran into a party of Lani travellers. Two men and two youths were coming from Ilaga, carrying salt and bird plumes to sell in the market in Wamena. They were magnificently dressed in traditional attire. Their skin glistened with sweat as they shouldered their load, while their long penis gourds and extravagant cassowary plume head-dresses surpassed anything I had seen.

The salt they carried had been made into rectangular cakes, each of which was carefully wrapped in immaculate pandanus leaves. The wrapping alone was a work of art. The salt had presumably been obtained from a brine soak somewhere in the mountains. The bird plumes, mostly from parrots and birds of paradise, were wrapped in sheaves of dried leaves, then placed into bamboo tubes.

It was sad to think that, if Indonesia's plans for a road network eventuates, these men may well make their next trip to Wamena in a crowded minibus, dressed in dirty European cast-offs. Their salt no doubt will be manufactured in Java and wrapped in plastic.

We met these men where the *Jalan Raya* passes through a

miniature montane heathland growing on sand. Small orchids, rhododendrons, dwarfed *Podocarpus* and celery-top pines, wild raspberries and native blueberries grew scattered across the landscape, separated from each other by bare patches of fine, white sand. A bright orange and yellow orchid was particularly common, its flowers growing in bunches which looked like small flames from a distance. The travellers had picked these and thrust them in bunches through their pierced nasal septa, or woven them into their head-dresses.

We picked blueberries and raspberries, which were delicious to munch on as we moved along. This vegetation type is characteristic of much of the higher elevation country in Irian Jaya. Here it occurred at lower elevation and seemed to be maintained by the fires which were often lit by travellers beside the track.

Within an hour or so, the vegetation changed abruptly and we passed into a tall, cathedral-like forest of southern beech and southern pines. The *Jalan Raya*, here a raised, broad and well-maintained footway, ran through the stately trees in a straight line. The effect was one of sublime beauty. Not since seeing the redwoods of California, or the mountain ash of Victoria, had I experienced such magnificent trees existing in such harmony with a human roadway.

The Antarctic beech which formed most of the forest were clearly a mature stand of even-aged trees. They must have established themselves centuries ago, following some catastrophe, possibly a landslide, which destroyed all prior vegetation. Now they were towering giants, at least a metre in diameter and fifty metres in height. Strangely, there was virtually no understorey except for a carpet of ferns and a few bushes. One rarely encounters forests like this in Melanesia.

Emerging from the forest we turned south and began to ascend the flanks of the Prinz Willem V Range. The track rose steeply through a dense tangle of mossy upper montane forest, until finally, at about midday, we left the trees behind and emerged into true alpine heath. To my chagrin, my old foe altitude sickness was beginning to affect me, producing headaches and general weakness, so I was grateful to discover that the track flattened out here. After a few more hours stumbling through a boggy but beautiful tundra-like environment we arrived at Billingeek.

The rockshelter is a long, undercut recess which sits on the side of a crater-like depression. At one time this may have been a glacial tarn (the point where glaciers originate), but the ice had melted long ago, leaving a miniature landscape of small lakes and rises.

The roof of the rockshelter was formed of a hard layer of limestone. It formed a shelf a metre or two thick, and on its upper surface grew a profusion of flowering plants, including dwarf umbrella trees, rhododendrons and many other species. Bloom-laden branches overhung the entrance, partially shielding the interior from the wind and rain. Even when it was bitterly cold outside, Billingeek could be as warm as toast.

As I levelled the floor in a far recess in order to set up my tent, a layer of ash and old animal bones was revealed in the sediment which comprised the rockshelter floor. Gingerly, I picked out a few pieces of charcoal with my Swiss army knife for radiocarbon dating and placed them, along with a few bones I had displaced, in a plastic bag.

The bones, I discovered, were almost entirely from Long-beaked Echidnas, tree-kangaroos, and pademelons. I was extremely excited by this, for neither living pademelons nor tree-kangaroos had ever been recorded from this part of Irian Jaya. I had high hopes that I might find them still alive in this remote area.

Billingeek was a magical place to stay. Each morning, after the hunters had left with their dogs, the birds would visit to feed on the flowers and berries of the plants overhanging the rock-shelter mouth. Because of the darkness of the interior, they could not see us, and I watched them, enraptured, for hours as they fed and quarrelled just a few feet away.

By far the commonest visitors were the Crested Berrypeckers (*Paramythia montium*). These are bold birds about the size of a starling. They are largely blue, but with a black crest, yellow rump and white eye-stripe. Nearly as common were several species of honeyeaters, including a lovely blackish bird with a short white beard: the Short-bearded Melidectes (*Melidectes nouhuysi*). Streaked Honeyeaters (*Ptiloprora* sp.) with bright green eyes abounded, as did a large, grey-green honeyeater with bluish patches of bare skin around the eyes. This was Belford's Melidectes (*Melidectes belfordi*). Robins, wagtails and a great variety of other birds also lived near the cave and sometimes visited. One day I was lucky enough to see the beautiful Painted Tiger-parrot (*Psittacella picta*), while on another occasion I saw my old friend, Macgregor's Bird of Paradise, in a *Dacrycarpus* pine growing just a few hundred metres from the shelter.

The animals which the hunters obtained intrigued me, for they were different from those represented by the bones I had found in the sediment. The species by far most frequently caught was the Coppery Ringtail. Near Billingeek, this large and usually arboreal possum was living in alpine scrub, where it often nested on the ground. Curiously, despite the fact that we caught about a dozen, there was not a single bone from this species in the ash-bed in the cave.

Day after day went by with no sign of wallabies being reported by our hunters. After much frustrating discussion with the Lani, using only my inadequate Bahasa Indonesia, I learned that they only ever encountered wallabies in the forest at lower elevation. It seems that the single species they were familiar with was the diminutive Mountain Dorcopsis (*Dorcopsulus vanheurni*).

The pademelons (genus *Thylogale*) I was looking for, which inhabit alpine grassland, were clearly long gone from the area. And hopes of finding living pademelons were ultimately dashed when, many months later, I received news from Geoff of the radiocarbon dates obtained from the charcoal of the deposit. It and the bones were 3,000 years old.

The news was almost as bad for tree-kangaroos and echidnas. The hunters said that no tree-kangaroo had been caught near Billingeek for more than a generation, while the last echidna caught in the area was obtained more than a decade previously. What could have caused these dramatic changes to the mammal fauna living around Billingeek? Clearly, the larger, slower species had suffered most. The pademelons (of which there were two species) had disappeared prehistorically, while the echidnas and tree-kangaroos had suffered local extinction much more recently. And how was one to account for the curious recent increase in ringtail possums?

As I pieced the evidence together many months later, it became clear that the pademelons had probably disappeared from Irian Jaya about 2,000 years ago (the time that dogs had been introduced). Hunting alpine pademelons with dogs is a ruthlessly efficient method. The tree-kangaroos and echidnas had apparently followed the pademelons into extinction much later, when the frequency of hunting visits to Billingeek increased. This had occurred only over the past forty years, perhaps the result of changes brought about since European contact.

It is possible that the possums extended their distribution because of the increase in 'empty niche space' these extinctions created. I was saddened by this evidence of extinction in what had appeared at first to be such a pristine environment. Added to the extinction at a much earlier date of the marsupial giants *Maokopia* and *Protemnodon*, it meant that Irian's alpine regions had lost almost all of their larger mammals.

One afternoon at Billingeek, the hunters returned bearing the gunny sack I had given them to carry live animals in. It looked to be very full, and I was abuzz with anticipation at what they might have found. They set the sack down before me, clearly expecting me to look inside. Peering in, I found to my horror that it was full of bones: hundreds of bleached human bones.

Aghast at the thought that they might have ransacked an ancestral cemetery in order to obtain this bounty, I voiced my disapproval, explaining as clearly as I could that I was interested only in animal bones, not human ones. One man told me not to worry, for there was indeed one animal bone in the bag. He emptied the sack in front of me, and a cascade of human bones spilled onto the ground. After fishing through the pile for some minutes, he came up with a solitary tree-kangaroo jaw-bone.

This jaw-bone, as insignificant as it then seemed, was to prove crucial to my future researches in Irian Jaya.

My immediate concern at the time, however, was to return the human remains to their original resting place. I explained this to the Lani, but they did not seem at all interested. They told me that the bones had come from a cleft in the rock some hours' walk away, and that it was just too much effort to carry them back! I was more than a little dismayed at having my camp turned into an instant ossuary. Despite my protestations, the bones were casually kicked about until they were scattered throughout the rockshelter.

On our last morning at Billingeek we decided to walk to the very summit of the Prinz Willem V Range. My altitude sickness had subsided and, although it was a misty morning, I was delighted at the prospect. We set out across the alpine tundra, which became increasingly bare of vegetation as we approached the 4,000-metre-high summit of the range. At one point our path crossed a vast pavement of limestone which had been scraped almost completely smooth by glacial action. Deep grooves had been cut in the otherwise smooth pavement by boulders as they were dragged along by the ice. Some grooves looked as fresh as if they had been gouged out yesterday, rather than 15,000 years ago. Indeed, in a few cases, the stone which gouged the track was still lying at the end of the groove, just where the glacier had left it 15,000 years before. As I gazed at this evidence of ice, the bitterly cold wind bit into me, and I could well believe that the glacier still lingered somewhere nearby.

Some remarkable and truly enormous boulders had been left behind by the glaciers on the sides of the valleys. One of these was as large as a suburban house, and sat perched precariously on a ledge high above the valley floor. We followed the valley as it rose gently towards the crest of the range until we saw, looming through the mist before us, another huge boulder, at least ten metres in diameter. Behind it was empty space, for it was perched on the very summit of the range. We had finally reached our high point.

By holding onto some bushes, it was possible to climb the great erratic block. From there, I beheld a most spectacular view—the southern side of the range as it dropped away almost vertically for hundreds of metres. Through the swirling mist I could make out, way below, the trees of the upper montane forest of the southern slopes of the range. Below them lay a steep jumble of ridges and valleys. Beyond that everything was obscured by cloud, yet I knew that just a little further to the south lay the lowlands of the Marind and Asmat peoples. And beyond that, four vertical kilometres below us, was the sea.

I raised my camera to capture the scene on celluloid, but was dismayed to find that all I could see was a blur. The autofocus mechanism of this expensive new high-tech camera had jammed on a focal distance of about one metre when I had used it to photograph some minute alpine flowers a few moments before.

So I simply sat, enchanted by this scene, and thought about the ice age which left this great boulder in its wake, and the marvellous bushwalk that could have been made long ago when ice gripped the planet. So much water was locked up at the poles then that the level of the sea had dropped dramatically, exposing the continental shelf. A person could have walked from the glaciers of Tasmania to the point I was sitting on. Meganesia, that vast landmass, was then a single entity, inhabited entirely by Aboriginal and Melanesian people.

It was only when my gaze dropped from the majestic view that I found evidence I was not the first person to sit meditatively on this spot. For there, on a small clear space atop the boulder, a fire had been made. Beside it, on a shelf at my feet, lay the carefully arranged skulls of four Pygmy Ringtail possums (*Pseudochirulus mayeri*). They had been picked clean and lined up after a leisurely and perhaps solitary meal. I wondered at the thoughts which preoccupied that hunter as he enjoyed his meal in the sun. Had he been here days, months, or even years ago, and did he leave the spot feeling as refreshed in spirit as I did?

When the morning of our departure from Billingeek came, I found it difficult to leave its glorious, bitterly cold mountains. As I walked down the track towards the valley of gardens, I vowed to return.

TWENTY-FIVE

Arfak, Fak Fak

Four years passed before I could revisit the Maokop.

Between 1990 and 1994 much of my time was taken up by two research projects. The first, an ecological history of Australasia, became a book, *The Future Eaters*. The second, far more demanding in terms of time and resources, was a faunal survey of the mammals of the south-west Pacific and Moluccan islands. In order to complete this second task I needed to assemble and arrange funding for a research team which would survey every major island group in this vast archipelago, and find time myself to visit most of the island groups.

The substantial funding necessary to carry out this work was made available from a bequest from the estate of Winifred Violet Scott. Miss Scott bequeathed her fortune to a trust which sponsors endangered species research. Posthumously, she has achieved more for endangered species than most researchers achieve in a lifetime. Several species have been rescued from extinction, largely as a result of her will.

There were five researchers, all with considerable field experience in tropical regions. To each I assigned a section of the south-west Pacific region. I myself surveyed New Caledonia, the north and central Moluccas, and the islands lying off Irian Jaya and Papua New Guinea. I also visited several of the other survey sites, to gain an idea of the nature of each island group and to assess the difficulties which the other researchers encountered.

So I did not go back to the mountains of the Maokop for four years. When I did return, however, I was much better equipped, for during my island work in the Moluccas I developed fluency in Bahasa Indonesia. This proved to be an invaluable asset in highest Irian.

I did, however, make one visit to the Irian Jaya mainland during the period of my island survey. This was in 1992 when my itinerary took me through the town of Manokwari on the Vogelkop or Bird's Head Peninsula. I had been surveying the islands of Geelvinck Bay with Boeadi, a senior Indonesian researcher from the Bogor Museum, and Alexandra Szalay, a member of the research team.

The team we formed was particularly well suited for work in Irian Jaya. Boeadi is one of Indonesia's most respected and senior biologists. He has worked at the Zoology Museum, Bogor, for much of the post-colonial period, undertaking research in virtually every province of Indonesia. He served as a zoologist on the Indonesian military expedition which climbed Mt Jaya in 1963 and has worked on many other major projects involving animals as diverse as Sumatran rhinos, tigers and bats. He has trained generations of forestry and wildlife workers, and his contacts within the Indonesian bureaucracy are extraordinary. Indeed, many senior forestry officials almost bowed down before him when we visited their offices.

Boeadi is also an excellent camp cook who can turn the toughest dunghill croaker into delicious *ayam goreng* in an instant. As well, he is a shameless bargainer who is not averse to beating the most impecunious-looking grandmother down a few rupiah in price, and rarely comes off the worse in such dealings (an exception being a long-remembered paraplegic rooster which somehow slipped past his guard on Halmahera). In contrast, I have probably purchased every wormy durian and rotten egg on offer between Java and Jayapura. In frustration at my ineptitude in this area, Boeadi finally banned me from attending markets and bazaars, and always kept himself between me and street vendors.

Alexandra is an anthropologist with wide experience in Melanesia. Her insights into local culture are invaluable in interpreting the information I collect about mammals. She always seems to ask the crucial question at the right moment. In contrast to Boeadi and me, she also has a memory like a steel trap and, where Boeadi and I tend to spread chaos in equipment, Alex restores order.

From our dingy hotel rooms in Manokwari we could see the majestic Arfak Mountains rising a short distance behind the town. We were going to have to spend a few days there anyway waiting for aircraft connections. Soon, we decided to make a brief visit.

The Arfak Mountains hold a special place in the annals of New Guinea zoology. For it was there, on 6 September 1872, that the Italian explorer and zoologist Luigi Maria D'Albertis first penetrated the mountainous interior of New Guinea and encountered and collected its unique mountain fauna. In his splendid account of his travels in New Guinea, *What I Did and What I Saw*, he records living off a diet of rice and birds of paradise during the three weeks he stayed there. Every shot seemed to bring down a species new to science. D'Albertis walked from Manokwari to a village called Hatam, and there, in addition to his birds and insects, he made a modest but important collection of mammals. Nearly all of the high elevation species were new. Since that time, very few additions have been made to our knowledge of the mammals of the Arfaks, and some of the species collected by D'Albertis have not been recorded since. In fact it is fair to say that the mountains have remained, almost to this day, a virtual *terra incognita* as far as mammals are concerned.

One of the frustrations of working in Irian Jaya is the impossibility of obtaining accurate maps, for the Indonesian Government is so security-conscious that it refuses to make available even those few maps which have been recently drawn. This forces one into reliance on archaic sources of information (often dating to before 1941 when the Japanese invaded)—and can lead to disaster.

We decided to follow Luigi's example and walk from the coastal plain into a conveniently located village in the mountains. The village I had settled on for the work was called Hing, and my Dutch map, printed in the 1930s, showed it to be at most a day's walk from the coast. It looked to be more conveniently located than Hatam, and from a scientific point of view it was preferable to sample another locality instead of returning to D'Albertis's old hunting ground.

I sent out word in Manokwari that I wished to employ some youths to carry our equipment and to act as guides on our trek to Hing. After several days there assembled, on my verandah, a rather motley-looking crew, whose main accreditation for the job was that they all claimed to have been born in Hing, and thus knew the village and the track which led there. Our main helper was a young man named Agus who, it turned out, came from Fak Fak, a town on New Guinea's south coast. Little did I know how many times during our trek I was to take the name of his birthplace in vain!

We set out very early one morning with sufficient food for just one day, as our carriers advised that we would reach Hing late that afternoon. The walk was not steep, but the track rose continuously, passing through the magnificent hill forest which still clothes part of the lower slopes.

We lunched under a break in the canopy of an extra-ordinarily diverse forest. All about us lay fallen fruit of types I had never seen before. Particularly conspicuous were the pale silvery-blue, ovoid, double fruits of a large tree. The seeds were about five centimetres long and, as one was always slightly larger than the other, they resembled nothing more closely than a pair of testicles. I was delighted by this evidence of an unusual forest full of endemic trees which were fruiting. Endemic plants (those unique to an area) often support endemic mammals. The fact that they were fruiting suggested mammal activity should be at a peak.

By late afternoon we had left the lowlands behind and were entering a forest of *Araucaria* trees. This suggested that we had gained about 1,000 metres in altitude, as *Araucaria*s occur no lower in New Guinea.

When we had not reached the village by late afternoon, I decided to look for a convenient spot to camp. We entered a small patch of open ground just before dusk. Below us lay Manokwari on its arc-shaped bay, its lights twinkling against the glow of a tropical sunset. Later that night a crescent moon, reflected brilliantly on the water, transformed the entire scene with silver.

Our carriers had brought neither warm clothes nor shelter, yet they seemed not at all perturbed at the idea of spending a night in the forest in such diminished circumstances. They quickly erected a hut from bush materials, and soon had a roaring fire going. They sat around happily scoffing the little food we had carried with us. Alex, Boeadi and I set up our rather cheerless tents, shared our remaining meagre supplies, and fell into an exhausted sleep.

At dawn next morning the grass was damp with dew and it was with some difficulty that I unbent my stiff limbs and began to collect firewood. Boeadi (who was then sixty and perhaps should have been enjoying a cosy retirement instead of traipsing around New Guinea) had even greater difficulty in warming up. A steaming mug of *kopi bubuk* (a coarse but aromatic Indonesian coffee) improved everyone's outlook, and we were soon packed and set out, expecting to arrive at Hing within the hour.

My concern turned to deep worry when, by mid-afternoon, it became clear that there was still no village nearby. We continued to climb all day and were by then entering a forest of Antarctic beech. This tree typically grows at about 2,000 metres elevation. This was getting to be too high for a village in the Arfaks, and the forest we were now passing through was in that virginal state which one only encounters far from humanity. Despite these signs, our carriers continued to insist that Hing was only a few hours away at most.

Concerned at the toll the walk was taking on Boeadi (who later referred to the expedition as the journey which half-killed him) we broke our march early that day. We spent the last hours of daylight setting rat-traps and mist-nets in the forest in the hope of catching something to feed our by now famished carriers and ourselves.

As we explored the adjacent forest, Boeadi made one of those discoveries that allows even such a dismal trek to seem worthwhile. While setting traps he found what he first took to be a miniature hut built by human hands. It was an exquisite structure, rather like the top of a Dani hut in shape—but its round thatched roof reached all the way to the ground. It was about a metre high, and the roof of twigs had been built around a central pole. There was a low, door-like entrance, and in front of that, a carefully manicured lawn on which lay a variety of brightly coloured fruits and flowers. Most remarkable of all, just inside the door, on an immaculate lawn of moss, lay a ball-point pen.

This extraordinary structure, we realised, was the work of the Vogelkop Bower-bird (*Amblyornis inornatus*)—the *burung tahu* or 'knowing bird' of the mountain people. Male birds (of which there are over eighteen species) build a variety of structures called bowers in which they woo their females. That of the Vogelkop Bower-bird is by far the most complex, and this was a splendid example. The pen, the sole man-made item present, was clearly the bird's prized possession. Some fellow traveller (perhaps a researcher from the World Wide Fund for Nature, who some years before had assisted in the establishment of reserves in the area) must have dropped it.

That evening as I sat in my tent pondering our predicament, there was an inexplicable noise. At first faint and apparently distant, it sounded for all the world like the kind of noise a flying saucer is supposed to make in a B-grade sci-fi movie. Alarmingly, this strange sound grew louder and louder. An approaching jet from the Indonesian armed forces? But soon the noise became so urgent that I rushed out of the tent and looked up into the canopy, half-expecting to see a silver disc floating above the trees.

The sound suddenly faded, then ceased. It was only then that I discovered the culprit: a great cicada which flew off a branch next to my tent and into the mist-net. It was a 'six o'clock cicada', so called because it emits its remarkable call for just a few minutes each day, at about six in the morning and evening. I had heard them before, but never a species with such a quality of sound as this one. In the high Arfak forests, it seemed, you could set your clock by them.

That evening I went to bed without eating, yet satisfied. The night was clear and bitterly cold, and it was only after some time that I drifted into a fitful sleep.

In the wee hours of the morning a low, humming sound woke me. At first, through the veil of sleep, the sound seemed an echo of the six o'clocks, but then it swelled and began to assemble itself into tune. Our carriers were singing—in four-part harmony. The hauntingly beautiful melody went on for hours, rising and falling through the night. I must have drifted off again, for I awoke at dawn cold and hungry.

In the morning the carriers said that they had sung in order to keep themselves warm and to stop thinking of food.

Although the tune was clearly Melanesian, missionary-inspired words had surprisingly been put to it. What they were singing over and over again was this: '*Don't drink spirits, don't smoke cigarettes, and don't trust Chinese...*'

Thankfully the traps had secured a cornucopia of about ten Moss-forest Rats overnight. I measured and skinned these and gave them to our carriers to roast over a fire. After getting about half a rat each, we felt somewhat strengthened and set off yet again, this time with assurances that Hing was *really, absolutely*, only an hour or two away.

By midday we reached the podocarp forest which grows only on the highest peaks of the Arfak Mountains—here approaching 3,000 metres elevation. We stopped, and found to our horror that Boeadi was no longer with us. We raced back down the track.

He had taken a wrong turning and, by the time we found him, had been wandering, lost and alone, in the forest for some time. He was exhausted and it was clear that he could not go on.

Angered by the constant misinformation I was getting, I sat the carriers down in the misty, cold forest, and sternly asked our guides if any of them *had ever been to Hing!* Finally, one ventured that he had seen the place as a small boy—and was sure that it was at least one or two days' walk further on!

The others scowled at his perfidy, although Agus, the Fak Fak man, seemed to be genuinely shocked at the revelation. Their deceit had been based on the theory that it was better to be paid for a five-day walk to nowhere, rather than reveal that they knew nothing about Hing, and not get the job at all.

Disgusted, I ordered a retreat. Boeadi was clearly too ill to continue with the expedition, so I suggested that he return directly downhill to Manokwari with part of the carrier line. Alex and I determined to take a path which led down an adjacent ridge, at the base of which I had seen disturbed forest that resembled an old garden. From there we might locate a village where we could obtain supplies and begin our work.

The Arfaks are one of the most rugged mountain ranges in New Guinea, so it was not surprising to find that this alternative path plunged abruptly over a near-vertical 1,500-metre drop. The cliff was formed of crumbling sandstone which gave little reliable support.

We set off gingerly down the slope, but after a few steps Alex lost her footing and began a fatal-looking tumble downslope. At the last possible instant she grasped a bush which broke her fall. Trembling now, we continued even more cautiously.

Descending such a slope is far more painful and difficult than scrambling up it. Your knees ache, shake, then turn to jelly. There is nowhere to sit and rest, and every step is an effort to resist the fatal attraction of gravity. Carrying a pack adds immeasurably to the difficulty.

After about four hours of tortured descent, we reached a more gentle slope and found that we were indeed in an area of old garden land. We followed a path through the undergrowth and soon came upon a village which appeared to be deserted. We flopped onto the springy grass on the edge of the compound.

As I lay exhausted by a hut, a woman and her daughter, who were returning from their garden, walked into the village square, unsuspecting of any visitors. But on catching sight of us they took fright. It was only quick action by our carriers that prevented them from rushing off, screaming, into the forest.

We made the nature of our unexpected visit clear to the fast-assembling villagers. All except one were women and children. The able-bodied men, it seemed, had all gone off to attend an important meeting in the lowlands. The sole remaining male inhabitant was an old man whose crippled legs were permanently folded under him, and who got about by walking on his hands. He introduced himself as Benjamin, and invited us to sleep in a vacant hut.

We elected to spend a day or two in this village (called Je'ute) to recover from our walk. Alas, the hut was full of fleas, and the nights we spent there were even more uncomfortable and sleepless than those in the forest. We cooked, ate, scratched and rested, and in between I talked to Benjamin about the mammals of the Arfaks. He explained that before he became crippled he was a hunter of renown who knew where to find every beast that lived in the mountains. For hours we sat together, my book *Mammals of New Guinea* open before us, discussing the photographs. Pointing to a tree-mouse, Benjamin would say *Choy-woi-be-a* with the beautiful sing-song inflection so characteristic of the Arfak languages. I would attempt to pronounce the name. When I had performed this to his satisfaction, he would tell me all that he knew of the animal, then go on to the next species. Within a day I had a workable list of Hatam mammal names, as well as a great deal of local knowledge about their natural history.

After a couple of days we left Je'ute and walked to Mokwam, a larger village. Mokwam has an airstrip and a trade post, as well as a population of hunters. Now we were able to settle in to a week's highly productive work. By an irony it turned out that Mokwam is only about six kilometres from Hatam, where Luigi Maria D'Albertis had done his work 120 years before. Hing, on the other hand, was now located on the far side of the mountains. Its inhabitants had pulled up stakes and moved, people thought, at about the time of the Second World War.

At Mokwam we stayed with the *kepala desa* (head-man) and his family. They graciously gave us a room in their humble house, in which we erected tents to give a semblance of privacy. Unfortunately, the place was infested with a healthy population of the Himalayan Rat (*Rattus nitidus*), which had somehow reached this remote place so far from its original home. The Himalayan Rat is a robust, noisy animal with little respect for sleeping humans. It soon developed the sides of my tent as a murine ski-slope and resort.

If we were discomfited by the non-human inhabitants of the *kepala desa*'s house, I'm afraid that the human inhabitants were even more dismayed by us. After we requested specimens from the local hunters, animals both dead and alive arrived at every hour of the day and night, much to the distaste of the *kepala desa*'s wife. She (in common with other women of the area) had a particular loathing of young marsupials. She could doubtless stare down with equanimity the fearsome Himalayan Rat, but show her a young possum, fresh from the pouch of its mother, and she would recoil with one hand over her mouth, the other pushing in the direction of the tiny marsupial. Once I learned of this phobia I was discreet in my handling of these creatures, for I'm sure we were on the point of being ejected from the house when the first one was given to me.

Despite these difficulties, the work in the Arfaks paid off. We documented the existence of about five species of mammals which had never been recorded from the mountains before, and also resolved a long-standing taxonomic mystery. This concerned the D'Albertis Ringtail (first collected by Luigi Maria himself at Hatam in 1872). The species seemed to come in two sizes, and these had been given different scientific names earlier this century, only to be lumped together again in the 1940s. After examining the large series of trophy jaws retained by hunters (which we collected), as well as a couple of whole specimens, we discovered that there were indeed two species. We christened the new one the Reclusive Ringtail (*Pseudochirops coronatus*) to commemorate its having remained undetected by western science for so long.

Among the species from the Arfaks never previously recorded was a giant rat, resembling De Vis's Woolly-rat (*Mallomys aroaensis*), but whose exact identity I am still uncertain of, and the Western White-eared Giant Rat (*Hyomys dammermani*)—which made a wonderful consommé. The remarkable Long-fingered Triok (*Dactylopsila palpator*) was also present. This black and white possum smells like a skunk and has the fourth finger of each hand elongated into a great, slender probe which it uses to hook insect larvae from their hiding places.

Our impromptu trip had made a contribution to the

zoology of the region after all. When we met up with Boeadi (who had by now recovered) in Manokwari, he was also delighted with the result.

Looking back now, I can see that Mokwam was one of the more successfully Indonesian-influenced mountain villages in Irian Jaya. After 1969, the Arfak Mountains were the focus for a vigorous resistance movement. This had died down, however, and while I was there, I heard nothing of the Irianese resistance, the OPM (Operasi Merdeka Papua—Free Papua Movement). The OPM remains strong (and is growing) elsewhere in the province. But at Mokwam I saw little resentment of Indonesians from outside the province. The people of the village and the surrounding mountain areas had all been given land in a large transmigration settlement in the lowlands near Manokwari. There, they would plant and harvest dryland rice, then return to the mountains when they wished to resume their traditional life.

PART VII

SNOW MOUNTAINS

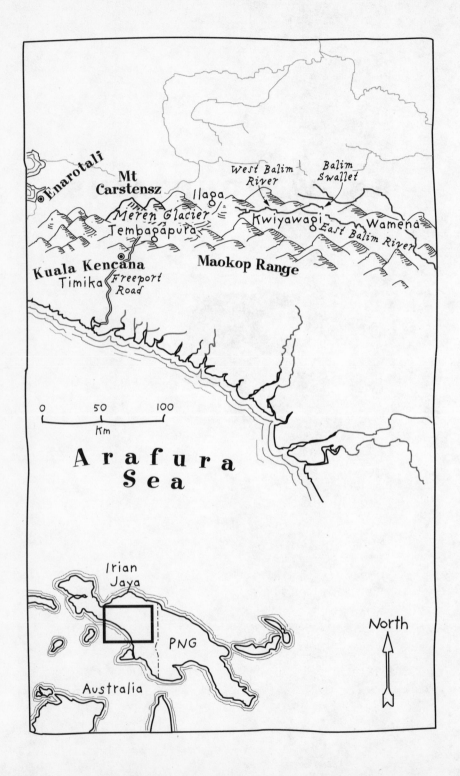

Enarotali

Mt
Carstensz

Ilaga

*West Balim
River*

*Balim
Swallet*

Meren Glacier

Tembagapura

Kwiyawagi

East Balim River

Wamena

Kuala Kencana

Maokop Range

Timika

*Freeport
Road*

0   50   100

Km

**A r a f u r a
S e a**

*Irian
Jaya*

PNG

Australia

North

TWENTY-SIX

The discovery of *Dingiso*

One day in late 1993, at about the time that work on the Pacific islands faunal survey was winding down, I received a telephone call from an employee of a mining company called PT Freeport Indonesia. Freeport is one of the largest mining companies in the world. Based in New Orleans, it runs the world's most profitable gold and copper mine, which is located in Irian Jaya.

The distant voice at the end of the crackly line informed me that the call was coming from Tembagapura, Freeport's town, in the heart of Irian Jaya. The man explained that he thought he had discovered a very rare kind of possum known as the Great-tailed Triok (*Dactylopsila megalura*). This remarkable possum resembles the Long-fingered Triok, except that its bushy black and silver tail is so enormous that it appears to be larger than the rest of the animal combined. The man had read my book on New Guinea mammals; he was wondering if I would be free to come to Tembagapura to confirm his identification, and to talk to the local community about wildlife.

The Tembagapura area is one of the least explored regions in Irian Jaya, at least as far as mammals go. It was somewhere I had always wished to visit, but had hardly dared hope to be able to do so, for Tembagapura is not the kind of place one visits without an invitation.

Tembagapura lies just 120 kilometres west of Kwiyawagi and is adjacent to Mt Carstensz, the very highest point on the Maokop range. Atop Mt Carstensz is a glacier. This remnant of the ice age is one of only a handful of equatorial glaciers on the planet, and due to global warming it is shrinking rapidly. Indeed, at its present rate of decline, it will probably die before I do.

Another factor which influenced my desire to visit Tembagapura was the tree-kangaroo jaw-bone which I had picked from among the pile of human remains at Billingeek. It still eluded identification. A piece of tree-kangaroo fur I purchased at Kwiyawagi, which had originally been fashioned into a war bonnet, remained similarly mysterious. It was unique among all the tree-kangaroo fur I had seen in being black with a flash of white on the chest.

To top it all off, since leaving Kwiyawagi I had received photographs of a tree-kangaroo joey which had been taken near Tembagapura. They showed a very young animal that was boldly patterned in black and white. It seemed now that yet another undescribed species of tree-kangaroo was waiting to be discovered in New Guinea's mountains. Perhaps this visit to Tembagapura would provide the opportunity to gather more evidence.

By mid-1994 I had convinced the Freeport management that I should incorporate a faunal survey into my visit. I was also able to gain permission for Boeadi and Alexandra Szalay to accompany me, and together we hoped to continue our work successfully. Alex and I flew to Cairns, then boarded a charter aircraft flying directly to Timika in the southern lowlands of Irian Jaya. On arrival, we were met by our Freeport hosts and whisked into a Land-cruiser for the two-hour drive from Timika to Tembagapura. Boeadi was to join us a few days later.

The road linking the towns of Timika and Tembagapura is one of the engineering marvels of the world, for it traverses about 100 kilometres of some of the most difficult terrain on the planet. In 1910 the English explorer A. F. R. Wollaston took eighteen months trying to struggle over the route. He spent nights in camp flooded up to his neck in water and weary weeks stumbling through the relentless swamp and jungle. He lost many of his companions to beri-beri, malaria and drowning on the way. After all this, he reached a maximum elevation of only 1,400 metres. In just thirty minutes, now, a traveller on the road reaches the point where Wollaston was forced to turn back.

The construction of this fabulous road took several years, many millions of dollars, and a number of lives. Its design is highly innovative. Part of the section traversing the lowland swamps is built on old tyres so that it floats atop the vast morass. It passes through extraordinary, primaeval-looking swamp forest. Enormous numbers of birds, insects, orchids and ferns give the scene a sense of superfecundity. Bright orange fungi ornament stumps and stilt roots projecting from the morass. Wispy moss, which covers every branch, is eloquent of decay.

After passing through this amazing forest, the road ascends a rise, then continues its way atop a flat, forested terrace which lies about 600 metres above sea-level. To a biologist this is a fascinating place, for it bears greater affinity with the high-elevation forests than the lowlands. The last time I had seen some of the species here was above 3,000 metres elevation at Kwiyawagi, almost five years earlier. This forest grows on infertile, poorly drained peat and experiences almost perpetual cloud and exceedingly high rainfall—eleven metres per year.

Beyond the terrace, the mountains rise abruptly, and from

this point the road winds its way up what appears to be an impossibly steep, knife-edged ridge. Miniature bulldozers about the size of ride-on lawnmowers were used to scrape the top off the ridge, allowing larger ones to follow in their wake. More and more of the ridge was removed until the flat space on top was wide enough to function as a road. It is the steepest road I have ever seen. I stopped at one point to take a photograph, only to find that I couldn't keep my balance.

As one follows the road upward the temperature drops and mists close in. The trees have smaller leaves and are more stunted. The hornbills and cockatoos of the lowlands are left behind and new sounds are heard, including the mechanical-sounding calls of the mountain-dwelling birds of paradise.

At one point the road enters a tunnel a kilometre or more long which bores through the heart of a mountain. Water drops from the roof in a subterranean cascade. The tunnel exits beside a precipice, and the road continues under towering vertical walls, until it reaches 3,000 metres in elevation. Here, one often encounters freezing rain and dense fogs. It is a terrifying experience at this point to meet a massive mine truck looming out of the almost impenetrable fog just a few metres ahead.

The road then begins its descent into the little mountain valley which shelters the town of Tembagapura. Tembagapura was built in the 1970s to house the staff of the PT Freeport Indonesia Mining Company. It has expanded enormously over time, and now even has its own dormitory suburb, Hidden Valley, which is perched on the range above it. It is prettier than your average mining town, largely due to its incomparable location, but also because of its compactness and good planning.

Life in Tembagapura is luxurious by Melanesian standards. With its population of more than 10,000 people, it has most of the facilities available in a small rural centre in the USA. There is a bank, supermarket and specialist shops, sports facilities, a club with restaurant and bar, and first-rate accommodation for workers and visitors. This is a very different environment from those I found when working elsewhere in Irian Jaya.

To my dismay, the Amungme people, traditional landowners of the area, were, at the time of my visit, largely kept outside the town by a vigorous security force. Even the jungle was kept at bay, for the rainforest had been cleared from the site, and someone had planted Monterey Pines (*Pinus radiata*) in its place. Most of these, doubtless imported at great expense, were dead by the time I visited again six months later.

The difficulty in contacting local people was a great impediment, for I needed to work with them as they hunted. This problem was overcome, however, when I met John Cutts.

John is perhaps the greatest asset that Freeport has in its effort to develop a strong relationship with the dispossessed landowners of its mining lease. American by birth, he was adopted when four years of age by a missionary couple who worked among the Moni people of what was then Netherlands New Guinea. Raised both by his Moni neighbours and his foster parents, John came to know Moni language and traditions intimately. In many ways he is as much Moni as he is American. The Moni have their territories just west of the mine and many of them live in the villages around Tembagapura, so this connection is highly useful to the company.

John was then community-liaison officer at Tembagapura, and it was through him that I was introduced to some local men, foremost among whom was Vedelis Zonggonau, a well-educated Moni man in his thirties.

I took out the fieldcopy of *Mammals of New Guinea* and opened it at Doria's Tree-kangaroo.

'*Ndomea*,' Zonggonau said, giving its Moni name.

'*Naki*,' the Amungme hunters said.

Next I showed them the photograph I had been sent, of the black and white joey.

'*Dingiso*,' Zonggonau said.

'*Nemenaki*,' the Amungme chorused.

After some discussion we formed a plan to explore the high forest above the town, in search of these species.

We decided to work in the forest along the road at between 2,500 and 3,000 metres elevation. There was good beech forest growing at this elevation and it looked like prime habitat for tree-kangaroos. We chose a campsite on a spur which was covered with heath, thus giving us a little sun. This was an important consideration, for the forests around Tembagapura are among the wettest on earth, and life can become unbearable unless you have a chance to dry out.

It was a beautiful place, and one which our hunters assured us had been used in times past by the OPM. It commanded a view over the Singa Valley to the east, encompassing a vast sweep of primary rainforest. The various shades of green in the canopy below suggested enormous botanical diversity, while a variety of bird calls rang out from the forest all day long.

The small patch of heath we camped in was very mossy, with orchids and rhododendrons making up most of the ground cover. One particularly spectacular orchid had a white flower which it produced in abundance. Its spent petals, scattered on the mossy ground, looked like a fall of new snow.

Over the first few days we camped in the heath we were puzzled by a strange and whimsical call, resembling, I felt, the sound that a slightly tipsy maiden aunt might make were she pinched on the bottom by a favourite uncle at a family party. '*Oooh,*' it went, at erratic intervals. The mystery caller was found on our first sunny day, when Alex spotted a tiny pink and black frog crawling over the sphagnum moss. It was no larger than the nail on my little finger, and was—needless to say—completely unknown to science.

We sent our hunters out each day with dogs in order to locate tree-kangaroos, and soon had our first specimen. I was disappointed to discover that it was not the black and white animal I hoped to secure, but belonged to a subspecies of Doria's Tree-kangaroo which I had originally described from specimens collected in the Star Mountains in 1987. I was nonetheless intrigued to discover this species living so far west of its known range. Over the next week we located several other Doria's Tree-kangaroos, but the black and white animal remained elusive.

Frustrated, I decided to try again at higher elevation. By following the road, which rises towards the mine site from Tembagapura, then turning into the bush, we reached an area with steep slopes rising to 3,700 metres elevation. There, scrubby plants grew in dense clusters among the rocks. I was deeply sceptical about the possibility of finding tree-kangaroos in this area, for there were not even any trees of a reasonable size for them to climb in. Our hunters, however, insisted that they could be had there, so I deferred to their plan to base ourselves at this bleak spot.

My worst suspicions seemed confirmed when, after three days' hunting, we had failed to locate any sign of tree-kangaroos at all.

Then, early one morning, a dog emerged from the mist and approached our camp. It was followed by another, then two men and two women. I introduced myself to the taller of the men. He said that his name was Yonas Tinal, and that he was a Lani man from Ilaga. He owned the two dogs and the women were his wives. The other man he introduced as his friend. He had come to this high forest, he told me, to hunt tree-kangaroos.

Despite my increasing misgivings, he seemed confident of success. His dog, named Dingo, was, he told me, a four-million rupiah hunter: it was so good at finding game that Yonas valued each of its canine teeth at a cool million rupiah (about seven hundred Australian dollars) apiece. Dingo's companion, Photocopy, was a less able animal and, as his name suggests, resembled a hunting dog more in appearance than action.

Yonas and I hit it off immediately. He is a big, open-hearted and generous man with a delightful sense of humour. He has a typically large Lani nose, the septum of which has been wonderfully perforated. He offered on several occasions to perforate my own nasal septum, claiming that the mountains were an ideal place to operate, as the cold air would make it a relatively painless ordeal.

Yonas liked Australians. At one time he worked for an Australian engineer engaged in road construction near the mine. The pair had become firm friends and still occasionally wrote to each other. Yonas had named the renowned hunting dog Dingo in honour of his Australian friend.

Yonas explained that until recently he had four wives, but because one fought with the others he reluctantly returned her to her parents. Polygamy clearly suited him, however, for he had plans to enlarge his little family. A fondness for the policeman's daughter at Nabire had blossomed into romance, and Yonas was now saving for the brideprice.

Yonas is almost unique among the more traditional younger New Guineans I have known in that he displays open, physical affection to his wives. He could often be seen nestled among them, holding the hand of one and smiling at another. For their part, they seemed happy and contented in his company.

After I'd explained to Yonas my desire to obtain a specimen of the black and white tree-kangaroo, he continued on his way even higher up the mountain, promising to return with one in a few days.

I would have loved to follow Yonas to his camp, but our nets and traps were already set out and our hunters were scouring the bush at this lower location. It would take at least a day to reorganise ourselves, and Yonas could not wait.

Our hunters found nothing and I was losing hope.

But at last one morning I saw Dingo emerge from the forest. A smiling Yonas, holding up two fingers, followed behind. As he opened his *noken*, I divined from this gesture that he had captured two tree-kangaroos.

As the contents of the *noken* were revealed, I was all but overcome by near-simultaneous sensations of exhilaration and despair. Yonas had captured two tree-kangaroos—but they had been eaten. All that he had brought were pieces of skin and bones!

Nonetheless, the remains were sufficient to confirm that the black and white tree-kangaroo was a very curious and hitherto unknown animal. The skins were incomplete and miserably torn, but it was clear from them that the new species was a largish creature (we learned later that females, which are smaller than males, weigh nine to ten kilograms). The back was indeed black, the belly white, and the tail patterned variously in black and white, but usually with a white tip. The face was very unusual, for a band of white fur surrounded the base of the muzzle, and a white star stood in the centre of the forehead. These features were not evident in the photographs of the joey, and nothing like this pattern is seen in any other marsupial.

The distinctiveness of this strange creature was also apparent from the bones. The skull showed some similarities to that of Doria's Tree-kangaroo, but was more gracefully shaped and differed in details of its teeth and foramina (holes in the skull). The limb bones were also dramatically different from those of any other tree-kangaroo I had examined. The major limb bones of tree-kangaroos are exceptionally thick and robust. They need to be, for many species leap as much as twenty metres downward from the rainforest canopy. The limb bones of the new species were, in contrast, gracile, and similar in proportion to ground-dwelling kangaroos. Clearly, this animal could not make such great downward leaps.

I would discover eventually that this new species was unique among tree-kangaroos in that it spent much of its time on the ground, among the stunted shrubs and bushes of the alpine region.

Meanwhile, our largely unsuccessful hunters had gone off up into the higher country with their dogs once more, while we proceeded at a more leisurely pace behind them, collecting frogs, examining plants and looking for traces of smaller animals.

In this venture, Yonas and I formed a team of sorts which specialised in searching under fallen timber for frogs and invertebrates. We worked rather like Jack Sprat and his wife, for Yonas had an unholy terror of all things amphibian, while I recoil at large, hairy spiders. Whenever a frog was exposed under a log, it was I who leaped on it, while Yonas had no compunction about casually stooping down to pick up the most terrible-looking spiders.

I did not realise the depth of Yonas' revulsion of frogs, until we watched a video together in our quarters in Tembagapura. A few days earlier I had taped Yonas and our other helpers while they worked. Now they were crowded around the television excitedly talking about themselves as movie stars—when the scene cut suddenly to a close-up of a toad. Yonas leaped vertically into the air and landed on top of a couch. From there, he attempted to scramble out of our third-storey window! When he had calmed down, he explained to me that while the look of such an enlarged frog was terrible enough, to hear its croak *amplified* was almost unthinkable.

Sadly, it was not Yonas, but another Lani hunter called Obert who brought in our long-desired specimen.

On this particular day Yonas and I were doing quite well at our double act when our hunters appeared through the mist, led by Obert—who was triumphantly carrying a tree-kangaroo on his shoulders. It was, he said, only recently dead.

As Obert carried the creature towards me seated upright on his shoulders, it looked more like a bear or koala than a kangaroo. It seemed such an adorable, gentle creature. Later, when I encountered a living animal, I would learn that its temperament is indeed mild. Lani have often told me that, when hunters find it, they offer it some choice leaves, and it approaches them—then they simply slip a noose over its head and lead it away.

This extraordinary animal is well known to hunters living high on the Maokop. The Moni people, who inhabit the western edge of the range, know it as *Dingiso*, a name which we eventually bestowed upon it as its English common name. We did this because we were tired of the clumsy, double-barrelled English names (such as Goodfellow's Tree-kangaroo) given to other species of New Guinea mammal. We wanted to bestow a native name, such as the Aboriginal *koala* or *wombat*, which would, in time, become familiar to western ears.

We also gave the scientific name *Dendrolagus mbaiso* to the creature. *Mbaiso* means 'the forbidden animal' in Moni, and we used this name as a tribute to the traditional Moni conservation practices which have been crucial in allowing it to survive to the present.

Dingiso remains common in Moni territory. Many clans revere it as an ancestor and refuse to hunt it. When they meet it in the forest, they say, it throws up its arms and whistles, which they take as an indication that it recognises its shared ancestry with the Moni. Even their dogs, Moni say, recognise the sacred nature of this creature, and when they see one will slink away on their bellies. Biologists, who are a more prosaic bunch than the Moni, view *Dingiso*'s behaviour differently, descrying in it a typical tree-kangaroo threat display. They have no explanation, however, for the behaviour of Moni dogs.

The Western Dani know the creature as *Wanun*. In their territories, which lie to the east of the Moni, it is not protected by traditional beliefs and is, as a consequence, extremely rare. It has already been exterminated within a few days' walk of most Dani settlements.

Now I had sufficient evidence to describe the species. With the discovery of *Dingiso* I felt that I had hit the high point in my career as a biologist. During the decade or so I had been investigating the mammals of Melanesia, I had discovered sixteen other species which were unknown to science, as well as fourteen new subspecies. Among these were bats, possums, bandicoots, wallabies and giant rats, as well as three other kinds of tree-kangaroos. None, however, was as unusual as *Dingiso*, and none had such an interesting evolutionary and cultural story to tell.

Prior to my departure to Australia I spent several days in the lowlands around Timika. The management of PT Freeport Indonesia were so pleased with the results of our survey that they put us all up at the newly opened Timika Sheraton Hotel. It is an extraordinary place to find in the middle of the Irian jungle, for the facilities boast the last word in luxury and one can hear and see (if one is lucky) from almost every room in the place several of the half dozen species of birds of paradise which inhabit the surrounding jungle.

The construction cost of the hotel was apparently stupendous. I heard rumours that eighty million dollars went into building the forty-seven room facility. Still, one has to have adequate accommodation for visiting dignitaries and heads of state. Other rumours suggested that among the hotel's customers were some Indonesian politicians seeking a quiet place for a weekend with their mistresses.

The grounds surrounding the hotel are exquisite. Trails have been cut through the forest, and myriad insects, birds and other wildlife can be seen in the regrowth along the paths. Brilliant butterflies of many kinds hover around flowers on creepers and vines, and skinks with brilliant blue tails dash from every log.

One does not have to travel far from the Sheraton, though, to be thrown into the reality of present-day Irian Jaya. The village of Kwamki Lama was created for displaced Amungme, who originally lived in the Tembagapura–Singa area. It lies barely a kilometre from the hotel. In 1995, nearly a hundred of the Amungme living there died of cholera. They are a mountain people and they fare just as poorly, health-wise, in the lowlands as do Europeans.

The Kamoro are the original inhabitants of the lowland swamps. Prior to the coming of the mine they were semi-nomadic, and some continue in a remarkably traditional lifestyle today. Despite the enormous disruption to their lives caused by the mine, they manage to take advantage of the situation in unexpected ways.

One day I was taken out to see the tailings levee. This is a large, dam-like structure which has been built to the north-east of Timika to contain the mine tailings which are dumped into the headwaters of the Aikwa River. The tailings consist almost entirely of crushed rock as, thankfully, no chemicals are used in the mineral extraction process. Nonetheless, the sheer volume of sediment being discharged is causing some environmental concern.

Where the sediment builds up it smothers the roots of nearby trees, causing vast tracks of forest to die. The area around the tailings levee looks awful. On its southern side, thousands of hectares of forest lie dead or dying. To the north lies original swamp forest, inhabited, I discovered, by a considerable population of Kamoro. Why had they come to live adjacent to this devastation?

The answer was provided by a couple of women who were returning to camp as I arrived. Strung from their heads were huge net bags full of freshwater prawns. These jumbo-sized crustaceans are delicious and nutritious. They are normally not common and I wondered how the women had managed to collect so many. The answer, it seemed, lay in the devastated forest.

The water under the dead and dying trees abounds in prawns. This is because the sediment which smothers the trees forms a highly fertile bed for the growth of algae and bacteria. This is prawn food par excellence. With the leaf fall and the sunlight reaching the forest floor, an incredibly fertile environment has been created in which the prawns and other aquatic life flourish. The women harvest the prawns by removing plugs set in the levee wall and placing their nets over the hole. Within minutes they are full.

The Kamoro are not the only ones attracted to the bounty. Fat crocodiles abound, while wild pigs and forest wallabies, attracted to the regrowth occurring under the trees, are seen in large numbers. All of these animals provide further food for the Kamoro who, while political stability lasted, were selling smoked meat at some profit in the Timika market. I have never seen a lowland people as sleek and healthy as the Kamoro living on that levee.

It is just as well that the tailings area has provided an alternative source of food for the Kamoro, for their traditional fare including the fish and mudcrabs which once abounded in the river estuaries, are now sadly depleted. Tailings have smothered many, while Buginese fishermen compete for those which remain. These aggressive people have recently discovered the near-virgin fisheries of southern Irian Jaya. With a ready market in Timika and Tembagapura, they have ransacked the region. In a few years' time, the gigantic barramundi and abundant mudcrabs still seen in the markets will be a thing of the past.

The forest damage caused by the tailings will eventually affect many square kilometres. It will be visible from space. But in the context of the lowland forests of southern Irian Jaya, the area of impact will be small. The greater damage to the forests is revealed as one flies out of Timika, for it is then that the logging tracks can be seen snaking out in all directions. When I first flew over the forest in 1990, there was not a logging track in sight. Today they seem to cover the region, reaching almost as far as Etna Bay in the west.

The damage which logging does to the forest comes with no side benefit to the local people and the extent of the area affected is staggering. There is no way that these operations will be curtailed, however, for the military and other wealthy Javanese are making far too much money from them. It is logging, not mine tailings, which will cost southern Irian Jaya its precious forests.

TWENTY-SEVEN

The high point

Camping in the forests around Tembagapura provided an opportunity to talk openly with the mountain people. In villages and towns, the locals were reserved, wary of eaves-droppers. I soon became aware that the mountain people are, without exception, deeply bitter at the way they have been treated over the past few decades by both the Indonesian Government and PT Freeport Indonesia.

In order to understand their point of view, one must try to see the world as they do. Members of the various tribal groups (including the Ekari, Moni, Amungme and Dani) see them-selves as a free and independent people whose lands have been recently occupied by foreigners. They regard their land and all it contains as belonging to them and no-one else. It is a land which they and their ancestors have fought for and jealously guarded for millennia. Most view the activities of PT Freeport

Indonesia, with its alienation of land, pollution and extraction of mineral resources, as outright theft. Many mountain people can hardly conceive of the idea that they are citizens of Indonesia.

Miners and government officials view things differently. Thus all 'unoccupied' land, officially at least, belongs to the Republic of Indonesia, although it can be given back to tribal people to live on.

The miners argue that they abide by the laws of Indonesia and that without their efforts there would be no wealth. They believe that they are contributing to the development of the province in ways which will eventually benefit the people, and that they are also contributing greatly to the economy of Indonesia. Most see the kind of development which they bring as being inevitable in any case, and that it might as well be them doing it as other, possibly less ethical people.

During the time of my first visit, few Irianese had jobs at the mine and, of those that did, several I spoke to complained of harsh treatment at the hands of some of the Indonesian supervisors. Things are now a little different, and an increasing (though still small) number of Irianese are finding employment with Freeport or affiliated companies.

It is hardly surprising that the situation has led to social unrest. The only way in which the Indonesian Government has been able to maintain authority in the area (and thus allow Freeport to operate) is through a large and increasing military presence. The result has been a smouldering civil unrest, which occasionally breaks out into small-scale war.

Although I heard many stories about things that have happened to Amungme and other tribal people, it was not until I became embroiled in an incident myself that I fully understood their situation, and the anger of the mountain people at it.

The management of PT Freeport Indonesia were generous to me during my visit. They supported me in all my requests for travel and other assistance, were candid and open with me concerning their operations and gave me freedom (in what is otherwise a highly regulated environment) to pursue my research.

I, on my part, assured them that they would be the first to know of my findings, but made it clear that I could promise them nothing more. I'm certain that they would have liked more control over the information I collected, but I could not agree to remain silent about the work I did or what I saw while doing it.

Freeport's support was particularly important for my plans to climb to the Meren Glacier, as permits to enter the area are strictly controlled by the Indonesian Government. Indeed, without support from the highest levels of the company, I doubt that I could have obtained permission to make the ascent.

I intended to ship our equipment into a camp in the Meren Valley by helicopter, to spend four or five days working at 4,300 metres elevation (mostly to study rats) and then ascend to the foot of the glacier to determine which mammals (if any) exist in that hostile environment. To see the Meren Glacier with my own eyes was a life-long ambition.

We awoke before dawn and assembled our equipment at the helipad in the pale light. We were the first job on the schedule, so after a rather extensive safety briefing we loaded up and lifted off. The excitement of helicopter travel in such places is not easily communicable. The high whine of the starter motor, the smell of leather and sweat in the thin cold air, the helmet with its radio—then the uncanny feeling of the lift-off, the short ascent and the swooping departure to places unknown.

The morning we flew into the Meren Valley was crystal clear. Before reaching our destination we had to fly over the mine site itself. It is an awesome spectacle, highlighting the power of the modern transnational economy to extract resources from wherever they might be.

In 1936 a Dutch geologist discovered a 300-metre-tall mountain of copper. The trouble was that it stood atop this great
limestone range in the most remote and inaccessible corner of
the earth. In the 1970s American capital financed a road, the
construction of which defies the imagination. Where even it
could not go, American engineers constructed the world's
longest aerial tram to link the roadhead with the mine itself,
which is perched at nearly 4,000 metres elevation. Travelling on
this tram, suspended in an iron box high over a great chasm on
a mile of steel cable, is an unforgettable experience.

The infrastructure needed to support the mine is enormous. A town of 10,000 or more, an airline and shipping line,
not to mention the extensive equipment sheds, dumps and
mining materials, are all financed by this powerful machine.
It, in turn, is fed by a flow of ten million dollars worth of minerals every day.

In 1994 the annual budget of PT Freeport Indonesia was
larger than that of most of the Pacific island economies. The
programs it ran were almost as comprehensive as those of a
national government. Today the company has divested itself of
many of its peripheral businesses, such as airlines, caterers and
shipping, in order to concentrate on mining. It is still, however, an awesome enterprise.

As we passed over the yawning pit, I thought of a story I
had heard about an Amungme leader who believed that
wealth beyond reckoning lay locked inside a mountain. He
could gain access to that wealth, he claimed, by the use of a
magical rodent tooth. Of course his cargo-cult came to nothing, but the man had been right. Vast wealth did reside in
mountains—the Amungme's mountains. It's just that
their technology could not unlock it, and they have been
dispossessed of it.

In a few moments' flying we had passed the mine site and
were ascending a steep rocky slope which led to the Meren
Valley. As we crossed the tussocks and rhododendrons of the
barren landscape I felt at home once again, surrounded by

the mountain scenery I know and love. And then, only a few seconds later, I was standing in a boggy alpine meadow, the helicopter already gone, with near freezing water seeping into my boots and an icy blast on my face. The quiet was divine.

We were set down beside an almost luminous green lake which is fed by glacial meltwater. Below it lay a smaller, bright blue lake. The ecology and chemistry of each of these glacial waters, which impart to each its particular colour, opacity and luminosity, are unique.

A few hundred metres away a huge limestone overhang reached out across the valley. The sheer wall, over a hundred metres tall, rose at an angle of about eighty-five degrees from the horizontal. For a distance of about five metres, the ground at its base was completely dry and sheltered from the rain. This extraordinary feature, which was to serve as our camp-site, must have been cut by the Meren Glacier during the last ice age. Countless millions of tonnes of rock must have been carved up and carted away by the ice, only to be dumped kilo-metres away. I wondered at the sharpness and power of ice. It dwarfs even the might of a mining operation to wreak change.

On reaching this campsite, we were dismayed to find the ground littered with sheets of silver foil and food scraps. Some very messy people had clearly camped here a few days before. At that time, take-away lunches wrapped in foil were available to Freeport employees who were working away from a canteen, and I took the mess (wrongly, as it turned out) to be the result of insensitive littering by company employees.

After we set our traps and nets in the surrounding alpine scrub, the hunters fanned out from the camp with their dogs. I set to exploring the valley and organising our equipment, and did not see the hunters again until evening. When they returned, they brought the disturbing news that they had found two people camped in a rockshelter a few hundred metres downslope. They were, I was informed, very sick.

Surprised and concerned at this news, Alex and I began to gather medical supplies and some food, then asked Vedelis and Yonas to show us where they were. The Meren Valley ends in a steep rocky slope composed of glacier-carried boulders. The slope is, I suppose, part of the terminal moraine of the great glacier which formed when it extended to this point some 12,000 years ago. There are hollows under some of the house-sized boulders, and it was to one of these hollows that Vedelis led us.

There, in the dim light, we made out two small, almost naked black figures lying in the dust. Their fire had gone out and they had nothing by way of food, blankets or extra clothing with them. Looking closer, I was disturbed to find that they were children.

As I stepped into the cave a girl, who at about fifteen was the older of the two, rose to her feet. It appeared from her dazed expression and disjointed speech that she was in shock. The boy, she said, was her brother, and he was badly hurt. He coughed as he sat up, then told me in a low voice that his name was Arianus Murip. He was a Lani from Ilaga, and he was thirteen years old. I offered the kids some chocolate biscuits, which they took, but to my great surprise did not eat. After treating a few superficial cuts and giving them some warm clothes, I asked them to tell me their story. This is what they said.

They had been part of a group of about ninety people who, after visiting the villages of Waa and Banti, near Tembagapura, decided to walk home over the range to Ilaga.

I knew that these villages act like magnets to people from all over the mountains. They come to see the mine and its white people, and perhaps to obtain some goods, such as food, clothing or kerosene, which, in Irianese eyes, the mine workers seem to discard in great quantity. The villages near the mine often become overcrowded. This is a problem for the Amungme inhabitants, for by tradition they must feed and shelter the visitors. When the crowding becomes critical, the village head-men come to Freeport and ask for help in relocating people who wish to leave.

Freeport organises the exodus by supplying buses which ferry the people from the villages, via Tembagapura and the mine site (which are normally off-limits to them), to a walking track which begins at the far side of the mine. This track, after crossing the range at almost its highest point, leads on to Ilaga.

On this occasion, the children said, the company supplied lunches to those who were undertaking the walk—which explained the piles of silver foil and uneaten food along the track. (The practice of wrapping take-away lunches in silver foil has now ceased, largely because of the visual pollution the cast-offs cause.)

Arianus and his sister had kept up with the group until they came to the steepest part of the track. There, Arianus had begun to have difficulty breathing. He also suffered frostbite on his right foot, which slowed him. His sister stayed with him, even when it became apparent that he could not go on. In doing this, she put her own life at risk. The path near the summit is strewn with the bones of people who were caught on the high pass during a cold snap without adequate protection. Melanesians are particularly susceptible to hypothermia, as they typically have almost no body fat and limited energy reserves. The scattered skulls, being slowly overgrown by moss, must have reminded her of the fate she risked in remaining with her brother.

It had become clear that their only chance of survival lay in returning quickly to Tembagapura, as a night spent exposed on the mountain would surely kill them both. They descended into the Meren Valley, and were about to enter the boulder-strewn slope which leads to the mine, when they encountered security guards in the employ of PT Freeport Indonesia.

These men had been posted at the end of the valley to ensure that none of the people being repatriated to Ilaga returned to the mine. As Arianus explained to them that he felt ill and could not go on, one of the guards (another Melanesian, from the island of Biak) lashed out with his fist and struck him across the face. The guards then kicked and beat him on the chest and the back of the head and left him, in the fading evening light, to die in the freezing grassland.

Yonas told me what happens to people who die in the high valleys. The wild dogs of the mountains come to feed on them. Yonas himself had once come across the remains of a group of thirteen people who had died of exposure following a rapid change in the weather. Their bodies had lain near where we were camped now. Yonas noticed that one appeared to have a long, hairy object protruding from its belly, which was moving grotesquely from side to side. On his approach, a wild dog, covered in blood, emerged from deep inside the body cavity where it had been feeding, and fled into the forest.

The victims had been recovered by Freeport and buried.

Arianus's sister was in shock after the assault, but she helped her brother to the crude rockshelter, where they spent the night without light, food or fire. The following day a few Lani men (who had heard about the incident) risked the wrath of the security forces to carry some firewood up to the children and light a fire for them. This action doubtless saved their lives.

It was now a day or two later.

The discovery of the children and news of their story posed a dilemma for me. It was clear that Arianus had to receive medical attention, and the sooner the better. He did not seem to be seriously injured, but I suspected that he had a bronchial infection and I was unsure how he would hold up after another day in the shelter.

I knew the children would be better off there, with a fire burning through the night, than at our freezing camp. We cut firewood for them, gave them some food, and promised to take them down to safety the next day.

Clearly the expedition had to be aborted. Yet I had waited a lifetime to see the Meren Glacier, and the chance to do so might not come my way again. All night I lay awake, wondering what the morning would bring.

Dawn spread into the valley and melted the ice on the ponds by our camp. I arose to the sounds of a very cold Boeadi claiming that the thin air and freezing conditions had doubtless taken a decade off his life—and that he needed a boiled egg for breakfast to restore his failing health. Yonas proclaimed equally loudly that his teeth had chattered so violently during the night they were now all loose in their sockets, while his waterworks had completely seized up.

I wandered out across the still frozen tundra to collect my traps. Each one had a rat in it. There were three species. One was my old friend the Moss-forest Rat, which I had encountered on my first trip to New Guinea. The second was new to me. It was a lovely rat. A little larger than the Moss-forest Rat, it had flesh-coloured tail, hands and feet, long, dense and fine bluish-brown fur, and a gentle disposition. It was the Glacier Rat (*Stenomys richardsoni*), which is only found in this region, and is a delight to handle. The third species was a small, chunky, short-tailed rat with a pinched face, the likes of which I had never seen before. With a million things to do, and some hard decisions to make, however, I lacked the time to examine it closely.

Back in camp, everyone's spirits seemed restored somewhat by the warmth of the morning light. Boeadi had eaten his egg and was at peace with the world, and Yonas's teeth had survived a breakfast of sweet potato. I gathered everyone together and announced my decision. Boeadi, Alex and all but one of the hunters would take the children and proceed down the valley to the security post at the upper end of the mine. I, along with Yonas, would make a dash for the glacier, and meet them at the post that afternoon.

Setting off up the valley, I felt a terrible guilt gnawing at me. Had I deserted the children just when they needed me most? But surely Boeadi, as a senior Javanese scientist, would be capable of pulling rank on the security guards if they obstructed our attempts to help the children.

My mind was in turmoil as I walked along, trying to take in the sublime beauty of the scene. The Snow Mountains rose all around, their icy peaks glinting in the sunlight. I could see cliffs, moraines and lakes everywhere. Tiny tussocks poked up through the boulders we passed.

Rice spilled out of discarded foil wrappings had attracted a multitude of birds to the side of the track. I saw the near-legendary Snow Mountains Quail (*Anurophasis monorthonyx*) several times, a great green honeyeater I had not seen elsewhere, and a number of other birds which are restricted to such high elevations. As we ascended the valley, we left the vegetation behind and began to travel over bare rock. Amid a pile of boulders near some glacial lakes I had a brief sighting of the Snow Mountains Robin (*Petroica archboldi*). This beautiful, red-breasted creature is unique to the area around the glaciers in Irian Jaya. It is, perhaps, the rarest bird in Melanesia and one of the rarest on the planet. It is a rather sluggish little creature, yet seeing it fulfilled what was, for me, another life-long dream.

The track now passed beside a recent glacial moraine, from which we could see a vast hanging wall of ice perched on the mountain to the left. The eerie milky aqua colour of the craggy ice face was mesmerising. Its size and luminosity dominated the scene. It somehow looked unreal, and I had to remind myself that we were just four degrees from the equator. We slowly advanced up the steepening moraine until I felt ice under my feet. A few metres more and we were standing on a solid sheet of ice: the farthest tip of the Meren Glacier itself.

I sat down on a rock. Between my feet, a strange shape in a greenish piece of rock caught my eye. It was the remains of a kind of sea urchin which had, I knew from my training in geology, lived at the bottom of a shallow, tropical sea some twenty-five million years before. Time, fate and the irresistible forces of plate tectonics had lifted it to the top of New Guinea, almost 5,000 metres above sea-level. It was exposed in just the right place for me to ponder its journey during the few minutes I spent on top of the world. It had probably broken free of the rock just a few weeks before. A few weeks longer and frost, ice and water would obliterate it.

Yonas interrupted my meditations with a concerned expression on his face. '*Rumah tuan tanah,*' he whispered, as he pointed to the side of the ice sheet. 'The home of an earth spirit.' What did he mean?

I followed him to the edge of the ice. Suddenly its colour changed below my feet, from a deep to a paler blue. Jumping off the glacier, I saw that we had been walking atop a ledge, below which was an ice cave.

I had never seen such a thing before, and was enchanted by the rounded lines and subtle blue, aqua and white of the backlit ice sculpture. Yonas was reluctant to enter the cave, but seeing me go first he jumped down beside me. We sat there in freezing contemplation of our very different worlds.

The sky was darkening. The time for our dash to the security post had come. We set out at speed down the slope with the weather quickly closing in. Yonas was suffering from a severe altitude-induced headache, but he continued to push on.

The last part of the walk to the security post led us through a ghastly quagmire of human making. Just above the mine site lies the once beautiful Carstensz Meadow. Beginning in the 1930s, this meadow was repeatedly studied by a series of researchers, and it and its adjacent glaciers are the only sites in the mountains of Irian Jaya with such a long history of documented environmental change. This, of course, makes them scientifically invaluable, for long-term changes to flora and fauna (such as those arising from global warming) can be measured there.

The problem is, the Carstensz Meadow no longer exists. It has been used as a dump site for mine tailings. Only a few hundred metres of the meadow at the very back—hard against the mountain wall—were yet to be filled. The tailings have impeded drainage and the tiny remnant of the once beautiful herbfield has become a morass. One day, I was assured by a mining engineer, the meadow will be buried hundreds of metres deep in mine waste. Then, perhaps, one will be able to step directly from the waste pile into the Meren Valley. The cave where the children suffered will be buried and forgotten.

I was told that by dumping the waste in the valley (rather than moving it further away), the company saved about as much money as its operation makes in five days.

It was already raining hard by the time Alex, Boeadi, our helpers and the children reached the morass. They ferried the equipment across, but first had to find a path through the bog. The carriers placed Arianus, who was by then coughing and shivering with cold, on the far edge of the morass. All they had to protect him from the rain was a towel, which they placed over his head.

As Vedelis and Marsellius (one of our hunters) crossed, carrying Arianus shoulder high, they sank chest deep into the freezing water of the drowned Carstensz Meadow. Two mine workers laughed at their predicament. Even as they approached the pile of mining waste which the post was built on, the workers did not lend a helping hand or throw down some planks which were lying about.

The security post was deserted. Vedelis hailed a bus on its way to pick up workers, which took our group to the Ertzberg first-aid post. A Lani head-man who worked for the mine met them there. He talked to Arianus, holding his knee to comfort him. Arianus answered quietly between coughs. Arianus was then placed on a drip. The girl was whisked away by the Lani head-man, who, before he left, held Alex's hands in his own, thanking her gravely for rescuing the pair. The departing girl nodded to Alex, and that was the last time any of us ever saw the children.

By the time Alex and Boeadi arrived back at the security post to await my arrival, a Biak guard was in occupation.

Boeadi took over the tiny guard house with its heater and commenced to skin the rats we had caught earlier. The guard was forced to stand in the rain. By the time Yonas and I arrived at about 4.00 p.m., Vedelis had a bonfire going despite the downpour. We then arranged for transport to the aerial tram, and were soon back in Tembagapura.

Upon arriving, I immediately called the hospital to check on Arianus's condition. I was able to confirm that he had been admitted, but the Indonesian nurse I spoke to would tell me no more, except that his condition was serious. Then I rang the American doctor on staff, in order to inform him of Arianus's history, and to ask for a report on the boy's health. To my astonishment, he said, in a formal voice, that he was not allowed to interfere with the 'Indonesian cases' and could not help me.

I called the hospital several times that evening, but always received the same response. Arianus's doctor, I was told, was unavailable to speak to me.

By morning I was sufficiently worried to call the hospital to arrange a visit. The voice at the end of the line told me not to bother, for Arianus was dead.

This news was devastating. Arianus had walked part of the way from the cave to the security post. He was a fit young boy who had smiled and chatted to me twenty-four hours earlier. His most serious injury, I learned, was a punctured lung. How could he have died so suddenly?

On several occasions since, I have described Arianus's injuries to medical professionals in Australia. They have been unanimous in their opinion that he was unlikely to have died had he been treated in an Australian hospital and that his sudden death from such injuries, given his condition and his survival for several days after they were inflicted, is indeed puzzling.

Sick at heart, Alex and I went to Banti village, where Arianus's sister was hidden away. The community was seething with rage. Arianus's relatives, including a number of senior men, had tried to go to the hospital to collect his body. The security guards at the town perimeter had refused them permission. When they were finally allowed in, there was a skirmish outside the hospital.

The following day, when I felt more composed, I related the entire incident to a senior manager in Tembagapura. He is a gentle and concerned American. He was distressed by my story, and gave me an assurance that, in future, medical checks would be carried out on anyone assisted to return home from the Tembagapura area.

I felt outraged. I wanted someone to take responsibility. I wanted a court case and, ultimately, jail for Arianus's assailants. Perhaps, in my heart, I wanted blood.

The truth of the matter, it seems, is that the Freeport management at Tembagapura have little control over Freeport security. Although paid for by the company, Freeport security seems to receive orders directly from ABRI, the Indonesian military.

That evening I sat in my room in Tembagapura, boiling with anger and frustration. There seemed to be absolutely nothing I could do to obtain justice for Arianus.

Desperate for a diversion, I remembered the rats I had collected in the Meren Valley. They were stored in the freezer. I got them out, and once again tried to identify the short-tailed, pinched-faced species which had defied classification. Then it struck me. It may well be new to science. If so, it was to be Arianus's Rat.

Months later, I found that the species was in fact named in the 1970s by a Belgian biologist. *Rattus omlichodes*—the fog-bound rat—he called it. Due to a changing taxonomy and a new common name I formulated for it, it is now *Stenomys omlichodes*—Arianus's Rat.

TWENTY-EIGHT

Kwiyawagi revisited

Arianus's death upset me so much that I left Tembagapura with relief.

I returned to Kwiyawagi, to continue the work I began four years earlier. Due to the strong anti-Indonesian feeling expressed by people there, I felt it best for Boeadi to stay in the lowlands near Timika, collecting bats and reptiles. Alex travelled with me, as she was interested in looking at Kwiyawagi to assess its suitability as a potential field site where she could undertake her doctoral studies in anthropology.

It was a delight to see my old friends Pastor Manas and Jot Murip again. The pleasure was doubled by the improvement in my Bahasa Indonesia—I could now communicate far more effectively than on my first visit.

My plan was to visit as many caves as possible in the area, and to carry out a full survey of the mammals of the valley.

Once people understood what was intended, I received enormous help from local hunters. People brought in bandicoots, possums and other mammals which they had collected in their traps or found in tree-hollows, and allowed me to weigh, measure and skin them before they cooked them for dinner. Various people volunteered to guide me to caves around the valley and, although none could compare with Kelangurr, I did find some interesting specimens.

Among the modern mammals, the most fascinating were the bats. One day a young boy brought me a tiny brown bat which he had found roosting in a hollow in a pandanus tree trunk. I recognised it as a Mountain Pipistrelle (*Pipistrellus collinus*). Its impressive penis (it looked to be a quarter the length of the animal's body) indicated that it was an adult male.

Over the following week, another five Mountain Pipistrelles were brought in by young boys. All were found roosting alone in hollows in pandanus trees, and all were male. My curiosity as to where the females might be was finally satisfied one morning when a young lad brought a bag stuffed full of tiny bats which he had found roosting together in yet another pandanus hollow. Examining them, I found that there were eleven females (which are larger than males and orange in colour) and a single male, whose impressive testes indicated he was in peak breeding condition.

This was a winged sultan and his harem.

The private lives of most species of bats are obscure, and it is only through chance encounters such as this that we gain insights into them. Had I arrived at Kwiyawagi a few weeks later, the harems might have dispersed; a few weeks earlier and they might not yet have formed. This was indeed a fortuitous discovery.

A second species of bat was found and brought to me by the tree-climbing boys of Kwiyawagi. This one was much larger than the pipistrelle, and had a rather bulldog-like face. It was the New Guinea Mastiff-bat (*Tadarida kuboriensis*)—a first for Irian Jaya.

I was particularly interested in obtaining a specimen of the Alpine Woolly Rat (*Mallomys gunung*), which I had never seen except as a museum skin, and also to determine if *Dingiso* still inhabited the area. So I dispatched a party of young hunters to walk into the high mountains. Unfortunately, they had not returned to the settlement by the time we left.

Our visit to Kwiyawagi was poorly timed in one sense, for an epidemic of dysentery was then ravaging the valley. During the first week of our stay, eight infants and older children succumbed to it. The disease killed with terrifying rapidity. Babies who one day looked happy and healthy were dead a day or two later. We had virtually no medication to offer and, in the absence of a diagnosis, did not even know whether the epidemic was amoebic or bacterial in nature. Without such information, it was almost impossible to guess at which medicines might help such young children.

But I would learn, in a rather peculiar way, that the epidemic had indeed been amoebic. During the writing of this book I suffered high fever and crippling stomach pain. I was hospitalised and diagnosed as suffering from a large abscess on the liver, full of *Entamoeba hystolitica*, the causative agent of amoebic dysentery. The disease, apparently, can migrate from the lining of the bowel to the liver if left untreated. I had probably been infected at Kwiyawagi in 1994.

The best we could do during the epidemic was to try to keep the children from dehydrating. Tragically, we had very little sugar and there was none available in the settlement. The only rehydrating fluid I had was a large bottle of Gatorade. We could not treat more than one or two children and, because Jot Murip shared our house, his baby received the lion's share. Thankfully, his adorable little girl survived the epidemic.

The deaths of infants, while a cause of deep sorrow to their parents, were not as traumatic to the community as those of older children. When a twelve-year-old boy succumbed in the village just a few hundred metres from our house, the entire community was inconsolable. Old men and women sat outside the victim's house for days, tears running down their cheeks. Other people gathered wood for a funeral pyre, and in the afternoon the corpse was placed on top of it and set alight. The following day, walking past the place, I noticed a circle of turf on the spot where the pyre had been lit. Into it was neatly cut the name of the young boy. Each day, as I walked from village to village, I saw the smoke of similar pyres, or people gathering in preparation for a cremation.

Although the epidemic rolled on virtually unchecked while we were at Kwiyawagi, I did manage before leaving to organise a drop of medical supplies into the area, which I hoped would put an end to it. The medicines were paid for by Freeport. John Cutts arranged for them to arrive with the helicopter which took us out. Unloading them from the helicopter, I thought that they looked awfully high-tech to be useful in such a remote area. I just hoped that the *mantri* (who is rather like a barefoot doctor) could make effective use of them.

Despite my manifest failure to stem the epidemic, my attempts to treat children gained me something of a reputation as a medical practitioner, and people would come daily for treatment. The saddest and most perplexing case concerned a man who should have been in his prime. Two years before, he had enjoyed a reputation as the finest hunter in the valley. His skill at catching wild pigs was particularly admired. But, when I saw him, he was a thin, twisted relic. His head was permanently turned to one side and his arms and legs were painfully contorted. He could speak, but do little else.

He explained that one day, while he was out hunting, he had sat down before his fire. A forest spirit had seized him and twisted his head round and round on top of his body. Ever since then, he had been disabled and had suffered fits. He was now near death.

At first I was puzzled about the nature of his affliction. Then I remembered pig tapeworm. Pig tapeworm invaded Irian Jaya from western Indonesia in the 1960s. It was first noticed when outpost doctors reported a higher than normal incidence of burns among mountain people. The people, it seemed, were fitting in their sleep and rolling onto fires.

The worm is transmitted through consumption of poorly cooked pig flesh. Unfortunately, pig meat is often consumed in a half-cooked state in Melanesia, and the disease has spread quickly in Irian Jaya. In humans, the worms can settle in various parts of the body. The greatest damage is done when they invade the brain. There, they form cysts which eventually cause severe fits and other symptoms. Our hunter probably had more access to pig meat than many others in the valley, and had suffered first.

During this second stay among them, my relationship with the Lani warmed considerably. Each day, friends from four years earlier would come to see me, and would often ask the most extraordinary questions.

One of our most frequent visitors was an old man named Tegiorak. He was, perhaps, the patriarch of the valley. He had converted to Christianity some years before, but was clearly worried about the effect of his pagan youth on his soul. One morning he came to me and with disarming simplicity explained that he already felt half-dead, and was sure that the end was not far off. He then asked, 'When I die, will I wake up in heaven?'

I hold no religious beliefs whatever, and was somewhat taken aback by this, yet I felt compelled to reply. After some thought, I said (with as much conviction as I could muster) that I was sure that when he woke up on the other side he would already be in heaven. A truly beatific look of relief came over his face.

This experience left me feeling rather uncomfortable. Simply because I had white skin, people assumed that I had expertise in this and so many other areas. Were I to stay any length of time at Kwiyawagi, I began to feel, I would severely disappoint their high expectations of me.

Not all of my relations with the Lani were so cordial, however. Like virtually all mountain people, they can view Europeans simply as a boundless source of wealth, and fail to accord them the common courtesy they would extend to anyone else. Some people demanded ridiculous prices for items such as vegetables, and then became angered when I refused to accede to their demands. Many, I am sure, thought that I acted out of pure selfishness by refusing to share my wealth.

On the morning of our departure we packed early, and by 8 a.m. were waiting on the airstrip for the helicopter from Tembagapura, which was to pick us up. But the weather conditions were appalling—dense mist filled the valley, and it soon became clear that our departure would be delayed.

As we waited glumly on the strip, the Lani arranged themselves into two teams (the Telenggens and the Murips, which appear to be the main clan names in the region), and began to play soccer on the airstrip with a tennis ball (sometimes two). Both males and females joined in, and there seemed to be no limit to the number of players allowed on each side. The men occupied the centre of the field and would call out to each other 'Telenggen!' or 'Murip!' in the hope that the ball would be passed to them. As these names rang out on each side (and as each member of a team bore the same clan name) I wondered how anyone could decide who to pass the ball to.

While the men were thus occupied, the women formed themselves into teams of goal-keepers. They stood three deep, each one crouched over holding a towel between outspread arms. Their role, it seemed, was to catch the ball as it was kicked towards goal.

In the midst of this spectacle I could sometimes catch sight of an umpire. As the game became more heated, however, he often joined one of the teams and the play became ever more chaotic. Finally, with shouting and screaming at fever pitch, the ball sped towards goal. At the last moment, one of the female goal-keepers scooped it up in her towel and raced from the field, squealing with delight. The rest of the players set off in hot pursuit. She was eventually caught and, after several playful thwacks on the head, was induced to release the ball, and play recommenced.

This riotous game was interrupted by the distant sound of a helicopter. Unnoticed by us all, the mist had cleared somewhat. As the helicopter landed I said my sorrowful farewells to my Lani friends. Within a couple of hours we were back in Tembagapura.

The following morning John Cutts came to us with amazing news. He had heard over the radio that the hunters I had sent out from Kwiyawagi in search of Alpine Woolly Rats had returned only a few hours after we left, with two specimens—as well as a *Dingiso*. It seemed that the chances of obtaining these specimens were about zero, but when I told Terry Owen (a senior administrator in Tembagapura, who was then looking after us) about them, he arranged for a helicopter to take me back to Kwiyawagi.

Those specimens must be about the most expensive which the Australian Museum has ever received, as they cost over a thousand dollars each in helicopter time alone. I paid Manas for them, then gave him a twenty-kilogram bag of rice—my contribution to the Kwiyawagi Christmas celebrations. This meant more to Manas, I think, than anything else.

At last this trip to Irian had come to an end. It was an expedition of the highest highs and lowest lows. My fragile illusion that Irian Jaya was somehow a better place than Papua New Guinea because it was less troubled by lawlessness, and goods were cheaper there, had been traumatically shattered. I had discovered *Dingiso* and climbed to a tropical glacier.

I should have been ecstatic, but I kept worrying about the cost. Could I have prevented Arianus's death?

TWENTY-NINE

A living *Dingiso*

In mid-October 1994, as I sat in my office at the Australian Museum, I received an unexpected telephone call from Terry Owen, who was by now a close friend.

'We have one of your tree-kangaroos,' he said. 'A live one. You'd better get up here in a hurry!'

Barely a week later, I was on a plane, once again bound for Timika before being whisked to Tembagapura. And there, in an enclosed balcony of a company house, I found that a miniature rainforest had been re-created.

As I opened the screen door to peer in, Ding, as I came to know the half-grown *Dingiso* which had brought me back to Irian once again, hopped out of the foliage and came towards me.

Ding had been cared for by the Owen family, and was in excellent condition.

The discovery of this animal was an unprecedented event. For years the people of Tembagapura had lived in ignorance of this wonderful creature, even though it inhabits the forests surrounding their town. Now, a living one had hopped into their midst. It was found in a disused machinery shed at the mine site. An Indonesian worker had entered the building so that he could relieve himself out of the rain. His micturition was cut short, however, when he noticed a black bundle of fur huddled in the corner. He ran to tell his American boss there was a bear on the premises.

Although no biologist, the American engineer knew there were no bears in Irian Jaya. Sceptical of the tale, he asked the man to retrieve the creature from the shed. A few minutes later the worker returned with a very cute, black and white animal in his arms. News of the discovery reached Terry, and soon thereafter myself.

Having handled a number of wild tree-kangaroos, I was surprised to hear that Ding had allowed himself to be picked up at his first meeting with a human. But it was further confirmation, if any was needed, of the stories told by Lani hunters about just how tame *Dingiso* is.

One can only guess at what Ding was doing in the shed. His coat was besmirched with oil, which is hardly surprising given that he had to cross a large industrial site to get to the disused shed. Perhaps he was moving out of his mother's territory. This is always a difficult period for young tree-kangaroos, and Ding was doubtless being given a hard time by adult males whose territories he was passing through. The forest surrounding the mine site seems to possess a particularly high density of tree-kangaroos. This is because hunters are excluded from the area. Ding had probably been chased from one territory to another, until he finally found refuge in a dark corner of the shed. The sheds and their heavy machinery may well be the only places in the vicinity of the mine which do not form part of the territory of an adult male *Dingiso*.

I spent several days photographing and observing this

gentle animal. Ding, I found, was most happy when he was munching on a fistful of young fern leaves. He was not a particularly fussy eater, and would take new leaves from a variety of plants. He appeared to have no clear activity pattern, but instead seemed to become animated whenever anyone entered his enclosure carrying fresh food.

After a few days I had done all I could, and the time came to release Ding. Terry arranged for a helicopter to take us to a high valley about three kilometres east of the mine site. It seemed to be equally distant from both mines and hunters, and Ding stood a good chance of surviving if he were released there. We carried him in a hessian bag, which he liked, feeling perhaps that it was akin to his mother's pouch. I had put a tag in his ear, just in case he should encounter a human again.

When we released him into the alpine herbage, Ding hopped away very slowly, sampling leaves as he went. He was in no hurry to leave us, and it was only after several minutes that he disappeared into a dense tangle of bushes.

Even though only six months had passed since my last visit, noticeable changes had occurred at Tembagapura by late 1994. For one thing, tension between the local people and both Freeport and the Indonesian Government had risen markedly. I was fortunate in being in a privileged position to hear both sides of the story, for by now I had excellent connections with the Freeport management and the community leaders.

Six months earlier, the local people had only spoken openly in the forest, away from others who might hear them. Now, they spoke out everywhere of their hostility. One village leader said to me, 'Everyone here, from the smallest child to the oldest man, knows that war [with Freeport and the Government of Indonesia] is inevitable.'

Every day in Tembagapura brought new alarums and rumours of hostile actions by the OPM. This was the week the war would begin, said my Dani, Moni and Amungme friends. The recent murders of respected men at Singa (by the Indonesian military), and all the deaths of the past for which compensation had not yet been paid, would be avenged. There were eighty armed OPM rebels hidden in the hills surrounding the town, they said. The water or electricity supply would be cut, or the town attacked. Maybe some Europeans would be shot.

Curiously, neither the Freeport administration nor the Indonesian armed forces seemed to be aware of the changes which were taking place in the local community. Indeed, they remained remarkably unconcerned, and life went on as always in the mining community. Whenever I raised the issue with people in authority I got a polite hearing, but also the distinct impression that they thought I was crying wolf.

One evening at dusk I was sitting in my room in Tembagapura, when I heard the strident notes of trumpet and snare drum approaching. A military detachment marched briskly by, and wailing fire engines and ambulances screamed behind them. These were followed by a long line of police and emergency vehicles. My heart was in my mouth. I expected to hear at any moment that the war had begun.

Then I saw a very strange thing. A fire engine drove slowly along the road, its siren wailing and all lights flashing. Something stood on top of it—it looked like Batman! This was followed by an even more bizarre sight, for behind came marching a strange collection of tiny devils, witches, lions and other creatures.

This, I suddenly realised, is how Halloween is celebrated in Tembagapura.

Watching the procession I thought incredulously of all I had heard over the past few days. How cosseted a world is this Tembagapura! Mist hangs over the forest and town like cotton-wool. The guard-posts which stand at each entrance keep Melanesia and its rumours of violence out. It is utterly cut off from the real world.

Tembagapura's lifeline is perilously thin. A single road, a pipeline, and an airfield. All are vulnerable. The flight to Timika often meets with massive turbulence. It feels like riding a bicycle over great angular blocks of concrete. One day a bicycle tyre will burst, and the steaming swamp forest might swallow a passenger jet. Maybe an earthquake will cut the road. Or a kilogram of semtex, or a few rifle bullets, will bring the flow along the lifeline to a halt.

THIRTY

Coming to a head

In January 1996 I again returned to Tembagapura. Alex had decided, based on what she had seen in 1994, that Kwiyawagi was indeed an ideal location for her studies. She intended to stay there for a year, and I decided to accompany her for six weeks or so in order to continue my research.

We had, through a great deal of effort and work (particularly on the part of my friends and colleagues in Indonesia), obtained visas which allowed us to reside in the country for twelve months, and to make multiple exits and re-entries. This seemed to be a victory over the Indonesian bureaucracy indeed. It turned out to be a perverse and short-lived one.

The day after I collected my sparkling new visa at the Indonesian consulate in Sydney, alarming news reached me. A team of young biologists working in Irian Jaya had been kidnapped by OPM rebels. Worse, they had been kidnapped from Mapnduma, a settlement just two days' walk from Kwiyawagi.

This news threw our plans into chaos. The military would be everywhere, and travel would be severely curtailed. Nonetheless, we decided that we must at least try to continue.

After a week haggling in Jakarta with officials (which was difficult, for it was Ramadan and Jakarta was grinding to a halt), we managed to get permission to enter Irian Jaya. But once in Tembagapura we found that virtually all of Irian (except for the mine site) had been closed to outsiders.

The special visa we had obtained was to subject us to further indignity. An unusual document, it was examined minutely at each government office we were forced to visit. The most intolerable inspection came in the immigration office at Tembagapura. There, a group of officials, all white-lipped and foul-breathed from their Ramadan fast, sat gathered around us, examining our strange visas. One possessed a claw-like fingernail at least six centimetres long on the pinkie of his left hand. With this, he scratched continuously at our passports, using its nail to flick over the pages. We sat there for over an hour as he contemplated his next move. All the while, I wondered about the previous use to which this extraordinary appendage had been put. The scratching sound reminded me of mice in a kitchen.

Finally, he asked us to fill out yet more forms, which resulted in our being issued with a mini Indonesian passport. In this was to be recorded every move we made in Indonesia, as well as a mass of irrelevant personal details. The final categories, complete with spaces for stamps, showed that one can never really escape the Indonesian bureaucracy. The penultimate one read *Meningal negri*—departed the country; the last was *Meningal dunia*—departed the world.

The atmosphere in the villages surrounding Tembagapura was now electric. My old friends welcomed us, but told me in no uncertain terms that this was not a good time to be a foreigner in Irian Jaya, and that, should anything happen to us, they would be helpless to intervene.

Through numerous conversations, I gradually pieced together the events which had led to the kidnapping. I cannot say that the story I reconstruct here is the only one, or even correct. It is, though, one which most of the Irianese people living around Tembagapura would believe to be true. Anger has simmered in their hearts for decades. This lies at the centre of the problem, and must be explained in some detail.

The Amungme and many other Irianese are angry both at the Government of Indonesia and at Freeport. The Indonesian military has admitted to having killed tens of people in the province. The true number killed since 1969 is almost certainly in the thousands. One estimate by a Dutch demographer puts the figure at 100,000.

Newspapers have reported that the Indonesian military has bombed villages, invaded and killed indiscriminately in remote areas, and has, in general, treated Irian Jaya as an occupied territory rather than a province of Indonesia. It has also tried to destroy Irianese traditions and culture.

Moreover, there are reports that individuals acting alone have perpetrated atrocities. Many members of the Indonesian military, particularly those holding lower ranks, see the Irianese as barely human. To a brutalised Javanese or Buginese private on duty at a guard-post, the wizened old black man in a penis gourd driving a pig before him is a demonic and deeply abhorrent being. He is a caricature of humanity, from whom the soldier withholds all contact except violence.

Yet I know that old man. He has an indomitable sense of valour, a sense of humour and a deep sense of humanity. He is the leader of a community who is respected for his wisdom, oratory and traditional wealth. He is a great man. The soldier is his inferior in every way. And yet the Government places a high-powered semi-automatic weapon in the hands of the nobody. He is now free to treat his fellow citizens with a barbarism and lack of respect that have led to an intense hatred in many Irianese of what they see as an occupying army.

The Indonesian Government has encouraged a flood of transmigrants into Irian. These people have generally settled in the lowlands, where land issues are not as keenly felt as in the highlands. By 1996, however, there was a growing awareness, at least among the better educated Irianese, that their very existence was being threatened by an ever increasing flow of migrants.

Irianese feelings towards Freeport differ somewhat. This is because the mine directly affects only the land of the Amungme and lowland Kamoro. Because of their opposition to the mine, the Amungme, who are a small group, have suffered horribly at the hands of the Indonesian armed forces. Among the survivors, many have been bowed into hopelessness by the events of the past twenty years. But a new generation burns with an anger which will not be easily placated.

When the geologist Forbes Wilson began exploration on the great Copper Mountain in the 1960s, Amungme tried to prevent the company from working there. The site, known to them as Tenggogoma, was considered sacred, the residing place of dead ancestors, as well as the now endangered Long-beaked Echidna—an important food item to the Amungme. Believing that violation of the site could have serious consequences, the Amungme erected *salep*s or hex sticks around it in an attempt to deter the company. They understood the implications of Wilson's work. But he told the Amungme, 'that the white men were not trying to appropriate the villagers' land. They just wanted to test the rocks. As evidence of their good faith...the white men would give the villages [*sic*] gifts of food and other items.'*

In reality, Freeport was given free rein by the Government of Indonesia forcibly to remove any people it needed to in order to get its operation going, and was in no way obliged to compensate them.

Soon, a great hole in the ground occupied Tenggogoma. A road and pipeline led from the mountain to the sea, and a city of foreigners was established on Amungme land. In the early 1980s the Amungme hit back by cutting the all-important pipeline which carried copper concentrate to the sea. Soon, bombs were falling onto their villages.

The Amungme have not forgotten the representations made to them when mine development began. They remember that Freeport helicopters and aircraft have carried Indonesian soldiers and equipment in raids against them. They know that Freeport workshops fuel and maintain army vehicles, which are in any case bought by the company for the use of the armed forces, and that Freeport engineers construct army posts and living quarters, and Freeport staff benefit, at least psychologically, from the exclusion of Irianese from their lives. There are also rumours that large sums of money have passed from the company to military commanders living in the area.

No wonder, then, that the Irianese have difficulty distinguishing between the actions of the company from those of the armed forces. Among those who do make the distinction, however, there is a feeling that they could deal with the company if only the armed forces were withdrawn.

A further issue for the Amungme concerns the security forces, which are paid for and maintained by Freeport. These security forces are, in reality, controlled at least in part by the Indonesian armed forces. The Irianese community living around the mine accuse the force of thirteen murders in recent years.

---

* Forbes Wilson, *The Conquest of Copper Mountain*, Atheneum, New York, 1981, p. 169.

The security forces add insult to injury by poorly treating mountain people who try to enter Tembagapura. They have, I am informed, publicly assaulted children, elderly men and women, and mourners who have come to the hospital to collect the body of a relative. The American wife of a senior mine manager was harassed, and finally had to leave Tembagapura, after intervening when she saw a security guard viciously kicking a ten-year-old Amungme boy in the street.

A final and more fundamental problem concerns the relationship between the local Irianese and the Americans who live in Tembagapura. There is a great cultural gulf between these two groups. Some Americans profess goodwill towards the Irianese, although a larger number look down on them. Freeport is based in America's deep south—in New Orleans. The enormous wealth derived from Irian has helped to revitalise that grand, if somewhat down-at-heel city.

I have heard the Irianese referred to as 'niggers' more than once at public meetings, and suspect that the term, and the contempt it implies, is used more frequently behind closed doors. But despite the feelings any individuals might have, meaningful contact between the two groups is severely inhibited by the structure of the town and the rules of the company.

It was striking, after I had worked at Ok Tedi, to see how black and white are segregated in Tembagapura. At Tabubil, Ok Tedi company workers eat in one mess, regardless of their colour. Papua New Guineans from all over the country eat side by side with Australians, Filipinos and visitors. At every level in the company, one finds Papua New Guineans working side by side with Australians. Indeed, a previous managing director of Ok Tedi was a Papua New Guinean. Social life, schooling and sports are all entirely mixed. In short, an environment exists which induces mutual respect and understanding.

At Tembagapura, in contrast, the Americans live inside their hermetically sealed enclosure alongside Indonesians from elsewhere around the archipelago. The Irianese are on the outside looking in. The situation reminds me of the gold rush in mid-nineteenth-century Australia, when small groups of Aborigines camped around the outskirts of growing towns such as Ballarat and Bendigo.

One other element makes inter-racial relationships at Tembagapura difficult. Fear. Any Americans who have thought at all about what they are doing, feel, I suspect, some unease at their situation. They know that the pipeline carries away ten million dollars worth of ore every day. Part of that wealth goes to the USA. It could, instead, have stayed in Irian Jaya, where it might have helped to build a prosperous Melanesian nation. How would the miners feel, I wonder, if the wealth of California were shipped to Indonesia?

They know that the Amungme have a valid moral claim to their land. They know that Freeport is providing the beachhead which will eventually see the replacement of the Irianese with Asian people. The guilt and fear (perhaps the most corrosive and unproductive of emotions) which this foreboding brings, cuts off completely whatever small connections there are between the groups.

A few Australian expatriates, and an even smaller number of Americans and Javanese, have escaped this psychological straitjacket. These people are usually workers on the periphery. They live in small exploration camps where there is no choice but to get to know the locals, or on community projects outside Tembagapura where they must interact daily with them. These are the people who feel comfortable in Irian. In them, perhaps, lies the only hope for meaningful change.

The rising levels of unrest between 1993 and 1996 culminated in a series of rebellious acts committed by the communities surrounding the mine. During 1994 an OPM flag was raised in the village of Singa. The military invaded the place, shooting dead both the village pastor and *kepala desa*. These deaths were a terrible blow to the tiny community, and will not be forgotten.

At Christmas 1994 the OPM flag was again raised, following

a church service in the village of Banti, just a kilometre from Tembagapura. The military opened fire, killing, according to my informants, seven people, including women and children. I was shown the spots where they fell. Some were in the public road, within easy viewing distance of Tembagapura.

By mid-1995 it looked as if the Amungme would be crushed yet again. Then an extraordinary thing happened. Bishop Munninghof, the Roman Catholic Bishop of Jayapura, released a document which reported on allegations made by an Australian aid agency. It accused the Indonesian military of gross abuses of human rights in Irian Jaya. This courageous act may have counted for nought, except that the matter was taken up by the Indonesian Human Rights Association, which had been recently set up and endorsed by President Suharto himself. This organisation forced an investigation of the bishop's accusations, and subsequently several privates and other junior army personnel were jailed for up to three years.

These events gave the people of Irian Jaya a sense of hope which they had never previously felt—and that hope precipitated a tremendous release of pent-up emotion. Amungme warriors invaded the lowlands town of Timika, where they danced in the streets for three days. The Indonesian immigrants wisely stayed indoors. Finally, it seemed, there was some check on the barbarous army, and the voice of the local people might be heard.

It was in this atmosphere that Kelly Kwalik and Judas Kogoya kidnapped the twenty-three biologists and their support crew at Mapnduma on 8 January 1996.

Whenever I asked about their motives or negotiating position, I always received the same answer from the Irianese who knew them. Kwalik, I was told, was *kepala batu*—stone-headed. He would listen to no argument about a release of the hostages except on his terms. And his terms were, and always have been, simply this: the hostages would be released when he received a document signed by President Suharto which guaranteed independence for his province. All other negotiating stances were simply ploys to gain time.

In January, a photograph purporting to be of Kwalik (which many of my informants claimed was of another man) appeared on the cover of *Gatra*, a leading Indonesian news magazine, and from that moment Kwalik was a hero to the Irianese, comparable in status perhaps to Australia's legendary bushranger Ned Kelly. In him, many saw a leader of the stature they had so long lacked.

These events galvanised the Irianese community. There was talk of all kinds of action against the mine. On the day I left Tembagapura for Australia, people were once more saying that tribesmen were gathering to attack the town's electricity or water supply, or to destroy the mill.

Two weeks later, riots rocked the towns of Tembagapura and Timika, causing millions of dollars worth of damage. Bulldozers were driven through company buildings and stones thrown through company windows. The mine ceased production for three and a half days. Riots have since followed in Jayapura and Nabire, and more kidnappings have occurred near Timika.

A few days before I left Irian Jaya in February 1996, I was given a vision of Irian Jaya's future as it was being moulded by Jim-Bob Moffet (CEO of Freeport) and the Government of Indonesia.

I drove out of Timika, a typically rambling, ramshackle Indonesian town, along a new dirt road to a great clearing in the jungle. There stood a scene of such enormity that my mind could not encompass it—Kuala Kencana, as the new town is known, virtually complete, but as yet uninhabited.

The site of Kuala Kencana has been cut out of the virgin lowland rainforest of southern Irian Jaya. It is a town of vast proportions. Designed for an initial population of 25,000, there were indications even before it was completed that rapid transmigration from other parts of Indonesia would soon swell its population to a quarter of a million, adding over 10 per cent to the population of the province.

Given this expansion, the land surrounding the site was clearly of commercial interest to those intent on making a quick buck. Under Indonesian law it does not belong to the Kamoro people who still live on it as they have for thousands of years. Instead, it has been acquired by extremely wealthy Javanese, who will bloat their bank accounts still further by selling it.

What struck me most about Kuala Kencana was its grandeur and silence. I stood on the edge of the expansive city square. Its immaculately manicured lawns and paths stretched seemingly forever in the burning tropical sun. In its very centre stood a copper sculpture. The size of half a house, it supposedly represented the *burung Cenderawasih*, the birds of paradise which had first drawn strangers to Irian's shore, and which are still seen as the quintessential symbol of the province. To my eye the sculpture looked like nothing more than a great green turban—an obscene authority symbol of a culture and religion entirely foreign to this place. In a land where fierce electrical storms occur almost daily, no-one had considered the advisability of attaching lightning rods to this monstrosity.

At the southern end of the great plaza lay a mosque—the most imposing and beautiful building in the whole town. To the north, barely visible, was the Christian church. To the east lay the building which would house the offices of PT Freeport Indonesia. Its architecture would not be out of place in New Orleans. It had already proved to be too small and an identical glass and steel structure was going up beside it.

All of this scene was entirely devoid of people. It was as if the town had been deserted, rather than waiting to be inhabited.

This surreal vision was surrounded on all sides by a crisp edge of newly cut rainforest. I knew, from studying its biology for over a decade, that this was not a benign edge. The forest was waiting, like a coiled spring, to reclaim the land taken from it. I could not help but speculate that one day it would shelter groups of angry Irianese, intent on the same mission. Perhaps then Kuala Kencana would resemble a Mayan city even more closely that it did on this day.

The suburbs of Kuala Kencana were constructed similarly to its centre. Each one formed a satellite community of a few tens of houses, all surrounded by the same towering forest, and each joined to the city centre by a system of sealed roads which would do a developed nation proud. The houses were all small-windowed block-houses, completely cut off from the outside world, and reliant on air-conditioning to make them habitable.

On the day President Suharto officially declared the city open, 3,000 members of the armed forces patrolled the surrounding jungle. Local Kamoro were removed from the area. The telephone services were restricted, and travel was curtailed. Hundreds of white doves were imported in baskets, to be released on completion of the presidential speech. The day was so hot, however, that many of the birds were prostrated. They refused to fly. Anxious assistants began throwing them skywards, and when this failed they tied helium-filled balloons to their legs. The peace they symbolised was off to a shaky start indeed.

This, then, was the beachhead into Irian which Freeport and the Government of Indonesia had jointly constructed. It would act very effectively, no doubt, in facilitating a rapid Asianisation of this particular piece of Melanesia. Yet it had more than one potentially fatal flaw. If the low-grade civil war which had rumbled on for decades flared once again, how defensible would Kuala Kencana be? What would happen if its electricity supply were cut? How safe would the inhabitants of Tembagapura, at present insulated from Melanesia in their high valley, feel here, dumped in the middle of a steaming jungle? Even clearing the forest would be no solution, for that would only create a suffocatingly hot and sodden plain, on which malaria and other diseases would proliferate.

Australians might recognise something familiar in this story of the conquest of Irian. Until the 1850s Australia developed slowly, and it was only in those areas where European-style agriculture flourished that the Europeans dominated. Just as environmental conditions in parts of Australia held back the European invaders, so those in Irian halted the eastward expansion of the Asiatic peoples. Then, in both cases, minerals were discovered. In Australia, gold provided the beachhead which Europeans used to make the continent their own. In Irian Jaya, it is the fabulously rich gold and copper deposit exploited by Freeport which will provide the fertiliser that the Asiatic lifestyle needs to flourish.

The dire predicament facing the people of Irian Jaya was succinctly put as long ago as 1957:

> Persons arrested under suspicion of 'disturbing the peace', which is the term traditionally used…for suspicion of involvement in democratic political activities, are none too kindly treated. There are reports that such people are sometimes beaten even before any investigation has begun as to their factual acts…
>
> There are other reports…of the summary shooting of 'disturbers of the peace', and it was stated…that entire populations of suspected villages were being rounded up before dawn, and marched off at bayonet point for the securing of 'confessions'…

These extraordinary allegations were made before the United Nations by the Indonesian ambassador to muster support for the removal of West New Guinea from Dutch control. Then, the human rights violations listed above were largely imagined. It was those who ostensibly strove for justice as they spoke these words who would make the violations real. The Indonesian Government still has time to avoid the catastrophe of genocide.

Envoi

Just before I left Irian Jaya that February in 1996, I visited a Freeport exploration camp at Etna Bay, on the southern side of the Vogelkop 'neck'. The camp is one of many in the province, which is fantastically rich in minerals. Etna Bay is a beautiful place, and I have never seen marine bioluminescence as I saw it there. To dip one's hand into the water at night is to ignite a vast, swirling universe of red and green sparks of life, some up to a centimetre across.

On land, Etna Bay taught me another lesson. At the village of Kiriru I saw my first Melanesian village without pigs. Instead, a dilapidated mosque stood in the middle of the town. It was adorned with multicoloured party lights which ran in strings up its cupola. I rarely heard local languages spoken in the streets. Bahasa Indonesia was the *lingua franca*. Kiriru has had contact with the rest of Indonesia for well over a century. Is this what the villages of the rest of the island will look like next century?

As I put the finishing touches to this book, I receive news from Kwiyawagi. The settlement which Geoff Hope and Bren Wetherstone walked 250 kilometres to reach is now connected to Wamena by road. Unless the Indonesian military have learned from their mistakes, there will doubtless be a military post there too.

Acknowledgments

When I first began working in New Guinea almost twenty years ago, I had no idea that anything except my scientific research could possibly be of interest to anyone. I was a poor note-taker. In coming to write this book I was reluctant to reconstruct events in my early expeditions from memory alone, so I sought recourse to the fieldnotes of my expedition partners (particularly Geoff Hope), and also asked them to read my accounts to ensure that my recollection of events broadly concurs with their own. I am grateful to Ken Aplin and Geoff Hope for their co-operation in this.

It was difficult to write the section which deals with Arianus Murip. Some may accuse me of duplicity, or at least complicity with Freeport, because I accepted funding from the company and enjoyed good relations with it, only to expose the ghastly events of 1994 to public scrutiny four years later. In this, as in all my dealings with the company, I have acted according to my conscience.

Above all, I have tried to give a feel for what it is like to undertake biological fieldwork in New Guinea. In some cases, the events of several sequential expeditions (particularly those to Telefomin and the Torricelli Mountains) have been discussed together, with no clear distinction drawn between the separate expeditions. For those interested in the minutiae of where I was and when, my fieldnotes are kept at the Australian Museum, Sydney.

In New Guinea I have accumulated many debts of acknowledgment for companionship and help. Assembling them here is a daunting task. Inevitably there will be some inadvertent omissions, but this should not be mistaken for ingratitude. All have my heartfelt thanks.

Lester Seri, Boeadi, Alexandra Szalay and Geoff Hope shared the trials of repeated expeditions into the remotest parts of New Guinea. To each I owe in large part what measure of success our expeditions met with; to one I owe my life.

Others have accompanied me on fewer trips, including Ken Aplin, Robert Attenborough, Hal Cogger, Tish Ennis, Hickson Ferguson, Eric Fruhstorfer, Don Gardner, Pavel German, Michael Holics, Martin Krogh, Roger Martin, Gerry Maynes, Rory McGuinness, Toni O'Neill, Richard Owen, Rebecca Scott, Gary Steer and Steven Van Dyck.

For their hospitality in the field, I thank Judy Ebsworth, Peter Ebsworth, Maria Friend, Tony Friend, Father Patrick MacGeaver and Father Alexandre Michaellod. I will always be indebted to Sister Cecilia Prestashewsky of the Franciscan Missionary Sisters of the Immaculate Conception.

Without the assistance of the personnel of the Papua New Guinea Department of Environment & Conservation, Puslitbang Biologi, Lembaga Ilmu Pengetahuan Indonesia (LIPI) and Departemen Kehutana Indonesia, my work could not have commenced or been completed. In particular, I thank Mahomad Amir, Iamo Ila, Karol Kisokau, Gerry Maynes, Sancoyo and Ucok.

I am grateful to Murray Eagle, Ross Smith, and Ian Wood of Ok Tedi Mining Limited for their invaluable practical help, and their trust in me. Several expeditions to central Irian Jaya between 1994 and 1996 were made possible by the support of PT Freeport Indonesia. For their generous assistance I thank John Cutts, Gordon Greaves, Howard Lewis, Bruce Marsh, Jim Miller, Paul Murphy, Terry Owen, David Richards, Charlie White, and Wisnu. I hope they will view my criticism of Freeport as being offered in a constructive manner.

My greatest debt, and deepest appreciation, is to the many individuals who shared their knowledge of the forests and wildlife of their lands. In particular, the following have been my patient teachers and friends: (in Papua New Guinea) Kaspar Seiko and the people of Miwautei in the Torricelli Mountains; Simon of Fas in the Bewani Mountains; Amunsep, Willok, Tinamnok, Seki and the people of the Telefomin area;

Anaru, Ambep and the people of the West Miyanmin area; Freddie, Serapnok and Fresta of Bultem in the Star Mountains; Peter Keno of Kosipe, Central Province; (in Irian Jaya) Benjamin of Je'ute in the Arfak Moutains, Bogaubau Ba Bolobau of Pogapa in the West Maokop; Yonas Tinal of Ilaga; Tegiorak, Pastor Manas and Jot Murip of Kwiyawagi; Julius Adi, Maria Magiu and Vedelis Zonggonau at Tembagapura.

Frank Rickwood read an early draft of the manuscript and offered invaluable criticism and comment. Eric Fruhstorfer, Lucy Hughes Turnbull, Malcolm Turnbull and Chris Ballard commented on vital parts of later drafts.

Finally I express my deepest gratitude to my son David and my daughter Emma. I was away far too often when you were growing up, yet you have continued to love me.

Index